LOVE SEX & COMMUNICATION

SKILLS FOR RECOVERY

by
JEANNE MILLER
and
PHIL LAUT

Illustrations by
George Longfellow

Cover by
William Johnson

VIVATION PUBLISHING CO.

AUTHOR PHOTO by George Longfellow

Illustrations by George Longfellow

"Vivation" is a service mark of Jim Leonard, Phil Laut, Jeanne Miller, and Anne Leonard, doing business as Associated Vivation Professionals. Only currently licensed members of Associated Vivation Professionals may use the word Vivation in advertising.

First Printing   January 1990

Printed in
United States of America

Vivation Publishing Co.
PO Box 8269
Cincinnati, OH 45208 USA
513-321-4405

Table of Contents
and Chapter Summary

PART II
TAKING ACTION BY YOURSELF

INTRODUCTION AND HOW TO USE THIS BOOK

Dear Reader,

This book has been a two year labor of love for us. We gained the information from our own personal recovery, through teaching our Love, Sex and Communication Weekend and through learning to grow together in our marriage. Read this book slowly — start anywhere, at whatever part is most pertinent to you now. Discuss it with your friends and family. We have included humorous illustrations to lighten up a subject that has been taken far too seriously over the ages. The methods in this book can be applied regardless of the current state of your love life. They will aid you whether you want a complete renovation or just minor repairs.

WHY RECOVERY?

Recovery means regaining the joy, creativity and capacity for love and feeling that you lost as a child (even if you don't remember having it). Recovery means reclaiming your birthright to the best that God can offer you. The essential first step is acknowledging this loss, rather than pretending that your life is already as good as it can be.

A NOTE ABOUT THE RECOVERY PROCESSES

In almost every chapter, there are processes, in order to take the information and actually apply it in your love life. In teaching our seminars, we have found that people learn best by doing. These processes are designed to be done in writing or verbally. The most important thing is that you do them.

The best way to use the Recovery Processes:
  Notice the answers your mind makes and notice your opinion about them.
  Notice how your body feels about the answer.
  Notice what your mind thinks about the way your body feels.

Used this way, you can actually have emotional recovery in action as you read.

WHAT THIS BOOK CAN DO FOR YOU

We teach you gentle yet direct communication methods (in some cases, we even suggest the words to say) and practical methods for resolving even the most troubling and deeply suppressed feelings that disturb your serenity. We think that the information in this book should be taught in all the junior high schools in the world.

Part I, Theories and Methods for Emotional Recovery (Chapters 1 through 8) may be different than you would expect in a book like this. In it we present essential information about the endlessly dynamic and yet often unnoticed interaction between your thoughts and your feelings. These chapters provide an essential starting point, because without this under- standing, there exists a strong possibility that you may use the methods we offer in the rest of the book in a manner so intellectual that they may be less effective than they could be in resolving the emotional aspects of your love life. We are pretty sure that the information in this book will bring to your attention long suppressed feelings about you. For this reason, we explain in Part I why your feelings are not verdicts about you and how to relate to them differently. Since this is a book about love, it's a book about feelings.

Don't take our word for anything in here. Instead try it for yourself. Nothing ventured, nothing gained. Write us and let us know of your results. We'd be delighted to hear from you.

GUARANTEE

Satisfied customers are the most valued asset of any thriving business. If this book benefits you, please tell your friends and associates about it. If you are not satisfied with this book for any reason, you can receive a full refund from the publisher by returning it to Vivation Publishing Co. within one year of purchase with your sales slip or canceled check.

DEDICATION

We dedicate this book to all the Graduates of the Love, Sex and Communication Weekend throughout the world. They have laughed with us and cried with us and trusted us enough to open their hearts and had the courage to feel their feelings in an honest way. And to all of you on the road to recovery, you have been a source of joy and inspiration and we thought about you often in writing this book.

We also dedicate this book to our partners who have brought us to their town by producing the Love, Sex and Communication Weekend for us. We couldn't have done it without you.

We also dedicate this book to Karen Regina and thank her for introducing us in 1981.

And to Jim Leonard, our friend, business partner and fellow Vivation Professional, who married us under the trees in our backyard in September, 1986.

ACKNOWLEDGEMENTS

Special acknowledgement to George Longfellow, artist, compadre and friend. We appreciate his patience and talent in creating the illustrations in this book. In many meetings around our coffee table, he never failed to amaze us with his ability to quickly turn our ideas into pictures.

Special acknowledgement to our friend and assistant Marilyn Zelcer, who kept Vivation Publishing Co., Miller Health Service and Miller/Laut Trainings open for business during our labors in writing this book.

People whose aid and support make this book possible:
Photography and Illustrations: George Longfellow,
Cincinnati, OH

Cover: William Johnson, Cincinnati, OH
Handy Print, Cincinnati, OH
Typesetting: Reporter Typographics
Printing: Delta Lithograph, Valencia, CA
Order Fulfillment: The Creative Source, El Toro, CA

PART I

LEARNING TO ACCEPT YOURSELF

CHAPTER 1 THE STRUCTURE OF THE MIND

Your mind is your closest and most enduring companion. Your relationship with your own mind began at birth (perhaps even sooner). It will never leave you. Learning to love and understand the workings of your own mind is the first step toward learning to love yourself and love and understand another person. As your life progresses, people come and go, you may change addresses and jobs, lovers and associates, but your mind will be there as long as you live.

We suggest you give up struggling to have a functional relationship with another person, without having a loving relationship with yourself. This could be called expecting someone else to love you more than you love yourself. Love is a FEELING. Loving someone else means accepting them just as they are and just as they are not and means accepting their feelings as they are. Loving yourself means accepting yourself as you are, accepting your feelings as they are (even though you may wish to change them) and giving up hope that hatred and condemnation will ever motivate you to improve. In this book, we teach you exactly how to do this.

Do not expect to have a good relationship with someone else if your mind is filled with self-condemnation, shame and unresolved feelings left over from your family of origin. You must work on yourself first. Having someone else love you can never take the place of self-acceptance. Even if someone were to love you more than you love yourself, you would tend to be suspicious of their motivation, want to protect yourself from them

or consider that they only love you because you fooled them, so you must struggle to keep up your act. In this book, we actually show you how to love yourself, by resolving the suppressed feelings that shame you into thinking that there is something wrong with you.

Usually thoughts like these are associated with uncomfortable emotions and body sensations. The discomfort leads us to suspend contemplation of the thought in order to avoid the discomfort. This is how our mind constructs the habit of denying our problems and maintains delusion. In this way, our neuroses are associated with uncomfortable emotions which motivate us to avoid behavior that would benefit us and to continue to engage in behavior that does not. Addictions and compulsive behavior are caused by this.

Your mind makes a wonderful servant and a tyrannical master. Our purpose in this section is to shed some light on the mysteries of the working of your mind so that it may become more of your servant and less of your master. The inner workings of the human mind remain unsolved at this point in human development. No one can claim to really know how anyone's mind functions. We however present useful models of how the mind works. The validity of these models lies in their effectiveness and ease of application; rather than in their intellectual impressiveness.

It is important to understand that your mind is not your identity, that you are not your mind; instead you have a mind. If you were in fact your mind, you would not experience your mind at all; in other words, you wouldn't know what you are thinking. Similarly, you are not the thoughts that inhabit your mind; your thoughts are something that you have, just as you have a pair of jeans or have a car.

IT'S OK TO BE CRAZIER THAN YOU THINK

A basic fallacy of much of the teaching about psychology is that there is such a thing as a normal person and that there is such a thing as normal behavior (or a normal appetite or a normal sex drive). This leads to the conclusion that anything outside of what has been defined as normal is abnormal. If you think about it, you will notice that everyone you ever met is different from you and each other. It is not normal to be normal.

All of us possess a part of our mind that is absolutely insane. We mean crazy—most likely crazier than the craziest person that you can imagine. This means that there is a part of all of our minds that is highly erratic, contradictory, senseless, foolish and which does not operate in our best interests. Ever heard anyone say, "I don't know why I keep doing this, but I can't stop!."? The question is not whether this part of your mind exists; but rather how you relate to it, whether you take it seriously, whether you believe it, worry about it or base your actions on what it tells you—whether you are its slave or its master.

To cite an external example, if a clearly mentally deranged person approached you in an elevator and began spontaneously to offer you investment advice about the stock market, it is unlikely that you would act on any of that person's investment tips, although you likely would acknowledge the presence of the deranged person by listening, or at least pretending to listen, until you reached your floor. The same thing applies to your mind, except that your mind is harder to escape.

All of us have a part of our mind that is this deranged. It is fine to let yourself know about the neurotic or disordered thoughts that you possess. Just because you have stupid thoughts, you are not necessarily stupid, just because you have murderous thoughts, you are not necessarily a murderer, just because you have crazy thoughts you are not necessarily crazy and just because you have confusing thoughts you are not necessarily indecisive.

Acknowledging the neurotic thoughts and letting them be that way actually provides you greater freedom. Suppressing them and hoping they will go away or pretending that they are not there or criticizing yourself for thinking that way or hoping you'll be better some day leaves you trapped by denial. In fact, acknowledgement of your own neuroses will bring you freedom from them and lead to new and powerful ways of perceiving your mind as a tool for you to use. This is primarily a result of the reduction in denial.

We trust that this information comes a relief to those readers who believe that their thoughts create their reality in an absolute sense or who are continuously haunted by the past. The purpose of acknowledging that our thoughts create our reality is to enable us to accept responsibility for our lives. The purpose of this is not so that you live your life in terror of what may pass through your mind. Instead the acknowledgement of the creative power of thought can aid you in discovering how the past has affected you.

Negative thoughts will have far less adverse effect on you, when you accept yourself for having them. This is obvious to anyone who has felt better after disclosing his uncomfortable, negative perceptions to someone in a loving way. For example, in our Love, Sex and Communication Weekend Seminar, (after this we refer to our Weekend Seminar as the LSC) we provide an opportunity for participants to verbalize their reasons for hating members of the opposite sex. There is always a gasp from the audience when we announce what we are going to do, and a sigh of relief, an explosion of laughter and a sense of compassion when it has been completed.

THE EFFECT OF YOUR MIND ON REALITY

That one's thoughts affect one's reality is evident to anyone who has engaged in the smallest amount of introspection; however, the belief that one's thoughts are the absolute cause of one's problems and results takes a good idea too far. Sometimes, the best cure for a cold is bed rest and plenty of liquids rather than trying to determine the thoughts that caused the cold. Clearly, it is better to think "positive" thoughts than "negative" thoughts. However, compulsive analysis of every event in your life to determine the thoughts associated with it is an unproductive neurotic obsession, usually resulting in denial of your feelings. The methods in this book will show you the power of using your thoughts and feelings together for your personal advancement.

We refer to the mind as having two major parts; conscious and unconscious. By the conscious mind, we mean the part that contains thoughts that we are aware of; and by the unconscious mind, we mean the part of our mind that contains thoughts that we are not aware and therefore do not think about. The conscious mind contains plans, internal chatter and the other perceptions we are aware of. The unconscious mind contains our unremembered personal history, habits and autonomic functions (digestion, growth of hair, respiration and heartbeat, to mention a few). Autonomic functions clearly require intelligence and yet we are not aware of the particular thoughts that cause and regulate them. Repetitive behavior, even of a reasonably complex nature requires little or no conscious thought once we have developed it into a habit. Saving regularly, getting dressed or driving your car require little conscious thought once the habit pattern is established, although considerable conscious practice and concentration may have been required before they became habits. So, our lack of awareness about the content of our unconscious mind, including our unremembered personal history, does not prevent it from having an effect on our life.

Some of the thoughts in our unconscious mind we keep from our awareness because they are conclusions that we made from past unpleasant events. Since the body sensations associated with these memories are

7

painful, our mind suppresses the thoughts related to the events in order to avoid re-experiencing the associated pain. Although your mind is convinced that it is doing you a favor by blocking the memory of unremembered upsets and tragedies, ignorance about or unwillingness to consider your past prevents you from learning from it and making the changes that you desire. Your past may be buried, but it is buried alive, enabling it to control you without your awareness. Memories may hurt, but they won't hurt YOU; such is the difference between pain and the memory of pain.

Demanding to know the reason why you are feeling what you are feeling, (or what your feelings mean or how or when they got there), before being willing to feel them is in fact an excellent way to be sure that the feelings will continue to escape your awareness. For this reason, it is almost impossible to increase your understanding of your mind without some willingness to experience uncomfortable feelings. Therefore, therapy and counselling techniques that rely solely on talking and analysis take a long time and may produce less than satisfying results, unless the therapist can aid you in resolving the emotions at a feeling level. Uncomfortable feelings may hurt when they return to your awareness; but they won't hurt YOU. A common cry of those who refuse to examine their history is "I don't want to think about it. It's too painful." Nothing changes until you let it be real. Vivation, which we will describe later, is a process about learning to accept what you are feeling without being overwhelmed by the intensity. By enabling you to feel your feelings in an honest way, they become far easier to resolve.

All of us know people who understand and even admit the reasons for their problems, yet persist in doing nothing about them. In this book, we describe proven methods that do not involve hypnosis, drugs or constant talking for gaining emotional access to past conclusions and will empower you to make the changes you want. Since the methods we describe work at the feeling level, they will enhance whatever methods you are already using. You can recover your true self-worth, personal authority and creativity.

YOUR MIND IS REDUCTIVE

An important characteristic about your mind is that you do not have a total experience of your mind. The mind gives and receives information about various experiences, sensations and ideas. Although this information is processed at very high speed, and sometimes the speed is so great that we do not notice all of the thoughts we may have on a particular topic; the thoughts are experienced one at a time. In other words, the mind is reductive. Your mind reduces its awareness of any item so that it can it can reach conclusions quickly.

For example, if you were asked to describe the Fourth Grade, you could probably come up with 500 words or so on this topic. Your answer to the question IS the Fourth Grade for you at this point. Your answer, however, is a greatly reduced version of everything that happened in the Fourth Grade, which would take nine months or so just to relate the events that occurred, not to mention how you got there, the feelings you experienced, the development of education through the centuries that caused the teaching to be done the way that it was and how you may have applied what you learned in the Fourth Grade. In most instances, you would not want your mind to spend many months contemplating the Fourth Grade every time something brought that subject to your attention. So, whether we like it or not, our minds are reductive as a result of a million or so years of evolution (based on the Big Bang Theory) or 6000 or so years of development (if you prefer the Creation Myth).

It is most important that we are aware of this reductive property of our mind. Thus, the first thoughts we have about something are not necessarily the complete truth about it. They may be simply our first impression, or they may be based on incomplete information and surely are colored by our current emotional state.

As applied to our love life, this means that what you now think about your relationship situation is not necessarily the complete truth about it. At best it is the partial truth. Knowing that your mind is reductive frees you from the bondage of insisting that you are right, allows you the opportunity to reconsider your views and search out new information, and provides you with the freedom to change your mind and thus change compulsive behaviors. The rest of this book will provide lots of new information for your mind's earnest consideration.

CHAPTER 2

THE OPERATION OF YOUR MIND
Content and Context

The reductive property of the mind leads us to the distinction between context and content. By content, we mean the thing itself or reality itself. Thus, your bank account, your house, the characters on this page, the thoughts in your mind and the sensations in your body are all content. By context, we mean the way that you relate to to reality. Context could also be described as your point of view, the meaning or interpretation that you give to something, your attitude about something, your outlook, your opinions about something, or the frame of reference in which you hold something. Thus, love and hate are contexts; good and bad are contexts; happiness and despair are contexts. Your mind reduces the content of any experience to some context so that it can perform its function of distinguishing between one thing and another and making decisions.

The mind could be described as a library of contexts, with opinions about everything. The socialization process to which your family of origin, church, school, government and other authority figures subjected you could be described as educating you about the benefits of adopting THEIR

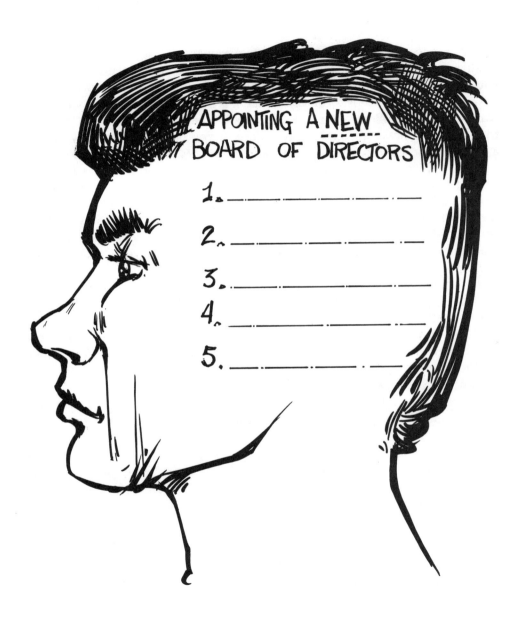

contexts, instead of the contexts that you might have preferred. Whether the contexts you hold are supportive of your well-being, of your wealth or of the happiness of your love life is the determining factor in your behavior and in the results that you experience.

Since your mind will tend to continue to hold any particular content within the originally selected context, it is important to develop a willingness to reconsider those contexts which are not supportive of what you want. Your mind already has contexts about everything, even about things that you have never thought about before. If you do not consciously choose a context for the on-going events and situations in your life, then your mind will unconsciously adhere to the previously chosen contexts for them or will adopt the contexts of others around you whom you think know more. Common responses are compulsive rebellion or conformity to those we perceive as authority figures, belief in a vengeful, authoritarian God, or fear of punishment, or narrow-minded defiance; depending on our reaction to family upbringing. Clearly there is an infinite variety of contexts for any content.

Our mind does not relate to the content of our reality directly. Rather, our mind perceives reality through our personal lens of contexts which are chosen consciously or unconsciously. Beauty is in the eye of the beholder. Rejection causes some people to give up, others to become more determined and others to become enraged. Your behavior is determined by the context in which you hold the rejection. Thus, a narrow-minded person could be described as someone with a limited variety of contexts available to him and with little willingness to consider new ones. Conversely an open-minded person is willing to allow his mind to consider everything differently and choose a new context when it is to his benefit.

Another way to describe the library of contexts is to liken it to a your own personal committee meeting of mental advisors. They are in session 24 hours a day, 365 days per year, composed of different personalities that may disagree with each other, and who minute by minute profess judgment, offer advice, praise, warnings, threats or encouragement about everything that you think, say, do or feel. Knowing about this mental committee will aid you in consciously choosing which voices to heed and which ones to disregard. This results in a light-hearted, yet effective method for evaluating the thoughts in your mind. If this model of how your mind works makes sense to you, you may consider consciously adding new members to your committee who can offer you higher quality advice and choosing to ignore the clearly outdated advice of some others. For an interesting experiment, the next time you have a problem, ask yourself,

"How would _____ think about this?" In the blank space add the name of anyone whose experience and opinions you respect and trust. You'll probably get new and useful ideas.

CONTEXT DETERMINES HOW CONTENT AFFECTS YOU

Successful people (in relationship, in business, or in any kind of achievement) have consciously or unconsciously developed the ability to change contexts. In other words, they have the ability to make conscious choices about the WAY in which they think about what happens in their lives. Because of this they can rise to a challenge, use even an unpleasant situation to their gain, recover from the past, learn from each other and take their commitment seriously but not so seriously that they become a humorless, obsessed fanatic. They can accomplish their goals despite setbacks and mistakes, allow themselves to enjoy competition, give themselves and others another chance and generally act in a self-determined manner.

To be a winner in any field, what is required is sufficient mental flexibility to shift contexts when it is to your benefit. You must be able to see yourself as a winner; but if this is the only context you have about winning, then you may not take the action required to improve enough to win. Positive thinking alone is not enough. You must be willing to see what you need to learn and take steps to improve, which requires a change in context. If all you see are your deficiencies, it is unlikely that you'll win or enjoy it much if you do. You must be willing to allow setbacks to inspire you. A useful context for mistakes is mistakes are when we learn.

We could argue for a long time about whether we humans have choice about what happens in our life. Whichever view you take, it is, nevertheless, clear that we do have a choice about how events affect and motivate us. This means that the content of your mind (your thoughts themselves) matters a whole lot less than your attitude about the content of your mind. Your state of mind matters much more than what you are thinking.

The health, wealth, happiness and satisfaction of each of us is up to us. They are determined by the contexts or attitudes that we hold about external circumstances. Family conditioning, the balance in our bank account, the behavior and expectations of our partner or employer, germs, the weather and whole multitude of external influences clearly have an effect on us; however each of us is free to determine what that effect is. Context determines how content affects us.

15

Knowing that context determines how content affects you is very important. Knowing that the circumstances in your life (the content) effect you only as a function of the context in which you perceive them can set you on the path to freedom, happiness and power. This is because your freedom, happiness and power are internal resources that become independent of your external circumstances, once you know how to consciously shift contexts. All of us probably know people who are rich but helpless, who are married but unhappy, who are talented but frustrated and who are beautiful but lonely; demonstrating that external circumstances do not in every case affect our internal reality. In fact it works the other way. The powerful gift of this knowledge is that it frees you to CHOOSE the contexts for the circumstances in your life, thereby freeing you from destructive patterns of behavior and thought.

Everyone changes contexts all the time, although sometimes accidentally and sometimes unconsciously. Mood changes result from unconscious shifts in context about the circumstances in our lives. The ability to shift contexts about your emotions is essential to having a satisfying love life, because your love life, more than any other area, is an emotional experience. The person who bumps into you on the bus is a clumsy oaf until you turn around and notice that he is blind, or people often berate their parents for their shortcomings until they become parents themselves and find out that parenthood is not nearly so easy as they thought or a bitter argument can look like a hopeless problem until you discover a creative solution.

CONTENT VS. CONTEXT

It is very practical to know how to consciously change contexts in your love life when it is to your benefit. All of us come into a relationship with expectations and hopes of how it will be or how it should be. Clearly some of these expectations and hopes are reflections of our conscious desires and others are the unconscious result of rebellion or conformity in response to family upbringing. Even our fondest dreams about our love life could be called contexts that we have pre-selected. A couple comes together with individually, pre-selected contexts about how a relationship should be. These pre-selected contexts are about who we are as a lover, how our lover should be, how we treat each other, how to best maintain the relationship, what is acceptable and not acceptable behavior in our mates and what a perfect relationship would be to us. Obviously the list is almost endless. People often jump to erroneous conclusions about their partner's behavior by judging their partner in accordance with their own pre-conceived contexts. Examples of this are: Since he didn't call me, it must mean he doesn't love me or since she wants time by herself, she must be is planning to leave me.

All conflicts are battles of context. This means that there is no right way for a person or a relationship to be. You have your preconceived contexts and your partner has theirs. It is a waste of time to discuss conflicts in terms of who is right. Knowing how to change contexts enables you to receive what your partner has to contribute, while at the same time maintaining your individuality. Disagreement represents a difference in contexts and does not necessarily mean betrayal or disloyalty. Maintaining your independence does not require emotional distance from your partner. Closeness does not require sameness of thinking. We will show you how to find out what matters to you and to your mate before you commit yourself. For example, a devil-may-care attitude about finances may be endearing in a lover you have chosen for a summer fling; but later as your spouse, may become a source of constant conflict.

CHAPTER 3 THE MIND AND THE BODY

Although it is obvious that our mind and our body are different, they are highly related to each other in important ways. In fact, it is impossible to affect one without affecting the other. At the risk of trying to explain romance, you could say that you love your partner because you associate him or her with pleasant sensations in your body and because that person lives up to a sufficient number of either your conscious or even your unconscious expectations. Thus, some people will stay with partners that abuse them if enough of their other standards are met or if abuse has become unconsciously expected from childhood experience.

In this book, we emphasize the relatedness of the mind and the body, rather than the differences. Every thought feels like something and you have certain thoughts about each body sensation. Sometimes you are more aware of what you are feeling than what you are thinking and sometimes it is the other way around. It is to everyone's benefit to develop the ability to shift the focus of their awareness back and forth from thoughts to feelings depending on the situation. If you are balancing your checkbook and feeling unsatisfied sexual desire, then your body sensations will serve as a distraction from what you are doing. Similarly, if you are making love and worrying about the state of your checkbook, then the thoughts in your mind are a distraction. Thinking about your first date brings about a certain pattern of energy in your body. Thinking about your mother causes a different pattern of energy and thinking about eating pizza brings up yet another sensation. We could go on and on about this, because we have thoughts and feelings about all of our thoughts and feelings.

As products of the post-Industrial 20th century, the educational system has subjected our minds to extensive training, emphasizing rationality and logic, and in most cases the training for our emotions has been under-emphasized. In most families and schools emotions are completely neglected and feelings are not OK. We are told to control or hide our emotions rather than to feel or talk about them or to let others know how we feel. Many of us have been taught to rely on our mind for logical answers to questions that have no logical answers.

Regarding your love life, your emotions are SENIOR to your intellect. What we mean is that your emotions have greater impact in motivating your behavior than logical thoughts. (Examples are being so in love that it is difficult to concentrate on what you are doing, acts of jealous rage, or the fear of rejection that prevents people from taking steps to get what they want.) A high quality education or a high IQ does not guarantee a happy and fulfilling love life, nor do good looks nor wealth. It is only necessary to look at the tabloid newspapers near the supermarket check out stand to know this.

Just as white light is a mixture of all of the colors, love is a mixture of all emotions and being in love requires the willingness to FEEL any of your emotions. If you hate feeling angry and it seems that your partner did something to cause the anger, then the tendency is to create emotional distance, until you either accept your anger or suppress it.

If it is not OK for you to feel angry, then it won't be OK for your partner to feel angry, for example. Conversely, if you can accept your anger, then you create an environment where it is OK for your partner to feel angry (or any other feelings).

Emotions matter a whole lot more in your love life than intellect. THIS IS GOOD NEWS. It means that anyone can start using the ideas we present immediately without extensive additional education. A satisfying love life is available to everyone; butchers, bakers and candlestick makers and anyone who is willing to claim responsibility for his feelings, even the most humbling and shameful ones. You can have a love life where you support and contribute to the success, well-being and happiness of your partner and enjoy the love, sexual intimacy and companionship of a lover who is your best friend. Your personal willingness or desire is the only pre-requisite. Not only is willingness the only pre-requisite; without it, there is little that this book or anyone else can do to help you.

4 DOING vs. FEELING
How our mind perceives time

Our mind perceives time in two different, yet related ways. These are linear time and momentary time. All accomplishment, activity and doing occur in our perceived context of linear time. The mental experience of linear time is referred to as Left Brain thinking. In the context of linear time, we perceive the past as real, that it actually happened the way we think it did and that the future will actually occur, and that there is a flow of time which constantly brings the present closer to the future and further from the past.

Feelings, emotions and all other kinesthetic sensations occur in momentary time. The mental experience of momentary time is referred to as Right Brain thinking. Nothing HAPPENS in momentary time. In momentary time all that exists is your experience of the current moment. Happiness, love, satisfaction, pleasure and all pain and suffering and our feelings and emotions exist only in the moment that we feel them. Although the future and the past may be contemplated in momentary time, our emotional or subjective experience of memories, dreams, goals and plans exists in momentary time. Commitment for example occurs in the current moment and is carried out through linear time. The momentary time experience is what matters, because how committed you were to your partner last month doesn't matter much now.

For many people, men especially, undue problems in your love life can be caused by inexperience and fear about dealing with the current moment and its emotional content. Much of this book relates to increasing your comfort with the inevitable emotional content of your love life and enhancing your ability to come into the present moment of being in love. All of us can probably benefit from some degree of greater comfort with our feelings, enabling us to become more of a human being and not quite so much of a human doing.

DIRECT ACTION WON'T RESOLVE YOUR FEELINGS

Direct action (which occurs in linear time) cannot be relied upon to change your emotions which exist in momentary time, except temporarily. In Modern society there is a wide variety of direct actions that people use to avoid pain and other unpleasant feelings. Clearly these are effective, but only temporary and often lead to a compulsive addiction, wherein the direct action becomes self-motivating. In other words our emotions exist in the moment whether we like them or not and in the current moment we have the power to choose different contexts about them. In some cases, it may seem to you that direct action is the only solution to a problem. Many problems do in fact require direct action to be solved, but not all. Staying home and reading this book and learning about how to have the lover you want is a good thing to do, but it is not enough, direct action is required as well.

If you have only negative contexts about taking actions to find the lover you want, then it is unlikely that you'll ever do it. By itself, direct action is not enough either. If you have looked high and low for the lover you want without success, then you will discover that examining and changing the pre-conceived contexts you have adopted about your love life will benefit you more than another futile evening at the singles bar or another one night stand.

The distinction between linear time and momentary time leads us to what may be obvious, but nevertheless essential conclusions about the relationship between happiness and direct action. Happiness is the result of acceptance of your situation in life, including the sensations in your body, because happiness is a momentary time context. This means that it is foolish to rely on struggling with direct action, which occurs in linear time, to increase your happiness, without acceptance of the sensations in your body. This statement challenges a great deal of common human behavior and conventional wisdom designed to increase happiness. We refer to relying on marriage, divorce, children, a new car, more money or a better job, moving to California, having more sex, doing more drugs, or any other change that occurs in linear time for example, will make you happy. It is fine to do these things (although we surely do not recommend drugs); however, none of these changes produce the internal changes on which happiness depends.

The good news is that it it not necessary to wait for anything to HAPPEN for you to feel good about your love life. Anyone can do this right now by choosing to give up the fight with the feelings present and accept them as they are. Additionally, accepting your feelings will increase the effectiveness of any subsequent direct action that may be required because you won't be expending energy to suppress the feelings, leaving more energy available for your conscious use. We are not talking about laughing your troubles away or pretending in any way. Instead we are talking about realizing that insisting that you SHOULD feel differently has never worked and realizing that the effect of any circumstance or condition of your love life depends solely on the context you give it.

5   SUPPRESSION

Regarding the mind and the body, we have identified two general types of contexts in which the mind holds content (thoughts or feelings or events) of any sort. We refer to these kinds of contexts as <u>suppressive contexts</u> and <u>integrative contexts</u>. Suppressive contexts are the result of making-wrong the sensations in your body and then suppressing them in order to experience relief. Making something wrong involves comparing some particular content, the sensations in your body for the purpose of this chapter, to how that content SHOULD be. Suppressive contexts are contexts in which you view yourself as a bystander or victim. They are based on the frame of reference that power or control resides in people or things that are outside you, and that you have little to say about your lot in life or power to improve it. The bottom line belief of co-dependency is that your feelings are subject solely to how other people feel.

Our dictionary has fifteen definitions for suppression including, to press under, repress, crush, subdue, put down, overpower, overwhelm, restrain, conceal and smother. We will refer to suppressive contexts as negative contexts or make-wrong contexts.

In suppressive contexts, the best that one can expect is temporary relief from the agony and suffering in your life. People who habitually hold their lives in suppressive contexts tend to believe strongly in the power of luck or fate or karma that they place in charge of how their life turns out. Suppression is therefore a choice or decision that will affect our future behavior.

An important characteristic of suppression is that it is FAR less selective than we think. It can become a habit, because your mind's conditioned **suppressive response to intense feelings produces a signal your body to shut down.** Thus, suppression of unpleasant feelings over time can lead to the suppression of all feeling, even pleasant ones.

THE MECHANICS OF SUPPRESSION

Suppression is caused by two desires that everyone's mind seems to have. These are the desire to be right and the desire to feel good. Whenever any particular content in your experience, (your partner's behavior, for example) fails to live up to imaginary standards that you have about how these things SHOULD be, you will then experience a corresponding unpleasant feeling in your body. (Because every thought FEELS like something, as we described above). The only way to be right and to feel good about a situation that you don't like is first to make the feeling wrong and, then suppress it, thereby removing it from your

THE BODY ARMOURS

awareness. Since you experience temporary relief from the discomfort, there is a tendency to believe that you were right and obviously did the right thing.

Once your mind has decided to make-wrong any sensation, and suppression has begun, it is maintained by the following behaviors although it is quite likely that you do not notice yourself doing these things:

1. YOUR MIND DISTRACTS YOU FROM IT AND CONTINUES TO DO SO.
2. THE BODY ARMORS AND STAYS THAT WAY.
3. THE BREATHING BECOMES AND REMAINS INHIBITED.
4. AN INTERNAL STRUGGLE IS CREATED AND MAINTAINED.

We will explain how each of these suppressive mechanisms work.

THE BREATHING BECOMES INHIBITED...

1. YOUR MIND DISTRACTS YOU FROM IT

If you are upset about your love life, you may throw yourself into your work or into caring for your children or drinking or cruising in bars in order to avoid feeling the upset. If you are really working hard at suppressing the feelings about your love life, then your mind will probably create all kinds of very good reasons why it is essential that you devote your attention to your work or to your children, or turn into the neighborhood couch potato champion, in order to maintain the suppression.

Other times people simply dismiss the thoughts from their mind, refuse to talk about it or pretend that it doesn't matter.

2. THE BODY ARMORS AND STAYS THAT WAY

Stress is both the armor that shields you from your feelings and the experience of the struggle to keep them suppressed. Any stressful event can be perceived as a delightful challenge if you are willing to embrace the feelings associated with it. When you suppress something, your body expends effort to keep the sensation suppressed, although it is likely that you are unaware of this happening. Common effects of body armor are jumpiness at any sudden sound or movement, a tight jaw, or a chin-down, hunched shoulders posture. Common effects of body armor are jumpiness at any sudden sound or movement, a tight jaw, a chin down, hunched shoulders posture, digestion and elimination problems, lack of body awareness that results in spaciness and splitting off from reality. The more our body armors, the less flexible it becomes and even the gentlest touch can make us aware of the pain that is there.

3. THE BREATHING BECOMES INHIBITED

Full and uninhibited breathing makes us aware of the sensations in our body in a way that nothing else can. When we suppress, we inhibit our breathing in an unconscious response to greater intensity of sensation than we want, whether the sensations are pleasurable or uncomfortable. Examples of this are closing the throat and sobbing when there is intense sadness, counting to ten when there is intense rage, gasping when there is intense fear, holding your breath to concentrate better, or holding your breath during sex, especially to unconsciously reduce the intensity of orgasm. By breathing less, we feel less. It's very habitual.

4. AN INTERNAL CONFLICT IS CREATED

Suppression creates a direct conflict in your mind and body. This conflict is the struggle not to feel what you are already feeling. The desire for suppression causes unhappy people to struggle with their problems while at the same time refusing to do anything about them. Clearly, a certain amount of delusion is essential to convince oneself that you are feeling something different from what you are.

Suppression is just one method of coping with your feelings. For many people it is the only method that they learned from parental messages, such as:

Don't be a cry baby!

Don't talk back to me!

The subject is closed and I don't want to hear another word about it!

Stop it! Be quiet! Get down!

You'll get a spanking if you don't stop that!

You ought to be ashamed of yourself!

Go to your room if your going to act like that!

Act like a lady! Be a big boy!

Don't be a scaredy cat!

etc., etc., etc.

Suppression is a response learned from these messages or from any other messages that your parents gave you for the purpose of letting THEM avoid THEIR discomfort. Abuse can be defined as behavior that adults use to control children so that the adults feel better. The abuse usually continues until the child gives up and suppresses his feelings. In this way, suppression is caused by abuse. Suppression is associated with invalidation of what you are feeling. We learned to suppress to gain approval or to manipulate and control those who care for us. We learned to suppress in order to survive.

MULTI-GENERATIONAL LEGACY OF SUPPRESSION AND ABUSE

In most cases, suppression is something we first learned how to do from our parents and which continued in school, as the only way of dealing with our feelings that others didn't like. The parent abuses the child to force him to suppress feelings that are not OK with the parent. The parent does this because he was abused by his parents until he suppressed those same feelings. Regardless of your opinion of your parents, you can see how a family tradition of abuse and suppression is passed from one generation to another. Another way to say this is that parents teach their children to be "good little co-dependents" simply because that is all they know. You may experience a great deal of denial about the abuse in your family of origin, simply because they were the only family you knew, so they seemed normal.

It is essential to point out that only blaming your parents for your problems is a waste of time. Sure it's their fault; but it's your responsibility to work on yourself. It is more than likely that many of our problems are in fact caused by our parents; however, it is fruitless to expect someone else to fix our problems. It is essential that you allow yourself honest awareness of the feelings that you suppressed as a child and resolve them. We suggest that you let yourself feel as enraged and upset as you need to, for as long as you need to, until these feelings are resolved. This is especially important if your parents would disapprove of this. We are all dependent and helpless children to the extent we haven't done this.

Parenthood is the most difficult job in the world for which there has been the least amount of practical training available. Your parents probably did the best job they could; nevertheless you are left to resolve the emotional wreckage of their ignorance.

Without any information about your family of origin, we can say with certainty that there are feelings that you suppressed during childhood which you are still suppressing. We know of no one who did not endure emotional abuse at least. Emotional abuse occurs in families where feelings are given little importance, dismissed, discounted or never discussed.

Emotional resolution will result in better parents for future generations. Whatever you learned from your parents is far less important than how you feel about it now. It is greatly to your benefit to learn other methods of coping with your feelings.

Suppression produces the following results:
1. Usually provides temporary relief.
2. Sometimes allows you to rise to the occasion in an emergency.
3. May give you a chance to reflect on your feelings
4. The struggle to maintain the suppression results in inhibited breathing with attendant deterioration of health.
5. Your body must stay rigid (painful, too) to maintain the suppression.
6. You may avoid essential discussions of topics which may activate the suppressed feelings.
7. The internal conflict that results from the denial of your feelings may keep you confused about what you are feeling.
8. Suppression may motivate you to engage in unwanted addictive behavior that maintains the suppression by medicating the associated feelings.

POSSIBLE RESULTS OF SUPPRESSION IN YOUR LOVE LIFE

1. Unwanted emotional distance from your partner.
2. Difficulty in being honest with yourself and your partner. (Being more honest with your friends or therapist than with your partner.)

3. Reduced enjoyment of and desire for physical closeness and sex, because of the tendency of your mind to distract you.
4. A tendency to give up on the relationship and find someone else rather than deal with your problems.
5. Being controlled by or dependent on your partner.
6. Difficulty in making the adjustment from your work life to your home life.
7. The tendency to give up on your problems and arguments rather than feel the uncomfortable feelings.
8. Compulsively putting other people's needs and desires ahead of your own rather than taking responsibility for what you want.
9. Rationalization that you are avoiding discussion of difficult topics to protect your partner from feeling his or her discomfort.
10. Tendency to blame your partner as the source of the feelings that you don't like.

Suppressive Contexts can be recognized as being associated with:
1. Undue seriousness and gravity
2. Survival at stake
3. Being right
4. Avoidance of your problems or blaming others.
5. Defensiveness or criticism

CHAPTER 6

HOW SUPPRESSION CAUSES ADDICTION

Whether the context that you choose for any body sensation is one of suppression or acceptance determines your future action. Once you suppress any sensation in your body, your mind and body both must continue to work to keep it suppressed. Additionally, you will consciously as well as unconsciously tend to avoid situations that may remind you of what is suppressed. Since the intellectual awareness of the feeling is suppressed into the unconscious part of your mind, suppression is similar to freezing the action in a movie. Once you suppress something, the action stops until the feeling is resolved (sometimes decades later). This analogy explains the dramatic changes in behavior that occur in us when we resolve long suppressed feelings. The action in the movie picks up where it left off. For example, divorced people who begin dating after a long marriage feel teenage awkwardness and people who resolve a suppressed make-wrong about disappointing their parents as children give up the compulsive struggle to please others.

Continual suppression requires effort and leads to a wide variety of compulsive behaviors and addictions that maintain the suppression. At first, compulsive behavior and addictions are methods that we chose in order to suppress certain feelings and cope with the discomfort by medicating our feelings. Repetition of the behavior renders it self-motivating and without choice. Compulsive behavior and addictions, as devastating as some can be, are nevertheless <u>symptoms</u> of the suppressed emotions. Anyone who has tried to change a bad habit (either successfully or not) has experienced the feelings suppressed by the habit. Success with breaking destructive habits is more about our willingness and ability to deal with the related feelings than willpower.

FIVE CHARACTERISTICS OF COMPULSIONS AND ADDICTIONS

For anything to be compulsive or addictive it must have one or more of the following characteristics. The more of these characteristics it has then the greater likelihood that it may be compulsive or addictive.

1. **Euphoric, mood altering or distracting**
2. **Fast**
3. **Available**
4. **Conflicting or unclear social guidelines**
5. **Produces changes in tolerance**

These characteristics account for compulsive behavior and addictions related to:

1. **Thoughts**
2. **Activities**
3. **Substances**
4. **People**
5. **Feelings**

To name some examples:

1. **Thoughts**

Obsessive worry or fantasies are compulsive behaviors that involve thoughts, they distract us from what is really happening to what might happen. Worry is clearly available to everyone and within undefined limits, worrying can be a sign that you care.

2. **Activities**

Compulsive TV watching or overwork are compulsive behaviors related to activities, which are definitely distracting, fast, and available for most people.

38

3. Substances

Alcoholism, drug and tobacco addictions and eating disorders are addictions related to some substance that possesses all five of the above characteristics.

4. People

Co-dependency is a compulsion where your well-being depends primarily on someone else (forming the basis for all decisions); all of us suffered from this as children in relation to our parents, and some people transfer their dependency on to someone else when they grow up.

5. Feelings

Compulsive sexual behavior or fantasy relates to being addicted to the feelings associated with sex to avoid feelings of loneliness or isolation. People who rage out of control often do so to avoid feelings of shame. People with phobias are often convinced that their fear is required for their protection and thus focus all of their fear on to one object or event.

In the next chapter we will teach you about the benefits of accepting your feelings exactly as they are. This is a substantial improvement over denial or suppression.

7 ACTIVATION: YOUR PATH FROM DENIAL TO FREEDOM

Activation refers to any emotional state where formerly suppressed feelings have come out of suppression and to our attention and we are still making them wrong. Activation feels weird. The weirdness is what motivated you to suppress the feeling in the first place. Feelings, sensations or emotions come out of suppression into our conscious awareness. At the same time we experience discomfort caused by the negative context in which they had been originally perceived. The feeling in your body is the content of your current experience and the context is your attitude about it. When you are activated, your mind most often will let you know the make-wrong label or context that it is applying and at the same time you have an unpleasant body sensation. Your mind may refer to your condition as depressed, upset, bored, frustrated, anxious, confused, nuts, tense, agitated or one of many other labels.

ACTIVATION IS AN ESSENTIAL STEP IN RESOLUTION OF SUPPRESSED FEELINGS

Other ways to say this are: "Nothing changes until it is made real" or "If you are feeling it, you can be healing it." It is essential to remember that there is really no such thing as a negative feeling, only negative contexts. Our feelings are the CONTENT of our emotional awareness. The cause of feeling bad are the CONTEXT in which we perceive the feelings. Most of us grew up in a family and in a society where feelings are not OK and thus developed a habit of suppressing them. Emotional recovery begins with the acceptance of our feelings, no matter how deeply suppressed. For this reason, we emphasize in this book teaching you how to activate and actually resolve suppressed feelings.

Different people are comfortable with different degrees and different kinds of activation. In some instances the people who feel OK crying in the presence of their lover, would never let their lover know they were angry. Some people are comfortable allowing themselves to feel their most intense emotions about their favorite sports team, but not about their family. Activation only feels uncomfortable to the extent that you fight it, to the extent that you make your feelings wrong (insist on holding them in a negative context); the discomfort is really not about the feelings themselves, rather it is caused by the struggle to return the feelings to suppression.

People spend varying amounts of energy avoiding activation because of parental and society conditioning to look good, to avoid feeling confused, overwhelmed or out of control. Emotions don't necessarily make sense, so activation can be confusing. Others avoid activation because they think that certain so called negative emotions reflect badly on their character, their upbringing or their spiritual growth. Some people fear the loss of their power position or fear that they might hurt others. You can expect that allowing yourself to experience the emotions that you have suppressed will to some degree shatter long held self-delusions, as well as violate some sacred family rules.

When feelings are activated and begin to come out of suppression, your mind will naturally want to figure out why you are feeling like this in order to supply a reason or a justification. This necessity to justify our feelings is the result of family conditioning which shamed us for having them in the first place. In fact, all of your feelings are valid, whether or not you can find a valid reason for them. At first, the feelings may be there for no apparent reason, but you can be sure that they are related to some unremembered upset in your personal history. Everything is recorded. It is more than likely that you won't remember the event at first, but demanding to know the related event or cause of your feelings, instead of just feeling them, can often result in their re-suppression. Letting yourself feel activated will bring suppressed memories to your mental awareness. Your feelings can provide you with total access to your past and the memories of events which may be very surprising.

There is not necessarily a one to one correspondence between specific feelings and specific events. Let's assume, for example, you were beaten as a child. Seeing your neighbor beat his child may make you feel angry and it is likely that the anger is the same anger you suppressed when you were beaten and this may be obvious to you. However, the fear you experience from loud voices may be related to the same beating experience, but this connection could be far less evident to you. Our point is that is not necessary and may even be undesirable to immediately try to connect your feelings with reasons or with events. That you have feelings without reasons may cause you to think you are crazy. This does not mean you're crazy; it just means you are human.

Activation occurs because your mind and body contain built in natural urges for emotional resolution or for peace of mind. Anything that bothers you tends to keep coming back to your attention as a reminder that it is not resolved. This means that whenever you are activated your mind and your body have offered you an opportunity for improvement. Activation of emotions that you had previously suppressed is almost always associated with:

1. **Embarrassment or shame**
2. **Surprise**
3. **Insight**
4. **Permanent Relief**
5. **Reduction of internal conflict**
6. **Being out of control temporarily**
7. **Strong body sensations**
8. **Threat to your self-delusion**
9. **Suppressed memories**
10. **Discovery about yourself.**

Some of the items on the preceding list are considered to be ruinous and to be avoided at all costs, despite the problems caused by suppression. One could argue that if you lack skill to shift contexts and accept activated emotions, then it would be a good idea to avoid activation and continue to suppress your unpleasant feelings. Therefore, the next few chapters will teach you the skills required for emotional resolution. Once you have learned how to resolve the discomfort of your emotions, you will perceive activation differently. You will learn to welcome your emotional activation, not take it so seriously and reap its rewards.

REWARDS OF ALLOWING YOURSELF TO BE EMOTIONALLY ACTIVATED

1. **You can eliminate the disadvantages of suppression**
2. **You can be more honest**
3. **You can have increased energy**
4. **You can reduce denial**
5. **You can become more open-minded to yourself and others**
6. **You can have increased intimacy**
7. **You can have more patience and compassion for others**
8. **You can eliminate compulsive behaviors**
9. **You can have increased self-knowledge**
10. **You can enjoy feeling your feelings in an honest way**

If your love life is any good, it is an emotionally activating experience. If it is not, it is likely that you are suppressing your feelings and putting on an act for your lover (or for yourself). Sex makes you aware of the sensations in your body. Sex without emotional activation is mechanical. Non-sexual relationships where there is strong caring between people are emotionally activating also, as in your family. Caring relationships offer us our greatest opportunity to improve ourselves, because of the intense emotions, the honesty required to maintain them and the opportunity to support each other.

8 INTEGRATION: EMOTIONAL RESOLUTION

Without a method to resolve the emotions that are bound to be activated by your love life, the only alternatives you have are acting out the emotions or suppressing them. Clearly, neither of these alternatives has the remotest possibility of producing the enduring harmony and co-operation that we want in our love life. Integrating your emotions does not necessarily change them. Instead what you change is their MEANING to you; or said another way, the context in which you hold them. By changing how you relate to your emotions, integration changes the way that your emotions affect you, and the way that you react to them. This frees you from previously compulsive behavior that you had used to avoid feeling them. Integration or emotional resolution is an alternative for dealing with our feelings that anyone can learn, and it's time we did.

Integration means making whole by the addition of parts and offers a new way to deal with emotions that previously had been interruptions to your well-being and which you had struggled to deny. Integration empowers you to accomplish whatever you want to do, because you will no longer be wasting energy or engaging in suppressive behavior for the purpose of keeping certain emotions suppressed from your awareness. Even the emotions which you believe to be the worst; shame, guilt, rage or helplessness prove absolutely nothing about you, except that you are human. All humans have these emotions sometimes; that is not the issue. The issue is whether the constant suppression of the emotions controls your well-being and accomplishment.

Integration involves shifting contexts about a previously suppressed and now activated body sensation to an integrative context. (The sensation is one that had been held in a make-wrong or suppressive context.) An integrative context is any context where one is willing to be accept responsibility for the feelings that exist in the current moment. Integrating one's feelings does not necessarily mean that the content of your feelings changes (although sometimes they might). Instead it means that your perception or context about them changes.

FEELING GOOD WITHOUT DENIAL

Emotional integration will not turn you into a zombie or a robot. You'll still feel angry, sad and scared sometimes, (in fact, it's likely that you'll notice more feelings). The difference is that instead of struggling to avoid your feelings or to rationalize them, you'll accept them as they are. Integration is the result of being willing to shift the content of one's experience to a positive context, without denying the uncomfortable feelings, so that you relate to them in a way that no longer causes your avoidance of the discomfort to prevent you from taking the action you want.

Emotional resolution is different from positive thinking because an essential factor in integration is the willingness to acknowledge the make-wrong that has occurred and its attendant uncomfortable feelings, rather than simply glossing this over with some happy thought. Positive thinking is a good beginning for your self-development, yet it often fails to result in emotional resolution and stability. All of us know people who, whenever asked, claim they feel fine, but their tone of voice, body language and actions do not reflect this; or people who compulsively laugh at their own tragedy.

Emotional resolution can be recognized by its association with:
1. Humor and lightness

2. **Delighting in challenge**
3. **Joy and acceptance**
4. **Compassion for your problems and those of others.**
5. **Freedom and power**
6. **End of denial**
7. **Sense of humility**
8. **Increased recall of past memories**
9. **Serenity**

Vivation™ is the skill of emotional resolution at the feeling level. It offers an alternative to destructive suppression or uncontrollable outbursts of expression for coping with your feelings on a moment-to-moment basis, as you are feeling them. Vivation is infinitely portable and can be done anywhere, anytime, while you are simultaneously engaged in any other activity. The origin of the feelings that are activated is immaterial to integrating them with the Vivation process. That is, it doesn't matter if your feelings are the result of the impossibly long line at the bank today or whether they are the result of something that happened decades ago in your childhood. Additionally, it doesn't matter whether you can identify the cause of the feelings that are activated.

The precise definition of emotional resolution or "integration", which is the result of the Vivation process is when we allow emotional content to move from hiding in the unconscious mind to the conscious mind, and the content is experienced as sensations in the body (called activation) and at the same time, shifting the context from a make-wrong or negative context to an integrative context or a context of acceptance. The shift in how your body feels is instantaneous, obvious and significant and provides you with a permanently different outlook that is stable and peaceful, about what had been bothering you.

Integration almost always involves a sense of discovering something about yourself that you have kept hidden. Instead of withdrawing, pushing away or suppressing your awareness of the sensations that you have made-wrong, you actually feel and accept these sensations just as they are. Acceptance of your emotional reality eliminates the power of your feelings to govern your behavior or act as a source of upset. Integration is not trying to change what you feel, (the CONTENT of the sensations), instead

---

Vivation™ is a service mark and publishing trademark of Jim Leonard, Jeanne Miller, Phil Laut and Anne Leonard, doing business as Associated Vivation Professionals. Only licensed members of AVP may use Vivation in their advertising.

it is changing the way you interpret the sensations or changing what the sensations MEAN to you or about you (the CONTEXT of the sensations). Integration produces emotional recovery.

INTEGRATION IN ACTION

For example, if you feel guilty about how you have treated a former spouse, and you make yourself wrong about feeling guilty, then it will be very difficult for you to talk to them, apologize or enjoy a friendly relationship with them. Nor will you be able to learn from the mistakes that you made in that marriage and use the lessons to your benefit in a future or current marriage. This is because contemplating the former marriage brings to your awareness the made-wrong sensations and therefore makes you feel uncomfortable, inducing you to think about ANYTHING else. Once you integrate the guilt, it means that the guilt is OK with you. It is possible that you will feel guilty about it forever, but once the guilt is OK, it no longer governs your behavior and you can take whatever action you most consciously desire.

For another example, if you feel shy in social situations or with members of the opposite sex, and if you make your shyness wrong, you will tend to behave awkwardly and avoid social situations to avoid feeling shy. Once the feelings of shyness are integrated, as a natural human response, then it is far easier to behave the way you want to in social situations. You'll probably always feel a little shy, but this does not have to ruin your social life.

THE END OF SUPPRESSION

Integration results in the elimination of the self-destructive, make-wrong component of the emotions so that they no longer limit your freedom and happiness. This is recovery. Integration results in the elimination of the stressful effects of suppression on the body so that you can feel the pleasure in your body again and so that it becomes less painful to the touch and less rigid. Integration results in the increased natural habit of breathing more fully, rather than inhibiting one's breath and results in resolution of the mental conflict. Formerly upsetting emotions, situations, consequences and past traumas; instead of being verdicts about you, which you think you are powerless to change, can simply become expressions of your individuality and growth.

MAKING INTEGRATION RELIABLE

The Vivation process is not necessary for integration. Integration may occur in a hit-or-miss fashion, because of your mind's natural tendency to seek the stability of a resolved emotional state. (Your natural desire to feel good.) However, the Vivation process allows you to cause integration quickly and deliberately, instead of relying on hope. In Chapter 27, we describe the Five Elements of Vivation, which are the exact How To of causing integration. The Five Elements work together to allow the suppressed sensations from all parts of your life to come back to your awareness, so you can put them to rest once and for all in one easy to use process.

Telling the truth about your feelings and desires is a valuable method of integration, too, and one we have all known. Everyone has had the experience of "getting something off their chest" and feeling better. This means that you already know what integration feels like. Knowing that you can resolve your feelings eliminates the hopeless sense of permanence about them and makes it safer to feel them. In much of the rest of this book, we will be showing you how to do it in a far more reliable way that ever before. Integration is a skill; you'll improve with practice.

It's a little like starting an exercise program. For the first day or two, your muscles feel stiff from the unaccustomed work, but quickly, how good your body feels spurs you on to continue. Since you FEEL the integration in your body, there is no doubt about its power.

USING THIS BOOK FOR EMOTIONAL INTEGRATION

The next section, entitled Taking Action By Yourself, offers applications of the Theories and Methods to many of the problems that occur in human relationships. There are frequent Recovery Processes that you can do to learn about yourself and recover the power that you have been wasting in order to suppress your feelings. These can be done alone, in writing or in conversation with your partner, therapist or friend. It is likely that uncomfortable feelings will become activated by the material in the processes. The processes have been designed to activate suppressed feelings. The resolution of the feelings matters more than figuring out their causes and more than the actual answers to any of the questions.

Let your breathing be circular by connecting the inhale with the exhale, relax your body so you can feel it more, focus your awareness directly on the most prominent sensations, cease any struggle to change what you are feeling and let it be that way. Above all cultivate your willingness to resolve your feelings. Intellectual insights and memories about your personal history are sure to occur, in conjunction with the emotional resolution.

The exercises are not school assignements. There are no right answers and no one will grade you. We know that the methods in this book will work for you because we use them ourselves and because they work for the thousands of people we have taught in our seminars. The Recovery Processes are tools and just like any tool, they will work for you if you use them.

Remember if you always do what you have always done; then you'll always get what you've always gotten. Be bold. There is little to lose.

PART II TAKING ACTION BY YOURSELF

9 UNDERSTANDING YOUR EMOTIONS

It is not necessary to know what you are feeling, why you are feeling or even what your feelings are about in order to integrate them. Integration will even work for you if you know what you are feeling and are wrong about it. In other words, the names that we apply to emotions are nothing more than labels. Nevertheless, a better understanding of your emotions may eliminate some of the mystery about them and enable you to develop willingness to feel them more honestly. In this chapter, we will provide you with detailed information about specific emotions gained from our experience in teaching seminars and in using the Vivation process. It is possible that some of the statements that we make do not apply to you. Since the topic here is emotions, the emotions that are activated by reading this chapter are far more important then the information presented. (Incidentally, this is true of the entire book). Please notice how your body <u>feels</u> as you read and what you think that means about you.

By "understanding your emotions", we mean knowing <u>what they are about</u>, we do not mean knowing why you are feeling them. Sometimes we think we know why we have certain emotions (and sometimes our explanation is accurate); other times our emotions defy explanation. The same event can trigger different emotions in different people and that a similar occurrence can trigger different emotions in the same person at different times. Our mind naturally wants to know why we are feeling what we are and it just as naturally evaluates and compares our perception of how we are feeling to pre-established models about how we SHOULD feel. If our mind concludes that what we are feeling is outside preconceived standards of how it should be, then it goes to work to design a plan of action that will return us to feeling "normal", or at least better. Most peoples' minds are a lot less than 100% successful at this.

HOW, WHAT AND WHY?

It is impractical, perhaps even foolish, to expect that your emotions be reasonable or meaningful. Your emotions do not necessarily MEAN anything about you and they do not mean NOTHING about you. Your emotions are

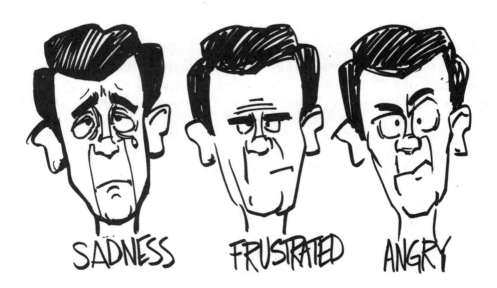

not in the realm of meaning. They are just the way they are. Because you feel angry sometimes does not mean you are an angry person and because you feel helpless does not mean that you ARE helpless. Realizing that your emotions don't necessarily MEAN anything about you will reduce the desire to justify them. All of your emotions are valid. This means you do not need a reason to feel angry or scared or anything else. The search for justification tends to place the blame on outside circumstances. Another way to say this is: your emotions are not final verdicts about you. Emotions are more like internal weather. They arise uninvited, change from moment to moment without rhyme or reason (despite our efforts to figure them out), and leave without saying good by.

Insisting that we know why we are feeling any emotion is one way that our mind suppresses our emotions, thus preventing us from experiencing them fully. In other words, using our rational mind to figure out our irrational emotions is about as practical as using a hammer to scrub your dishes.

In a similar vein, expressing or writing or reading about emotions is not the same as feeling them. Nothing in this book can replace your willingness to resolve the emotions that are uncomfortable for you.

Each of us experiences a cornucopia of emotions every day. Some we like and others we fight against and struggle to make different, justify or hide from others. Whether what you are feeling is OK with you (the context of what you are feeling) is FAR more important than WHAT you are feeling (the content).

The emotions that you have suppressed the most are the ones that will tend to be the most uncomfortable for you and the ones that you will have the most resistance about feeling and acknowledging. Often we hear from people that we work with statements like, "When I realized that I was angry at my wife, I became afraid that anger is all I had for her", or "When I finally began feeling all of the pent up sadness that I had pushed away for years, I was afraid that I would never stop crying." There is a tendency to fear that any long suppressed, intense emotion may become a permanent condition when it first comes to your awareness. We

HELPLESSNESS   RAGE   SHYNESS

have mentioned before that although activation of feelings suppressed in the past may hurt, they will not hurt YOU. In fact it is your struggle to keep them suppressed that puts limitations on your freedom and happiness.

Our language does not make it OK to have feelings. In English we say, "I am depressed" or "I am angry" as if to imply that depressed or angry were a complete description of us at that time. If you are a good cook, it is likely that you are a good cook even while depressed, although you may be unlikely to remember this at the time. In Romance languages, the method of describing emotions is more accurate than in English. In French, Spanish and other Romance languages, they say "I HAVE anger" or "I HAVE fear" or "I feel sad". English speakers tend to take their emotions more seriously.

WHO IS RESPONSIBLE FOR YOUR EMOTIONS?

If you are unwilling to accept responsibility for your emotions, you will be a helpless victim in your love life. You will tend to blame your lover

GRIEF   WORRY   DEPRESSION

59

for how you feel and try to change your lover so that you can feel better. The emotions that we will describe here are the CONTENT of your body when you are feeling them. Although we will discuss emotions that are almost universally made-wrong, it is not the emotions that are negative, it is the CONTEXT in which they are perceived that is negative and therefore suppressive. You have a choice about what your emotions MEAN to you, what they MEAN about you or what they MEAN about someone else.

Sometimes it seems that our thoughts create our emotions and sometimes it seems the other way around. For example, if you think about political oppression, child abuse, the high divorce rate or government corruption long enough, you'll begin to feel your emotions about it. For example, "The divorce rate makes me sick."

We have thoughts ABOUT our emotions, as well as emotions about our emotions: we can worry about our anger or feel envy of more out-going people. There are other times when the intensity of the emotion blocks out our thoughts and even other times when our mind is so engaged that

the emotions tend to fade into the background. It is greatly to your benefit to have the ability to focus your awareness on the thoughts in your mind, (when you are balancing your checkbook or reading a map, for example) and it is greatly to your benefit to have the ability to focus your awareness on the sensations in your body, (when you are making love or playing tennis, for example).

A WHOLE NEW PERCEPTION

Our thoughts and emotions are really the same thing PERCEIVED differently. If you sit in your kitchen while your partner prepares dinner, you can tell what is happening because you SEE him or her at the stove adding ingredients to pots and pans, you hear the noises of the sizzling food and you smell the aromas as they change and mix with each other. If you were to close your eyes, or block your ears or hold your nose, one at a time, you would still know that dinner was cooking, from the information that you were receiving from the senses that remained unblocked.

Our mind and our feelings are similar to this in that they bring us the same information that is PERCEIVED differently. How different emotions are associated with specific thoughts will be explained in the next section. Our purpose here is to provide you with a degree of understanding about your mind and a degree of acceptance about your emotions. There is an inherent sense of honesty and freedom about letting yourself feel exactly what you are feeling.

I'M OK, BUT ARE YOU?

Your love life is essentially about your emotions and the corresponding feelings in your body. Every day there is "new material" to deal with. One minute you can be wildly in love and happy and the next moment there is intense discomfort. If all of your emotions are OK with you then there is nothing that you will be unable to handle. However, if it is not OK with you or you don't like feeling jealous, for example, and then your lover does something to activate your jealousy, it will be very difficult for you to talk about your feelings or settle the argument. It's not really accurate to say "you made me jealous". People do whatever they do and it is up to you whether how you respond to their behavior and how long you allow it to upset you. Do you want to be right or be in love? Do you want to make your partner feel guilty or do you want to forgive them? Do blame your partner and shame them or accept their apology? Do you tolerate abuse or do you state your rights?

When upsets occur in romantic relationships the ability to integrate quickly and completely is obviously to your benefit. That way you can spend more time being in love instead of handling the endless stream of upsets which contain the same emotions but perhaps different words. You will discover that, even using the techniques in this book, you may not integrate every feeling that becomes activated right on the spot. However, having the intention to resolve it will at least remind you that the upset is a temporary condition and knowing that it <u>could be</u> resolved will reduce your attachment to justifying what you are feeling. We have found great comfort in knowing how to handle anything that limits our love for each other.

EMOTIONS AND HOW TO USE ALL OF THEM FOR YOUR BENEFIT

You can benefit from all of your emotions in several ways. Whenever any unpleasant sensation is activated, you have an opportunity to integrate the emotion or suppress it. Additionally you will be less reactive to the emotions of others, increase your compassion for and service to others with the same problem, learn something about yourself, and eliminate the restrictions that suppression places on your freedom.

Sometimes we know what we are feeling and not what we are thinking and other times it is the other way around. For each of the emotions that we describe, there is a table that shows emotions with their corresponding thoughts. Emotions tend to be related to each other like families with siblings, cousins, nieces and nephews. The emotion itself is NOT what causes problems, making the emotion wrong and suppressing it is the cause of suffering.

A NEW LOOK AT SOME OLD FEELINGS

SADNESS

EMOTION and relatives	CORRESPONDING THOUGHT
Sadness, remorse grief, loneliness	Contemplation of some change that occurred in the past (usually interpreted as a loss) and making it wrong. Often you can hear your mind thinking, "IF ONLY" or "WHY ME?"

Often, we pretend not to enjoy sadness, however tear jerker movies, tragic books and songs that bemoan the misery of life and love have sold well for centuries, because they provide a context in which it is OK to feel sad. In other words, sad books, movies and songs provide us with an acceptable REASON to feel our sadness. People commonly cry "tears of joy" at weddings. These tears are about the change that has just occurred and are frequently accepted as OK.It is not necessary to have a reason to feel sad. Some are secure enough to allow themselves to cry without apparent reason. If you demand a good enough reason to let yourself cry, it is likely that the habit of suppressing your sadness has or will become so strong that you will never find a good enough reason to justify your tears.

People who habitually suppress their sadness often experience a sense of dissatisfaction because they are unwilling to take any risks that might result in a loss. If your crying upset your parents, it is likely that you were conditioned to believe crying is a sign of indulgent weakness, resulting in punishment, ridicule or isolation. If you are not accustomed to crying, you may be reluctant at first because it seems that once you start, there will be no end to the tears. In our seminars, we tell the participants to never pass up an opportunity to cry, especially if you are a man, and cry as long as you need to.

GRIEF

The feelings of grief and the process of grieving are natural and essential parts of recovering your true identity. Some losses in life are irreplaceable. There is nothing we can do to replace the loss of trust that most people experienced toward their parents. If you lose a lover, sure you may find another, but there won't be another just like that. If you compulsively take action to replace the loss, without grieving about it, then it is likely that you'll experience profound fear of loss related to the replacement, which will greatly limit your enjoyment of it. An example is, using "I won't get close to anyone else ever again," as a defense mechanism against the feelings of loss. Do not expect yourself to be completely rational about grief. It is fine if you feel more intense grief about the loss of a favorite pet, than you do abou the loss of a loved one. The feelings in your body matter more than the reasons.

LONELINESS

The experience of loneliness does not occur only when you are by yourself. It is possible to feel lonely in a crowd. Although it is impossible for anyone to take the place of someone you have lost, it is important to know how to reach out for help and support, instead of allowing your loneliness to isolate you. It's fine to feel lonely. Unless you can resolve your feelings of loneliness, you will always be dependent on the acceptance and the company of others. Loneliness does not mean no one loves you or that you are not good enough. Insisting on thinking that way can prevent you from enjoying the solitude of your alone time and can prevent you from taking any action to make acquaintances. Acceptance of feelings of loneliness identifies an effective leader.

When we are apart, we miss each other, notice the absence of the other and look forward to our reunion. However, since our well being does not depend on our being together, we enjoy our separations, which support our independence, and have much to share with each other upon return.

Sadness feels bad ONLY to extent that we make it wrong. Integrating your sadness, about the loss of a family member, for example, doesn't mean that you won't miss them anymore, nor does it mean that you are disloyal or don't love them anymore. Instead it means that you stop allowing the suppressed sadness to affect your life in undesirable ways. When you integrate sadness, you most often end up with gratitude. Our aphorism about this is:

SADNESS IS GRATITUDE IN DISGUISE

For example, if a lover leaves you, you are left with their memory, instead of their physical presence. If you make your sadness wrong, you will bemoan the loss of their physical presence, avoid talking about it, or perhaps even rush out to find a substitute, often unsuitable, to avoid feeling the loss. When you accept the sadness as an OK feeling then you experience the gratitude for having known the person and your memories about them. Sadness is a natural response to any change that occurred in the past.

Here is an exercise that will aid you in resolving suppressed feelings of sadness. Although we describe it as a writing exercise, it also works well verbally with a partner. First take two minutes and make a list of 5 or so events that you feel sad about. Now for each event, write a brief statement describing exactly what you lost. Then, write at least one benefit that you COULD now derive from having whatever is remaining of what you lost. It is a good idea to continue to come up with benefits you could derive until you notice the feelings change in your body. For example, if you were thin and now you are fat, you still have the memory of your thinness and you could use that to inspire yourself to lose weight; or if you hurt someone you love, you can use the memory of how your relationship used to be to motivate you to apologize and ask for forgiveness.

ANGER

EMOTION and its relatives	CORRESPONDING THOUGHTS
Anger, outrage, disgust, hope, resentment, boredom, disappointment, blame, depression Helplessness, struggle and ignorance. Cynicism and sarcasm.	Intention contaminated with helplessness. Contemplation of your current situation and making it wrong.
Frustration and irritation are mild versions.	
Helplessness	"I can't." (most often really means "I won't"

Ignorance	"I am not willing to know." (I don't know and I won't do anything to find out.
Struggle	"I'll try." (most often means "I will do what I can; but if my helplessness comes up, then I won't go any further.
Blame	"It's your fault." Feeling angry and at the same time projecting responsibility for your anger on to someone else while trying to use shame or guilt to manipulate them.

People who compulsively suppress their anger often experience a lack of accomplishment because the energy required for suppression is substantial enough to produce stress and fatigue as well as a lack of patience and persistence. You can get as sense of this yourself by recalling the most recent time you were angry. Anger has a lot of energy to it. At least as much energy is required to suppress anger.

Most of us were conditioned as children to believe that anger was not OK. If your parents were uncomfortable with their own anger, they probably didn't like yours any better. Most of us concluded that anger was not OK whether our parents were the only ones in the family that were allowed to be angry or whether no one was allowed to be angry. People that are afraid of other people's anger often put up with a great deal of deprivation and unhappiness, because they refuse to speak up, thinking it more important to keep the peace. This is the essence of co-dependency. These are compulsive "nice guys" and "nice girls". Often these people have the idea that anger leads to violence. Anger and violence are different. Anger is a feeling and violence is an action. If you are in the habit of denying your anger, pay attention to it. Anger may be a sign that something is wrong or that someone is crossing your boundaries and abusing you. There is nothing wrong with feeling angry and letting people know about it. If you claim responsibility for your angry feelings, with practice you can express yourself clearly and without being abusive, no matter how angry you are. You and your partner can serve each other greatly simply by listening to each other when you are upset. This, of course, is impossible if one person blames the other for his feelings and/or the blamed person actually thinks it is his fault that his partner is angry.

We believe that SUPPRESSED anger is what leads to violence or some other undesirable result. We have noticed that whenever the authorities apprehend the perpetrator of a violent rampage like the massacre at the fast food restaurant in San Diego or at the Post Office in Oklahoma, which occurred in the mid 1980's, the TV news then interviews friends and neighbors of the criminal, in an apparent effort to discover how anyone could do such a thing. If you have watched such interviews, you have probably observed that the common reaction by the friends and neighbors is one of surprise and disbelief. The people interviewed often state that it is hard to imagine how a "nice, quiet guy" could have done such a thing.

Since anger is so commonly suppressed, it follows that there are many compulsive behaviors about it. A more common and less extreme version than the massacre example is seen in the child that grows up bullying the other kids in the neighborhood or who becomes a tyrannical boss or parent in an attempt to unconsciously get even with his parents. Another common symptom of suppressed childhood anger is the person who is fearful of anger and who habitually avoids any person or situation where anger or disagreement is likely to be experienced.

Expression of anger is not the same thing as integrating anger. Often when someone is angry, he expresses it by pounding his fist on the table or smashing tennis balls or screaming and finding fault with his partner. What happens in this situation is that the feelings of anger become so uncomfortable that the person engages in some expressive behavior in order to change the feelings of anger to something else. In the example of pounding a fist on the table, the person pounds the table until the feeling of his fist striking the table becomes more prominent than the anger. In the example of the tennis match, the person plays ruthlessly, until the feelings of fatigue or triumph (or something else) become stronger than the original anger. In the example of yelling, the person yells, until the feelings of guilt about yelling become stronger than the anger that was there at first or until the people around him change to his satisfaction.

In therapeutic situations, yelling or pounding pillows can be useful methods for activating deeply suppressed anger. The effort is wasted, however, unless a method is offered for resolving the feelings that have been activated.

In many circles, anger is the least socially acceptable emotion. You could probably cry at work and a few of the people would be uncomfortable about it, but most would understand. You could probably state your fears about your ability to complete an important project. But if you start telling the truth about how angry you are, people may ask you to be quiet or leave the room, until you calm down. Anger has nothing to do with attack, unless you are irresponsible about it. Blame involves the idea that someone else causes you to feel angry and involves attack as a method of controlling the other person to stop the behavior that you think is causing you to feel angry. Anger is as valid a feeling as any other and is nothing to be ashamed of.

Most people SAY they do not enjoy feeling anger. Behavior indicates differently. The Evening News is the longest running show on TV. It focuses on the most terrible events of the day, about which most viewers intend to do nothing, despite watching it religiously, claiming that it is important to be well informed. Have you ever noticed that you when you tell a third party how angry you feel toward someone, you feel better? Some people call this getting support; others refer to it as moaning and complaining.

Anger feels bad ONLY to the extent that we make it wrong. When you accept anger as merely a strong feeling in your body, it most often feels like increased intention or determination. Our aphorism about this is:

ANGER IS DETERMINATION IN DISGUISE

If you make your anger wrong, then whenever you experience a setback or make a mistake, you'll experience the helplessness more profoundly than the intention and have the desire to give up. Anger always contains an intention. To the extent that you accept the anger, the intention becomes stronger.

If someone treats you badly, you may feel helpless to do anything about the particular incident; however you can change contexts and use it to strengthen your determination to receive better treatment in the future and to actually increase your ability to get what you want by asking for it. Any setback tends to activate our anger. If you are habitually unwilling to feel angry, then you won't want to undertake big tasks, you will give up at the first setback, be unable to stick to your decisions or unwilling to argue in your behalf. If you have ever failed at dieting (or any other important project), surely you know what we mean. We all love come-from-behind stories because they are about people who have resolved their anger and have used their determination to get what they want.

Compulsively suppressing your anger in your love life can lead to disastrous results. Some people run from one lover to the next because they are unwilling to participate in an argument, which would activate the anger that often goes with arguing. Others resort to cynicism or sarcasm as covert and ineffective expressions of their real anger. Others suppress their anger until it explodes in a temper tantrum where things are said that are later deeply regretted or use it to scare others into doing what they want. What follows may come to a shock to those who are hopelessly self-deluded romantics: It is unreasonable to expect that you can be in love without having upsets and having an upset does not necessarily mean that there is something wrong with your partner or your relationship. Inability or unwillingness to resolve upsets is the cause of problems; not the upsets themselves.

In the table about anger, we stated that hope, helplessness, depression, struggle, ignorance and boredom are related to anger. This assertion requires some explanation.

HOPE

When we say that hope is a relative of anger, we mean that RELYING on hope is a kind of anger. By this we mean that believing that the passage of time ALONE will ease or solve your problems. The passage of time alone will not mend a broken heart, the passage of time alone will not increase your income, it will not increase your enjoyment of sex, nor will it stop your partner from abusing you. It is fine to have hope, but if you think that hope alone will make things better, then it is likely that, in fact, you feel helpless to do anything to create the changes that you want.

An example of people who rely heavily on hope are those who play the state lottery, for whom winning the lottery represents their most carefully formulated plan to become a millionaire, as a result of their sense of helplessness about their ability to use more traditional, active and proven methods of accumulating wealth. A similar situation occurs in relationships when one partner hopes that the passage of time alone will, by some unexplained miracle, change their partner into the person that they want or will cause their partner to begin treating them the way they want to be treated.

HELPLESSNESS

When we say that helplessness is a form of anger, we mean that the person is upset about the current situation and therefore possesses some desire to have it different, but feels powerless to do so. For example, people who habitually seek permission to do what they want, people who suffer with the same problem for years and people who resign themselves to dissatisfaction with their love life surely feel helpless about it. The thought that is most related to the feeling of helplessness is "I can't". If you allow your mind to continue to take seriously your thoughts of "I can't", you have given up all of your power to make the situation different and all of your power to accept it the way that it is. It is fine to feel helpless. Anyone would feel suspicious of someone who claimed to never feel helpless. However, if you replace "I can't" with "I won't", then you have reclaimed your power and responsibility. At this point, you are free to make a new choice to either formulate an effective plan to change the situation or to resolve to accept it as it is and do nothing about it.

STRUGGLE

When we say that struggle is a relative of anger, we must first point out that struggle is non-productive behavior with the sole purpose to suppress helplessness. In other words, if you are DOING SOMETHING (even something that has not worked repeatedly in the past), then you can convince yourself that you are not helpless. People who struggle a lot tend to tell themselves, "I tried" as a rationalization for their failures. Struggle could also be described as the insanity that leads us to believe that doing the same thing over and over will somehow lead to better results. Even rats in a maze know to change their behavior to get the cheese.

IGNORANCE

When we say that ignorance is a relative of anger, we mean ignorance about yourself. If someone were to ask you the name of the 14th President of the United States, you may be ignorant of the answer, but you could find out at any time at the library. What we mean here by ignorance is chronically allowing your mind to get away with saying "I don't know" to questions that are only about you, such as "What do you think about the election?", "What are you feeling?", "Do you want to get married someday?" We offer a humorous and effective method to point out to your partner that he is stuck in ignorance. In response to "I don't know", simply say, "Is there someone else I should ask?"

BOREDOM

When we say that boredom is a relative of anger, we mean that boredom is most often a suppressive technique to avoid feeling angry. In other words, boredom is an experience of the effort required to suppress a feeling that is partially activated and the partially activated feeling is most often anger. You can discover this for yourself the next time you feel bored by breathing faster and fuller than normal for a few minutes, thereby putting you in touch with the anger that is just below the surface of your

awareness. When we feel bored, we have allowed our mind to convince us that there is nothing to do or that life itself is boring.

List five things that you are angry about. Then list the actions that you have taken in the past about each issue. Then for each issue, ask yourself, "Am I willing to do anything more about this?" It is likely that you'll begin to resolve your anger, whether your answers are yes or no. You'll feel better in cases where your answer is no, because by acknowledging your unwillingness to take action, you acknowledge the degree to which the situation is already acceptable to you. In cases where your answer is yes, the determination to take action will become more prominent than the helplessness that was there before. For the situations that you are determined to take action about, write down as precisely as possible the result that you desire. Now ask yourself what specific steps could you take RIGHT NOW to bring about your desired result and START There is a magic in taking the first step.

DEPRESSION

Chronic depression can also be the result of a chemical imbalance that is caused by poor nutrition and is easily remedied with the help of a nutritionist. If you know or suspect that your diet could be improved consider seeking help from a professional.

Most people have experienced at least some amount of depression. In some cases depression is such an overwhelming condition that people take anti-depressant drugs for relief. That is not to say that this approach is a bad idea. Our objective here is to give our ideas and possible solutions to depression.

Depression involves a sense of helplessness to do anything about it. The resulting inaction tends to maintain the behavior of turning rage inside against us, sapping your energy.

When we are depressed there seems to be a total absence for the joy of living, resulting in uncomfortable body sensations. It has been described to us as "it feels like you are not living", "When I'm depressed I feel half dead", "I give up", "Why bother?" It is evident from the descriptions that depression is related to thoughts or premonitions about death. There is a fear of life and a feeling of complete hopelessness to do anything about it. If you have ever talked to someone who is depressed there often is nothing more you can do than listen, because they have convinced themselves of their futility.

People do all sorts of things to suppress their depression. They might overeat, become alcoholics, take drugs, have more sex, or become the compulsive jokester who is always trying to cheer up themselves and other people. The problem with trying to cheer up when you feel depressed is that it is fruitless. Anyone who is depressed can give you such a long list of reasons why they are depressed, that you will either agree with them or get tired of listening. Trying to convince someone that their reasons are not important enough to warrant such depression, will often make them more depressed. They may conclude that not only are they depressed, but they have just been told that their feelings are not legitimate, which makes them feel even worse.

When someone is depressed they say "I am depressed" as though that is who and what they are, and they are completely helpless or that the situation is totally hopeless. For most people, depression is temporary no matter how often it arises. Remember that if you suffer from frequent depressions, notice that you are not completely depressed, that there are times when you are happy. Depressed people sometimes use their depression to control others, who compulsively struggle to cheer them up. Our feelings change from moment to moment. For example: have you ever experienced feeling depressed, and then received a phone call or letter from someone you care about and suddenly felt great? Or have you ever felt depressed and then you do something to help another person and afterwards you feel good about yourself? At this point is is difficult to remember why we had been so depressed. We all have experienced such situations which show that depression integrates just like any other upsetting emotion. What is most important is to take 100% responsibility for how you feel and for feeling better. Oftentimes serving those who are more depressed or who are suffering more than you are is a highly effective way to gain perspective on your own suffering.

When depression integrates and you allow yourself to feel the rage you have been stuffing inside, you become aware of the preciousness and intrinsic value of life. There is nothing more valuable than life itself. At the extreme, people who lose sight of this, commit suicide as a result of thinking that life is too much to deal with and they are better off dead than experiencing what they are experiencing now or asking for help.

Here is a simple process that will begin some movement out of depression. Don't worry, we're not going to cheer you up. Write down your thoughts for fifteen minutes, without censoring what you write in any way. Obviously, you can think much faster than you can write. This does not matter. The important thoughts will come round again.

Now read over what you have written. If you have been honest, you may feel just as depressed, but you'll take it less personally, concluding, "No wonder I feel depressed. Anyone with thoughts like that would feel depressed."

FEAR

EMOTION and relatives	CORRESPONDING THOUGHT
FEAR Anxiety, jealousy, panic, terror, worry, impatience and shyness.	Contemplation of some possible change in the future and making it wrong. Jealousy is fear of loss with survival attached. When you are afraid, you may hear your mind thinking, "I have to", "I need to", "I'd better" or "I ought to".

There is a distinction between rational fear and irrational fear. Although this distinction is far from precise, fear can be considered rational when the danger is objective and threatens one's health, safety or financial well being. Fear can be considered irrational when danger is subjective and threatens one's feelings. The rationality or irrationality of any particular fear has nothing to do with its validity. It is fine and valid to have fears;

our point is that is not necessary to have your life run by fears. Knowing about your fears and learning to deal with them is a step in that direction.

Fear is the result of our mind contemplating some undesirable change that may occur in the future and making that result wrong. Then our mind busily sets to work to find a rule or a plan that will prevent the change from happening. That's why thoughts associated with fear often start with phrases like "I have to", "I need to", "I'd better", "I've got to" or "I ought to".

Irrational fears are fears about things that are scary, but not dangerous. Examples are fears about speaking in public, selling, asking someone how they feel about you, asking someone for a date or asking someone to have sex with you. Resolution of these kinds of fears add to the excitement and success in your life, especially if the fears have, in the past, prevented you from doing what you wanted.

RATIONAL FEAR   IRRATIONAL FEAR

Rational fears involve objective danger. When you drive on the freeway, you experience your fear of an auto accident more acutely than when you are at home; when someone whom you are not sure you can trust makes important promises to you, you tend to experience your fear of betrayal more intensely. These fears exist for your benefit and protection and serve to make you more alert and careful.

In some instances, there is in fact danger, but we have suppressed our fear associated with it. An example is that having a Soviet intercontinental ballistic missile pointed at the back of your neck is clearly dangerous; however, for better or worse, most of us have learned to live with nuclear terror and go for extended periods without noticing it.

Just to be clear about it, we are not, saying that you shouldn't be afraid or that you shouldn't worry. There is plenty to fear and plenty to worry about. By resolving the fears that you have, you can actually use them to motivate you to take action that will prevent the undesirable events that you fear from occurring and ensure your safety.

People who habitually suppress their fear tend to live their lives with the emphasis on staying safe and avoiding risks and change in general. Their desire to avoid feeling fear prevents them for asking for what they want or taking action to get it. In extreme cases of suppressing fear, people are unwilling to acknowledge that they are afraid of anything. Clearly, only a fool would not fear danger.

Some people seek more and more money, power and control to try to protect themselves from fear. A famous quote tells us, "The man who has the most fear carries the biggest gun", as if to imply that if one sufficiently protects himself from external danger or can completely control his reality, then he won't be afraid.

Some religions even teach that their followers should fear God, as if God were a vengeful scorekeeper, severely judging your every move. This way of thinking is not much more enlightened than pagan practices of human sacrifices to appease the angry gods.

Often people talk as though they do not enjoy fear, though their behavior proves otherwise. If you visit any amusement park, you can observe crowds of people, some who have travelled thousands of miles, standing in long lines in the broiling sun, waiting to ride a huge roller coaster that goes 85 miles per hour and will turn them upside down 10 times. Horror films, too, are another example; they draw large audiences and earn millions of dollars year after year. This proves that fear is not necessarily something to be avoided. These are examples of situations where it is OK and enjoyable to feel afraid and serve to demonstrate that it is not fear itself that is uncomfortable; but rather it is the MAKE-WRONG of the fear that causes the discomfort. When you learn how to integrate your fear, then it will no longer prevent you from accomplishing what you want or communicating what you really want to say. When irrational fear is integrated, it feels like excitement, which most people already enjoy. Our aphorism for this is:

FEAR IS EXCITEMENT IN DISGUISE

Rational fear integrates into alertness, which is at least physiologically similar to excitement. For example, if you are afraid that your lover might leave you, you will tend to worry or act suspicious or demand that your lover account for his time or struggle to make improvements in yourself for the sole purpose of keeping your lover around. If at the same time, you make yourself wrong for having this fear, it is very likely that it is an unpleasant experience for your lover, too. When you stop making yourself wrong for this fear and allow it to integrate, then it will be easier for you to talk about it and get assurance if you need it. People with an overwhelming fear of change tend to remain in jobs and relationships long after there is any realistic possibility of the situation giving them what they want.

SHYNESS AND REJECTION

The basic idea about shyness is that we are all shy to some extent! The question is not whether you are shy, but whether you allow your shyness to rule your social life. You inability to speak up and take action is cuased by making yourself wrong for having fear of looking foolish, making a mistake, being rejected, not to mention the weird and intense feelings in your body. Shyness is clearly an example of irrational fear. Nothing bad will happen if you announce your desires, or even if the other person notices your nervousness. The statement, "I'm too shy" is an example of the misconception that feelings are unchangeable verdicts about a person. Fear of rejection is the overwhelmingly predominant reason that people do not ask for what they want. It hurts to get rejected and it also hurts to reject others, despite frequent attempts to laugh it off. However, speaking up and aksing for what you want and saying yes when you mean yes and no when you mean no are essential skills for functional relationships. In most countries of the world, freedom of speech is a right enjoyed by their citizens. This right is limited by laws regarding libel and slander, but generally you can say whatever you want to whomever you want.

JEALOUSY

Jealousy usually FEELS the way the name implies, lousy. One way to define jealousy is that it is seeing someone else get what you want, and concluding that their having it stands in your way. It could also be described as a fear of loss with survival attached. If you think that your life depends on another person, (if she leaves me, I'll die) the tendency is to engage in foolish and irrational behaviors to keep the other person around. This way of thinking is often based on conclusions made in infancy, when our life did in fact depend on someone else taking care of us. This thinking pattern may be re-inforced through sibling rivalry, and into adulthood compulsions of keeping up with the neighbors.

Some people seem to be compulsively driven to feel their jealousy by continuing to engage in triangle relationships. Others perceive the jealousy of their partners as sure signs that they are cared about. It is unlikely that jealousy will ever feel really good to you; however, you can resolve the discomfort sufficiently so that you can discuss it with your partner, rather than being immobilized, addicted or enraged by it.

WORRY

Children often come to the conclusion that parents express their love by worrying. If you made that conclusion as a child, it is likely that you did everything possible to cause your parents to worry about you, thereby assuring yourself of their love for you. Worry can be described as generalized and pervasive fear that something bad and undefined will occur unless you take the right action to prevent it. As a relative of fear, some worry is rational and some is irrational. You can use worry to your benefit by allowing it to remind you to make a plan or a better plan, so that you can have the result that you prefer, rather than the one that you are worrying about. It's fine to worry. Do so with as much humor as you can.

Here is a writing exercise that will aid in resolving fear. Write down at least five things that you want to do, but are afraid to. Then list all of the possible dangers for each of them. Look over your list of dangers and see if there are some that you could perceive as exciting. For the rest, see if there is something that you could do to minimize the risk or danger and still do what you want to do. Another way to do this is simply to list all of your fears about any specific action you are planning, for example: "My fears about marriage", "My fears about becoming wealthy", "My fears about divorce".

GUILT, SHAME AND MISTRUST

EMOTIONAL STATES
Guilt, shame,
and mistrust.

Guilt and shame	Generalized make wrong; fear of punishment; fear of failing to live up to unconscious standards
Guilt	"I did something wrong and will be punished."
Shame	"I am wrong" or "There is something wrong with me." thereby proving my worthlessness or blameworthiness.
Mistrust	Blindly thinking that others know what is right for you to do, say and desire, instead of trusting yourself.

79

Guilt, shame, and mistrust are emotional states. They are far more complicated than the emotions that we have described so far but are the same in the ways that are most important. These emotional states have thoughts and body sensations associated with them. They are sometimes suppressed, sometimes become activated and can be integrated using the Vivation process. Just like the emotions that we described earlier, there is nothing wrong with any of these emotional states, the problem is rather that we make them wrong and hold them in suppressive contexts.

Guilt and shame are similar in some ways and different in others. Guilt could be described as the belief or knowledge that you DID something wrong in a universe that is unsafe and therefore deserve punishment. The memory of childhood punishment and abuse re-inforces this belief. Since the universe is bigger than you, the tendency is to beat the universe to the punch by punishing yourself. This we do by feeling guilty. Guilt is therefore self-punishment.

Whereas guilt is the belief that you did something wrong, shame is the belief that you ARE wrong. Not wrong in the sense that you make a math mistake or took a wrong turn, but that there is something basically wrong with you, that you have some inherent character defect that is beyond repair. SHAME GRAVELY DISTORTS YOUR PERCEPTION OF YOUR IDENTITY. The belief in original sin is like this. People bound up with shame struggle to suppress it by trying to live up to standards of others or by blaming themselves when they don't.

SHAME IS A DISEASE OF THE FAMILY TREE

Most parents have deeply ingrained contexts about right and wrong (imparted to them by their parents) and use guilt and shame to impress these contexts on their children to "keep them in line". Guilt and shame are intensified by moralistic religious beliefs where the punishment for misdeeds is taught to be eternal and goodness is proven by adherence to externally imposed standards and spouting carefully memorized phrases. Guilt and shame are also intensified by the criminal legal system which has dedicated itself to punishment and the civil legal system which is about placing blame.

As an adult, if you compulsively avoid feeling guilty, then your effort to suppress your guilt makes you easily manipulated or makes you tend to use guilt to manipulate others. Compulsively avoiding feeling guilty makes it almost impossible to say NO with any conviction. Compulsively feeling guilty makes it almost impossible to accept love, acknowledgement and other good things in life. Happiness and pleasure become only temporary reprieves from the pervasive underlying sense of how wrong you are. Those who use guilt to manipulate others can't seem to take NO for an answer and instead attack the thinking or motivation of the person who said NO. Phrases like "How could you do this to me?", "How could you think like that?", or "You ought to be ashamed of yourself!", "Who do you think you are?" are commonly, and often effectively, used by guilt and shame manipulators.

The benefit of guilt is that it puts one in touch with his conscience. Your conscience serves to remind you of your personal moral standards. When you act in opposition to your morals, your conscience will call it to your attention that you have violated your standards. People who are not in touch with their conscience are usually cold-hearted and ruthless in their behavior.

When guilt is integrated, you can extend your apologies and ask to be forgiven. Some people find it easier to forgive themselves rather than the other person, while others seem to forgive others long before they forgive themselves. Forgiveness is its own reward, and there is no one MORE deserving of forgiveness than you.

SUPPRESSING GUILT REMOVES YOU FROM YOUR CONTACT WITH YOUR CONSCIENCE.

INTEGRATING GUILT ENABLES YOU TO FORGIVE YOURSELF, FORGIVE OTHERS, APOLOGIZE IF APPROPRIATE, AND MOVE ON.

Recovery Process

Here is an exercise to help you resolve guilt. Make a list of three things that you feel guilty about. This exercise will be a stretch for some in their ability to shift contexts and see things differently. Choose one to work on first. For that chosen guilt, identify exactly who was harmed by what you did. Now figure out which "defect" in your personality led you do that act. Then figure out 5 ways that person (or persons) that you thought you harmed actually got benefit from what you did. Next figure out which good things about you led you to do that thing and create all the benefit for that person. Repeat this procedure for the other two items on list and any others that are still upsetting you.

SHAME

Recently many excellent books have been written on the subject of shame. Shame is the basis of all suppression. What we are ashamed of we suppress and all emotional resolution involves the resolution of shame. The belief that your shame is the truth about you is murder to your true spiritual identity. Shame is what holds destructive loyalty and unworthiness in place.

We live in a society that is based on shame. If you read any good book about motivating people, whether it is about child development, education, business or military leadership or about sales, they all tell you that praise and acknowledgement are more effective methods of motivation than criticism and blame. The motto of this way of thinking is "Catch someone doing something right." If this knowledge is so widespread, then why doesn't the world work more that way? Unfortunately the intellectual awareness that praise and acknowledgement work better does little to overcome the more deeply, emotionally ingrained lessons from childhood. As children, we learn shame in subtle and not so subtle ways. We are taught to be ashamed of our bodies, of their functions, noises and smells, we are taught to be ashamed of our sexuality, our accomplishments, our mistakes and our thoughts and our feelings. Some parents teach their children to be ashamed of themselves, purposely or not. "You ought to be ashamed of yourself." or "Shame on you." Unresolved shame makes ANY feeling you have uncomfortable. The profound unwillingness of some people to experience their suppressed shame causes them to engage in entirely irrational behavior for the so-called purpose of upholding their honor or saving face, or because they think they are bad.

INTEGRATING SHAME BRINGS YOU INTO REALITY AND ACCOUNTABILITY IN YOUR LIFE

Every time you integrate a pattern of energy or emotion, an integration of shame occurs also because if you weren't ashamed of the feeling in the first place, it would not have been suppressed. When shame is integrated, there is a profound sense of well being with any and all of your feelings accompanied by the experiencing your true identity as an innocent child of God.

Here is an exercise to aid you in resolving shame. It is different from the exercise about guilt because guilt is about doing wrong and shame is about being wrong. Make a list of 5 items you are ashamed about. Pick one item and write down what that MEANS about you. Keep doing this until you see the humor in it. It is very likely if you are honest with yourself, the gross over-statement of your judgments about what your shame means are so extreme that you'll laugh and take it less seriously. An honest perspective about your shortcomings is far more useful than compulsively believing the lies that your shame gives you. You can do this with the other shameful items as well.

MISTRUST

Our parents wanted us to trust them. Since they were the ones in charge of such a big part of our life during our childhood, we wanted to trust them too. As children we wanted to trust our parents to love us, to do what they said they would do and to tell us the truth. Too much loss of trust in a family convinces the child that there is no one that they can trust, leading to isolating himself from others. We wanted to trust that they would hold our hand when we learned to walk, that they would feed us, as well as not let go of the bicycle seat until we got our balance. It is fine to trust people. However, blindly trusting everyone in every situation is foolish. It was probably not acceptable for you to say "I don't believe you" to your parents when you were a child. If you are not a child any more, you can express your mistrust, when it comes to your mental or physical awareness. Some people lie most of the time and most people lie at least some of the time. Even when someone tells the truth, there is nothing wrong with requesting that he convince you so that you can find out for yourself. If you experience a substantial amount of disappointment in others or if you find yourself thinking "I can't trust them" or "People don't mean what they say", it is likely caused by your unwillingness to express or trust your feelings of mistrust. It is fine to speak up and ask people about their ability and willingness to carry out their commitments to you. Expressing your mistrust does not mean that you are paranoid. It means that you are secure enough to act on your feelings. We are suggesting that you allow yourself to feel your feelings about the commitments that people make to you and to put your trust in those feelings. It is always OK to say:

"Are you sure about that?"
"Do you really mean that?"
"Aw, come on"
"I don't believe you."

The people who demand that you trust them without question are probably the least trustworthy. It is fine to require that people earn your trust and it is fine to withhold or withdraw your trust.

Blindly mistrusting everyone will not provide you with much freedom either. When we fly we trust the pilot to exercise due care. We trust the local utility to provide us electricity when we purchase an electric appliance. Demanding that your partner account for his behavior in minute detail every time you are apart does little to promote harmony.

WHEN YOU INTEGRATE MISTRUST YOU GAIN A SENSE OF SELF-AUTHORITY, AND EQUALITY WITH OTHERS, WILLINGNESS TO ACT ON YOUR INTUITION AND WILLINGNESS TO DISCLOSE YOUR VULNERABILITY.

FORGIVENESS AND EMOTIONAL STABILITY

Forgiveness is the path to emotional stability. Forgiveness is not the end result; emotional stability is. Since nothing is healed until it is made real, forgiveness is an intense process of feeling the formerly suppressed rage, shame and all the other feelings. In cases where guilt and shame are pervasive, you may feel even too guilty use the remedies that we will suggest. A new willingness is required; a new willingness to see yourself and your past differently. Forgiveness can be called the return from guilt and shame.

Forgiveness is a particular change in context that integrates guilt and shame. Forgiveness does not necessarily mean that what happened is OK, instead it means that you give up your righteous claim to punishment of yourself or of others. The desire for revenge is based on the misconception that causing someone else to suffer will somehow make you feel better.

For example, if you suffered extreme abuse as a child and your parents beat you every day after school, then you clearly have uncomfortable, suppressed feelings about this. If you insist on making these feelings wrong and suppressing them, you are an ineffective advocate for preventing child abuse, simply because whenever you even think of the subject of child abuse, the feelings are so uncomfortable that you quickly think of something else. Perhaps you even justify your feelings of revenge by abusing your own children or by staying in an abusive relationship. Forgiving your parents for this behavior does not mean that you think that child abuse is a good idea. It DOES mean that you surrender your need to punish them and yourself.

We have worked with many people who have experienced childhood abuse and childhood sexual abuse. By using the Vivation process, they have been able to resolve their feelings about their childhood to the point where the childhood abuse is no longer any more especially upsetting to them now than any other unpleasant past event in their lives. In other words, they have realized that the memories cannot hurt them and that it is not happening now, which means that they are no longer struggling emotionally to suppress these feelings based on the past and are free to tell the truth about it.

Forgiveness is a process. It has a beginning, a middle and an end. It may take a long time. Forgiveness must be emotional to be meaningful. There are times when you will feel angry, foolish, perhaps even justified in your desire for revenge, and want to give up. At first, all that is required is your willingness. At the beginning, when you say, think or write, "I forgive myself for hurting others," you may not feel any different and you may think you are just fooling yourself.

We know some people who talk as though forgiveness were merely a quick and easy intellectual exercise. They write the statement, "I forgive my mother completely" a hundred times, without any emotion and then proclaim to themselves and others that they have truly forgiven their mother. Another deluded approach about forgiveness is to say something like, "My parents did the best job they could with the skills they had. It wasn't their fault, so I forgive them." This is intellectual rationalization without awareness of the associated feelings and as such is ONLY the beginning step of the forgiveness process.

True forgiveness begins with thoughts like "My mother neglected me when I was young. I hate her for doing it and wish she hadn't because it has messed up my life." When your mind begins to wonder about how your mother was treated as a child, a sense of compassion emerges that can develop into forgiveness.

You can be certain that you have forgiven if when you contemplate the event or person, the feelings in your body no longer cause you pain as before.

Here is a feeling based forgiveness process.
1. Write down what happened
2. Write down what it means about you
3. Write down your feelings about what happened
4. Write down what those feelings mean about you
5. Write down the benefits you can continue to enjoy by continuing to interpret your feelings this way
6. Write down the new benefits you could expect by interpreting these feelings differently
7. If another person is involved, could you surrender your claim to retribution even if they were never to acknowledge what they did was wrong in any way or never apologized or never talked about it.

CHAPTER 10

IDENTIFYING UNCONSCIOUS PATTERNS OF BEHAVIOR AND THOUGHT

People who are unwilling to learn from their past are enslaved by it, enslaved by the emotional struggle to forget. Like a stone in your shoe, it keeps hurting until you do something about it. Perhaps even more painful is that some people actually succeed at forgetting the unpleasant parts of their past by suppressing it into their unconscious mind. The problem with this method is that the mind then acts to re-create the patterns of the past over and over, seemingly without conscious choice and without remedy. We seem to do this as a natural urge toward peaceful resolution of the turmoil.

The past is a paradox. In one sense, the past is over, there is nothing you can do about it and so it doesn't matter what happened. In another sense, any unresolved events from the past are carried forward into the present as suppressed feelings and will so continue until the feelings are felt and resolved. In this way, our feelings provide the most ready access to the parts of our personal history that we have suppressed.

Some people refuse to review their personal history and others use the past as a constant excuse for their failures. Neither of these methods will

87

aid you in learning from and making peace with your past, and most likely will hinder you in creating the life that you want.

There is nothing you can do at this point about the CONTENT of the past. The context in which you hold the past, and, therefore, how the past affects you, is completely up to you and may be changed at any time. Memories may be painful, but they cannot hurt you. You cannot change the content of the past, however you can learn from it and use it to your benefit regardless of what happened by changing contexts about the residual sensations.

Our families were our first teachers of love, sex and communication. As children we obviously did not have any pre-conceived ideas about how men and women should relate to each other. Children learn by watching, listening, and mimicking grownups; this is how we learned to talk. Your patterns were formed by observing your family's habits and modes of behavior whether you were aware of this or not. Whether your family provided a good or bad example of a loving relationship, really doesn't matter now. What matters now are the beliefs and unresolved feelings that you have brought forward from your childhood experience. It is a good idea to contemplate those beliefs, feelings and actions and then choose which ones are beneficial to you and which are not.

Our mind tends to operate on momentum to a great extent. Mental momentum is experienced by anyone who has attempted (successfully or not) to break a long time habit or to begin a new project. In breaking a long term habit, the habit itself builds up mental momentum causing our mind to expect things to stay the way that they are and the way that they have been. Since every pattern represents learned thinking and behavior, every pattern can be changed by learning something different. Thinking about starting a new project frequently activates a degree of resistance, despite the fact that you may be excited about the project. Often people notice that once the initial reluctance is overcome and the project is begun, the excitement of the project is sufficient to overcome any reluctance. A generalization about this is everything seems more difficult before you start and becomes easier once you get going.

All of us have unconscious patterns of behavior and thought. Some of these patterns are positive habits that support our purpose in life and contribute to our well being, while others act to prevent us from accomplishing our conscious desires. To have what you want in life requires you to change the unconscious patterns of thought and behavior that prevent you from having what you want. For some, the previous statement is so obvious as to be meaningless; however, millions engage in behavior that has proven over and over to produce undesired results.

Some of our patterns, both positive and negative, operate whether we are in an intimate relationship or not, while others spring to the fore only in our love life. Our focus is on changing the patterns that effect your love life. Whenever someone successfully changes a pattern, the following three events occur:

1. Recognition of Pattern
2. Activation and resolution of feelings associated with the pattern.
3. Choosing different behavior.

These three events do not necessarily occur in the order listed and may occur in any order. This means that you can start wherever is most convenient in changing a pattern. In this book, we present several self-evaluation quizzes to enable you to recognize and identify patterns that may have previously escaped your attention and, in various places, we suggest certain steps that will produce different behavior for you. The Vivation process enables anyone to activate and resolve feelings associated with unconscious patterns. Additionally, there is a chapter coming up about Attitude Builders, which can facilitate the accomplishment of all three of these steps required to change patterns.

RECOGNITION AND IDENTIFICATION OF PATTERNS

A simple way to identify patterns is to pay close attention to your conversation, especially to the statements that you make that contain the words ALWAYS, ALL, EVERY or NEVER; and to statements that you make that are so general and definite that your mind has allowed no possibility for things to be different. During our LSC, participants often verbalize the thoughts that cause unconscious patterns. Some examples are:

"I always attract the wrong kind of men"
"I always meet women who tell me what to do."
"I never seem to get what I want."
"I have always had problems talking about my feelings."
"When I open up to my lover, it always starts an argument."
"All the men that I meet just want sex and are afraid of commitment."

89

"I've always been like this."

Another way to identify and recognize patterns is to evaluate your behavior in a systematic way so that the patterns become more easily observable.

Recognition of a suppressed pattern is almost always humbling, involving the realization that your behavior has produced nothing but a lack of value. When you discover that you are compulsively late to assure getting noticed, or compulsively early to avoid being left out, or compulsively alone to avoid being hurt, it is likely that you feel humbled, and perhaps even embarrassed, by what you have been doing to yourself. The patterns that seem to be the most suppressed, and therefore the most beneficial to resolve, are those associated with childhood abuse or neglect; since in these situations, our survival was at risk.

Here are a couple of examples to illustrate the point that all three steps are required to change a pattern. You may recognize a pattern from the self-evaluation quiz that follows. You may recognize that the partners that you attract are almost always married when you meet them. You might even realize that you are attracting already married people so that you can avoid commitment, or continue the struggle to take Daddy away from Mommy (or vice versa) or for some other reason. This realization by itself will do you no good whatever, unless you are willing to experience and integrate the feelings associated with the pattern. Because if you don't, when you next meet an attractive married (wo)man, you will give in to those feelings of yearning and for some reason, be unable to say no.

Another example is that you could integrate in a Vivation session your fears about speaking in public. This will not benefit you if you don't get up in front of a group and say something.

Another possibility is that you change your behavior but do not resolve the feelings associated with the change. This just adds more stress (this is known as the white knuckle approach) and makes the change uncomfortable, because the change is not complete and the battle continues. Diets are like this for many people.

Earlier we mentioned that the three steps to changing a pattern may occur in any order. We'll give you a couple of personal examples, so that you can see this.

An example from Phil. Before my first Vivation session, I was nervous speaking in front of groups (not just a little nervous, I mean the sweaty palms and churning stomach brand of nervous). I compensated for this by meticulous preparation, which did little to reduce the nervousness. At the presentation I gave following my first Vivation session, I noticed that the nervousness was replaced by a sense of excitement, which made speaking in public much more enjoyable. Nothing occurred in the Vivation session that I could associate with speaking in public.

An example from Jeanne: I had been doing Vivation for a year or so, when one day I realized that for the last week, I was the one who was doing the driving when my friends and I went somewhere. Before that, I had been very uncomfortable about driving with passengers in my car (a fear adopted from my Mom, who was nervous about driving) (her parents had been killed tragically in an auto accident when she was a child).

We conclude, in both these instances, that our fears about speaking in public and driving in public, respectively, were integrated at the kinesthetic level of awareness without our mental awareness of what the sensations were about. It is common for people to identify what was integrated in their Vivation session a week or so later. Both of these are examples where the resolution of the feelings was the final step in changing the pattern.

An example from Phil: I had a lot of resistance about physical exercise and had lots of reasons to avoid it, despite the fact that it was obvious that my lifestyle as an author and teacher didn't provide any exercise and despite Jeanne's loving encouragement and despite writing Attitude Builders about it. One day I drove to the local gym and purchased a membership. For the first week or so I went every other day and hated it. Exercise seemed like boring drudgery, punishment and an intrusion in my busy schedule. I kept at it anyway. One day my body felt great when I was exercising and I noticed that I was looking around the gym for other things to do. This has continued and I enjoy my workouts now. This is an example of choosing different behavior first and then integrating the feelings that become activated.

An example from Jeanne: During my 20's, the men that attracted me and whom I became involved with had similar characteristics about their income and purpose in life. They earned very little money and despite heads full of beautiful dreams had no clear ways of implementing them. After having relationships with about ten "starving artists", I got tired of constantly paying for our dates, while at the same time expending emotional energy to encourage them to find work that they loved. Contemplating a lifetime of this was unappealing to me, despite the fact that we adored each other and I felt like a strong woman. When I recognized this pattern, I realized that I wanted a partner who had work that he loved and who was willing to accept responsibility for his own development. In social situations, I noticed that I was still attracted to men who fit the earlier picture, and considerable self-restraint was required to prevent me from being seduced by my desire to rescue others once again.

An example from Phil: In my 20's and 30's, the women that I cared about the most were the ones that liked sex the least and who were the most afraid and least willing to take any action that might lead to improvement. Every once in a while I was attracted to a woman who did enjoy sex; however, these women served primarily as ideals that the ones that didn't like sex should be like. With the lovers who didn't like sex, there were frequent arguments mostly about what I thought they should do to solve their problem. One day I devised the sexual history quiz, which is in Chapter 13, and realized that as long as I stayed with women who did not like sex, then any sexual problems between us would automatically become their problem that had nothing to do with me. From then on, when I attracted women who were unwilling to enjoy sex, I broke off the relationship, instead of arguing about it. When I began attracting women who did like sex, my own sexual hangups (primarily performance anxiety), which I had successfully suppressed by having my partner to blame came to the surface.

An example from Jeanne: When Phil and I decided to write this book, I knew I had things I wanted to say, but was convinced that I couldn't write. Phil offered to coach me in a Vivation in Action Session. I wrote a letter to a friend, while Phil coached me in applying the Five Elements to the sensations I was feeling. At first I noticed that I was holding my breath and gripping the pencil very tightly. I experienced intense fear about making a mistake and sadness about my inability to express myself. I decided to write something every day and let all my feelings about writing come up. At one point I had a memory of the teacher standing over me in Third Grade penmanship class watching me write as I worried about time pressure, neatness and punctuation. Now I know that I can write at my own pace and that I can easily correct any mistakes that I make, and that it is easy to say what I mean. I also began to use the Attitude Builders, "People love to hear what I have to say" and "My mind is filled with creative ideas". This is an example of resolving a pattern by choosing different behavior that would activate emotions and resolving them.

An example from Phil: When I returned from Vietnam in the 1960's, I had lots of unresolved feelings about the War and my participation in it. At first these unresolved feelings manifested in nightmares and in spontaneously hurling myself to the ground when I heard any loud noise that resembled an explosion. Soon after my return, I learned how to suppress the feelings with hard work and by not talking about them. This method worked for over a decade. In the late 1970's, about the time I learned the Vivation process, movies started to come out about the Vietnam War. I went to "The Deer Hunter", "Apocalypse Now" and movies like them repeatedly, sitting in the closest available seat to the front row. Each time I went I would engage in the Five Elements, breathing, relaxing and resolving my feelings of resentment, sadness, shame and survivor's guilt. They were some very intense experiences for me with many tears and a lot of shaking. I realize that I may never completely resolve all of this, so I attend every new movie that comes about the War as a therapeutic experience.

An example from Phil and Jeanne: When we were first married, we noticed that we got along almost perfectly when we travelled but that our intense arguments occurred at home. Although this is still the case and we have not completely resolved this pattern, we have recognized its existence and its origin for each of us and can help each other with it. The following quiz will aid you in recognition of some of your patterns.

93

FORTY QUESTION QUIZ

INSTRUCTIONS: On the top five lines of the answer sheet, write the names of up to five past relationships,preferably sexual ones. You can include your current relationship. Questions number 15, 16, 17 and 20 do not apply to a current relationship. Force yourself to choose one answer that most applies for each question for each relationship and enter the corresponding letter on the appropriate line. There are no right answers.

1. APPEARANCE
Male
  a. Ordinary
  b. Extremely masculine
  c. Odd looking
  d. Handsome
  e. Cute

Female
  a. Ordinary
  b. Striking beauty
  c. Odd looking
  d. Country girl
  e. Cute

2. PERSONALITY
MALE CHARACTERISTICS
  a. Tough veneer, flexible
     underneath
  b. Rigidly masculine
  c. Neither masculine nor
     feminine

FEMALE CHARACTERISTICS
  a. Shy with a heart of gold
  b. Helpless female
  c. Neither masculine nor
     feminine

3. FAMILY BACKGROUND
  a. Lower middle class
  b. Middle class
  c. Upper middle class

4. EDUCATION
   a. High School
   b. College degree
   c. Graduate or professional degree.

5. WORK
   a. Salaried employee
   b. Hourly employee
   c. Self-employed
   d. House wife/house husband

6. ANNUAL INCOME
   a. Under $25,000
   b. $25,000 to $60,000
   c. over $60,000

7. MONEY MANAGEMENT OF OTHER
   a. They spent money carelessly
   b. They spent money frugal
   c. They spent money wisely

8. AGE DIFFERENCE
   a. They were one to five years younger than me
   b. They were one to five years older than me
   c. They were the same age as me
   d. They were more than five years younger than me
   e. They were more than five years older than me

9. FIRST MEETING
   a. Work
   b. Friends
   c. Accident
   d. Bar or singles event
   e. Other (specify)

10. MARITAL STATUS OF OTHER AT FIRST MEETING
    a. Never married before
    b. Divorced
    c. Separated
    d. Married

11. CURRENT MARITAL STATUS OF OTHER
   a. Single
   b. Married for first time
   c. Re-married
   d. Divorced
   e. I have no idea

12. RELATIONSHIP OF OTHER WITH HIS OR HER FAMILY
   a. They had a good relationship with their family
   b. They a poor relationship with their family
   c. I don't really know

13. ATTITUDES OF OTHER ABOUT PERSONAL GROWTH
   a. They were very interested in personal growth
   b. They were somewhat interested in personal growth
   c. They thought personal growth was a waste of time

14. DEFINITION OF GOALS
   a. They had definite plans for their future
   b. They were still considering their future
   c. They had no definite plans for their future

15. FUTURE ORIENTATION
   a. Both of us were future oriented about our relationship
   b. Other was; I wasn't.
   c. I was; other wasn't.
   d. Neither of us was future oriented about our relationship

16. CARING
   a. Other cared more for me.
   b. I cared more for other.
   c. There were no strong feelings either way.
   d. Caring was strong and equal.

17. RESOLUTION OF DISAGREEMENTS
   a. We argued a lot
   b. We rarely argued
   c. We never argued

18. COMMUNICATION LEVEL
   a. We were able to talk about our feelings easily
   b. We rarely talked about our feelings
   c. We never talked about our feelings

19. HONESTY
   a. Other was always honest with me
   b. Other sometimes lied to me
   c. I found out later that other lied to me
   d. I suspected that other was dishonest

20. SEXUAL EXPERIENCE
   a. We had sex on our first date
   b. We waited until we knew each other to have sex
   c. We never had sex

21. SEX ACTIVITY DURING THE RELATIONSHIP
   a. I always wanted more sex
   b. They always wanted more sex
   c. We were both satisfied with our sex life

22. COMMONALITY OF INTERESTS
   a. Little in common
   b. Some things in common.
   c. Great deal in common

23. INTENSITY OF NEED
   a. There was little intense need on either part.
   b. I needed the other more.
   c. Other needed me more.
   d. We both needed each other strongly.

24. DEPTH OF LOVE
   a. I loved other more.
   b. Other loved me more.

25. COMMITMENT
   a. Other was more committed
   b. I was more committed

26. CHANGE
a. We accepted each other fairly well.
b. I wanted the other change in important ways.
c. Other wanted me to change in important ways.
d. Both of us had major complaints and wishes for the other to change

27. HOW EARLY WAS TROUBLE DETECTED?
a. I knew from early on that it wouldn't work.
b. We had a long period when everything worked
c. I didn't know until the end that anything was wrong.

28. HOW LONG DID YOU STAY, KNOWING THAT IT WOULDN'T WORK?
a. I left as soon as I knew.
b. I left, but not nearly as soon as I should have.
c. I stayed much too long.

29. THE BREAK-UP
a. I precipitated the break-up.
b. Other did.
c. Basically mutual.

30. DIRECTNESS
a. I wanted to marry other and said so.
b. I wanted to marry other and never said so
c. I didn't want to marry other and said so.
d. I didn't want to marry other and never said so.

31. DIRECTNESS OF OTHER
a. Other wanted to marry me and said so.
b. Other didn't want to marry me and said so.
c. Other did not discuss intentions about marriage.

32. COMPLETION
a. I still long for other
b. I am still angry at other.
c. I could enjoy a meal with other once in a while.

33. COMPLETION FOR OTHER
a. They still long for me
b. They are still angry at me
c. They could enjoy a meal with me once in a while

34. PARENTAL APPROVAL OF OTHER
    a. My parents approved of them
    b. My parents disapproved of them
    c. My parents never met them

35. PARENTAL APPROVAL
    a. Their parents approved of me
    b. Their parents disapproved of me
    c. I never met their parents

36. REASON THEY ENDED RELATIONSHIP
    a. They wanted someone else
    b. They wanted their freedom
    c. They did not say clearly
    d. Incompatible
    e. Other please specify

37. REASON I ENDED RELATIONSHIP
    a. I wanted someone else
    b. I wanted my freedom
    c. I did not say clearly
    d. Incompatible
    e. Other please specify

38. FRIENDS OF OTHER
    a. I liked them
    b. I did not like them

39. MY FRIENDS
    a. Other liked them
    b. Other did not like them

40. TEMPERAMENT
    a. Hotheaded
    b. Cold blooded
    c. Warm/Caring
    d. Laid back
    e. Good sense of humor

ANSWER SHEET
Name of past relationship
(write names of up to five past relationships)

_____ _____ _____ _____ _____

Write the letter that most applies
  Question #
    1. _____ _____ _____ _____ _____
    2. _____ _____ _____ _____ _____
    3. _____ _____ _____ _____ _____
    4. _____ _____ _____ _____ _____
    5. _____ _____ _____ _____ _____
    6. _____ _____ _____ _____ _____
    7. _____ _____ _____ _____ _____
    8. _____ _____ _____ _____ _____
    9. _____ _____ _____ _____ _____
  10. _____ _____ _____ _____ _____
  11. _____ _____ _____ _____ _____
  12. _____ _____ _____ _____ _____
  13. _____ _____ _____ _____ _____
  14. _____ _____ _____ _____ _____
  15. _____ _____ _____ _____ _____
  16. _____ _____ _____ _____ _____
  17. _____ _____ _____ _____ _____
  18. _____ _____ _____ _____ _____
  19. _____ _____ _____ _____ _____
  20. _____ _____ _____ _____ _____
  21. _____ _____ _____ _____ _____
  22. _____ _____ _____ _____ _____
  23. _____ _____ _____ _____ _____
  24. _____ _____ _____ _____ _____
  25. _____ _____ _____ _____ _____
  26. _____ _____ _____ _____ _____
  27. _____ _____ _____ _____ _____
  28. _____ _____ _____ _____ _____
  29. _____ _____ _____ _____ _____
  30. _____ _____ _____ _____ _____
  31. _____ _____ _____ _____ _____
  32. _____ _____ _____ _____ _____
  33. _____ _____ _____ _____ _____

34. _____ _____ _____ _____ _____
35. _____ _____ _____ _____ _____
36. _____ _____ _____ _____ _____
37. _____ _____ _____ _____ _____
38. _____ _____ _____ _____ _____
39. _____ _____ _____ _____ _____
40. _____ _____ _____ _____ _____

WHAT DID YOU LEARN?

WHAT DO YOU WANT TO CHANGE?

In this quiz, the last two questions are the most important ones. By reading horizontally on your answer sheet, the patterns in your relationships will become apparent. It is likely that there are some patterns that you like and others that you don't. Many good books have been written analyzing particular patterns in relationships; however, analysis alone will not empower you to change the ones you don't like. Some people know all of the reasons for their problems, but don't know what to do about them.

As we mentioned earlier changing unconscious patterns of behavior and thought require three steps which may occur in any order.
1. Recognition of Pattern
2. Activation and resolution of feelings associated with the pattern.
3. Choosing different behavior.

Before we discuss interaction with your lover's patterns, in the next chapter, we cover the source of the vast majority of patterns, which is family upbringing.

11 YOUR RECOVERY FROM A GOOD UPBRINGING
Family dynamics as the source of patterns.

It is very difficult to write about childhood conditioning and bringing up children without sounding moralistic. It is not our intention here to shame or criticize anyone. Parenthood is the toughest, and one of the longest, jobs in the world (the human child is the most dependent creature on earth, for the longest period of time). Parenthood is also the job for which there has been the least amount of practical training available. (Our society offers and requires more extensive training for prospective accountants and truck drivers than it does for prospective parents.) The possibilities for errors in judgment and errors of omission abound even for the most caring and enlightened parents. The best of parents and upbringings will leave you with unresolved patterns.

For many people, the suppressed feelings left unresolved from childhood abuse and neglect render them unable to make the choices that they want in their life. Unresolved childhood abuse and neglect are likely to have a greater effect on your love life than on other areas, because your love life takes place in a kind of family setting involving closeness and loyalty, similar to what we experienced growing up. Generally, abuse refers to grievous mistakes of commission and neglect refers to grievous mistakes of omission.

In this chapter, we will discuss how an unresolved childhood may prevent you from applying the communication techniques that we will be describing throughout the rest of the book. Both of us and surely many of you acquired some useful patterns from our parents. Our focus here is on resolution of the patterns that are destructive to our well being.

First off, it may come as a surprise to some people to discover that their parents abused or neglected them. You may notice that your mind is providing you with emphatic denials that your parents ever neglected or abused you. Please consider the following question: "Would you raise your children *exactly* as you were raised?" If the answer is NO, then it stands to reason that you consider the treatment that you would not wish to duplicate with your children to be abusive or neglectful. We are not interested in presenting a universal condemnation of parents. We are very interested in adding to public awareness of parenting methods and their effect on all areas of our society. It is extremely unlikely that your parents abused or neglected you on purpose; many of them even thought they were doing the right thing. Your parents' treatment of you was most likely their delayed response to the treatment and instruction that they received as children. This doesn't mean that it is a good idea to blame your grandparents either, because traditions of abuse and neglect often stretch back for generations. It is also true that you are not to blame for the abuse or neglect that you received as a child even though you may feel ashamed about it, even too ashamed to talk about it. Although you are not to blame for your childhood experience, the responsibility for resolving the effect it has on your life is yours. These patterns will continue for generations into the future unless resolved by acknowledging their existence, feeling the associated feelings and choosing different behavior.

Most adults suffer from childhood amnesia. Even if they remember the EVENTS that occurred in their childhood, many have forgotten what it FEELS like to be a child. For a child, the most important thing in the world in his or her parents' relationship, almost as though the child knows that it is how he got here and that it is essential to his well being. Gratefully, today the subject of family abuse is far more "out of the closet" than any time in history.

Resolution occurs when you no longer require anything back from the perpetrator of the abuse, including money, understanding, admission of guilt, promises to change, apology, etc. Blame provides no satisfaction whatever. Acknowledging the feelings does.

Hating your parents and hating your parents' behavior are very, very different. Resolution of all this does not necessarily mean that their behavior was OK, instead it means giving up your claim to retribution and compensation, and giving up your past treatment as an excuse for your current condition or behavior.

In our LSC Weekends, we have observed various kinds of patterns resulting from childhood abuse and neglect. These tend to be the easiest to deny and the hardest to change. They are easy to deny because of the desire to forget, although it is unlikely that a happy childhood would be forgotten. They are hard to change because the feelings associated with acknowledging that your parents hurt you are often shameful and uncomfortable, causing you to fear that you may become stuck in hating them forever.

KINDS OF ABUSE AND NEGLECT

Physical Abuse and Neglect
Sexual Abuse and Neglect
Intellectual Abuse and Neglect
Cultural Abuse and Neglect
Emotional Abuse and Neglect
Spiritual Abuse and Neglect

PHYSICAL ABUSE AND NEGLECT

Physical abuse means violence and/or punishment in excess of the minimum required to get the point across (say this better). Since children learn by observing the behavior of their parents, the wife beater abuses his children as well as his wife, even if no violence is directed toward the children and even if the children neither see nor hear the beating. This is because there are really no secrets in families. A child will certainly know that SOMETHING is going on from his observation of the external emotional affect of his parents.

Most parents CLAIM that they punish their children because of the child's behavior. However, the vast majority of punishment that crosses the boundaries that most adults respect for each other is motivated by the parents' unwillingness or inability to deal with their own frustration. Common responses to a violent upbringing are: continuation of the abuse

105

on their children and others, lack of memory about childhood (people don't forget HAPPY childhoods), depression, substance addictions of any kind to alter or medicate the feelings, compulsion to please others or withdrawal in the form of de-personalization (referring to themselves always as YOU) or multiple personality or out-of-body experiences or development of the ability to go unnoticed by others. Sado-masochistic sexuality is often the result of eroticized violence. Parents who are violent with their children sometimes rationalize this behavior by claiming that they are toughening them up in preparation for the real world; however we think this is motivated more by the parents' unwillingness or inability to nurture their children, which results from their own unresolved feelings.

A rationally motivated adult victim of domestic violence would pack up after one or two incidents. However, many battered women that stick around do so because violence is a process of enslavement, resulting in a reduction of choices considered by the victim. Thus, the women who stick around were most often already enslaved as children to the extent that their shame about telling anyone about this makes even the consideration of taking any action uncomfortable.

There is a long way to go before we have a violence free society. The practice by public school officials of administering corporal punishment to school students has been upheld by the U.S. Supreme Court. Although eight states in the US passed laws prohibiting corporal punishment in schools during 1989, it remains legal in 31 States. This national Hall of Shame is:

Alabama	Kentucky	Oklahoma
Arizona	Louisiana	Pennsylvania
Arkansas	Maryland	South Carolina
Colorado	Mississippi	South Dakota
Delaware	Missouri	Tennessee
Florida	Montana	Texas
Georgia	Nevada	Utah
Idaho	New Mexico	Washington
Illinois	North Carolina	West Virginia
Indiana	Ohio	Wyoming
Kansas		

Do not wait until your child is abused by school officials. Write to your State Legislator today. Make your feelings about legalized child abuse known at your child's school. If your child is abused by school officials, we suggest that you protest this. Help is available from the National Coalition to Abolish Corporal Punishment in Schools:

614-221-8829

Although your child may not be the direct victim of abuse, simply witnessing or hearing about legally condoned brutality plants an indelible message that violence solves problems.

Violence (both real and dramatized) abounds on commercial television as a reflection of the violence that occurs in the family.

Physical neglect relates to parents' unwillingness or ability to provide for the material needs of their children. Children will grow up fine if they are deprived of the latest stereo system or a new skate board every Christmas, but prolonged malnutrition and lack of medical and dental care are certain to have long lasting effects.

If as an adult, you have not resolved any physical abuse that occurred in your childhood, then disagreements will be difficult to resolve simply because every disagreement will trigger the childhood emotional memories to which tend to activate the fear of being abused or being abusive.

SEXUAL ABUSE AND NEGLECT

Sexual abuse involves boundary violations that the victim can do nothing about. Sexual abuse can be perpetrated by a family member (incest) or anyone. Despite the fact that parents warn their children not to talk to, take money or candy from strangers, in 80% of the instances of childhood sexual abuse, the perpetrator was known to the victim. Incest is sexual contact between family members too closely related to marry each other. Sexual abuse involves sexual behavior of any kind related to someone who does not have the power to say no and stop the person. Regrettably, incest and sexual abuse are are far more common than most people know about.

Talking about these subjects is far more taboo than engaging in them. Lifting the veil of secrecy and denial can lead us to resolution. Great strides have been made in this direction; however, there is much in the way of public awareness left to do. If one person in 100 were infected with influenza, a national emergency would be declared, every kid in school would receive immunization at no cost and there would be hourly announcements on TV informing us how to identify the symptoms and where to go for help. Yet, instances of childhood sexual abuse far exceed

1 person in 100 (70 in 100 according to reliable surveys) and there is still no national public awareness campaign.

Reported survivors of sexual abuse are most commonly females, although this information may be distorted by socially induced difficulty of males in acknowledging their helplessness.

Sexual abuse does not have to involve intercourse, nor does it have to have occurred repeatedly. One betrayal is enough to damage you. Just a few examples of sexual abuse are: being touched in genital areas, rape, being forced to watch pornography or participate in pornographic photography, being coerced into oral sex, being fondled, kissed or held in uncomfortable ways, being told that sex was all you were good for, having your sexuality be the subject of intrusive or mocking interest by adults, being in a family where sexual abuse occurred even if you did not participate and having adults expose themselves to you.

Many parents believe that they have the right to IMPOSE their own standards about sex on their children. This is a highly unrealistic view and leads only to frustration for all concerned. It does not require saying that sexual desire is very strong — it is a manifestation of our desire for caring human contact, for self-expression and for the continuation of our heritage. Thus, your sexuality is a unique and spiritual reflection of your own individuality. By a highly perverted use of logic, parents, governments and churches take it as their duty and right to persuade people into thinking that sex is shameful. Being shamed for the natural sexual urges and functions of your body is sexually abusive.

If any of these events occurred, then you have been abused sexually. If you suspect they occurred, then we suggest that you honor these suspicions and investigate the associated feelings rather than insist that it could not have happened.

Incest Survivors Anonymous (ISA) has supplied us with the following list of symptoms that may indicate sexual abuse as either an infant, child or adult.

Sections of time blocked out and unable to remember.
Sudden personality changes and identity problems.
Hearing of voices.
Clinging fearfully to childhood possessions or events
Anti-social behavior
Job related problems
Bed wetting
Confusion or disorientation

Delinquency, stealing or runaway
Excessive jealousy or possessiveness
Fainting, migraines or respiratory ailments
Hyperactivity or stuttering
Promiscuity, prostitution, seductive dress or behavior
Punishing attitude
Rage, repressed tears or screaming
Change in school grades
Alcoholism, drug addiction, obesity, anorexia or bulimia
Battered or batterer
Damage to rectal, vaginal or mouth areas
Epileptic seizures with or without organic causes
Pelvic, back, hip, leg or feet injury
Stop in ovulation and/or in genital development
Terrified of pelvic or rectal examinations, dentist chair or medical examining table
Venereal disease
Claustrophobia and all other phobias
Fearful of doors, of being touched, of people, of medical uniforms
Infant fearful of diaper change
Cutting, hitting or mutilating oneself
Difficulty in listening, asking frequently for statements to be repeated
Suicidal fantasies
Psychosomatic illnesses and unnecessary surgery

RESOLUTION OF SEXUAL ABUSE

It is safe to say that you will never resolve sexual abuse if
1. You insist that it didn't happen (even though you may have told someone and they said it couldn't have happened).
2. You won't talk about it.
3. You are dedicated to protecting the perpetrator(s).
4. You are not committed to taking as long as you need to resolve it.
5. You insist on medicating your feelings.
6. You allow your shame to prevent you from feeling the associated rage.
7. The realization that it MAY have been enjoyable to you is something you cannot accept.

Talking about your experience of sexual abuse and investigating the feelings associated with it are essential, and painful steps toward resolution.

It is important to remember here that, although the memories can hurt, they cannot hurt YOU and that suppressing the memories is what hurts. There can be no resolution of your experience of sexual abuse unless there is verbal debriefing. Talking is essential. Sexual abuse is accompanied by dire threats of what will happen if it is discussed, for example, ("If you tell, it will kill your mother" or "If you tell, I'll do something worse"). The fear from these threats renders the victim helpless to do anything about it. Talking about what happened unfreezes the feelings for the victim.

The taboo about talking about sexual abuse makes it especially important that you discuss this part of your past with your lover, whether you are a survivor or were a perpetrator. Approximately half of the people who have attended our Love, Sex and Communication Weekend Seminar have known they are survivors of sexual abuse and there began the process of regaining their personal power. Additionally most Vivation Professionals have been trained to assist you in resolving sexual abuse. For a list of the ones nearest you, call

TOLL FREE 1-800-829-2625.
A world wide listing of support groups is available from Incest Survivors Anonymous by calling

213-422-1632.
There are several books suggested in the back about resolving sexual abuse.

SEXUAL NEGLECT

Sexual neglect means that your parents failed in their responsibilities to provide you with useful and appropriate information and education about sex, sexuality and your body functions. In our LSC Weekend, we always ask participants, "Please raise your hand if you are satisfied with what your parents taught you about sex". So far we have done this for over three years and in six different countries, and have never had more than one person raise their hand. Since a dysfunctional family is one in which the important issues are not discussed, then almost all of us grew up in sexually dysfunctional families.

What children require most is parental openness that allows discussion of sex, but reliable information about sexuality, birth control and menstrual cycles is essential, too.

Sex is a personal topic whose discussion requires privacy and trust. For this reason, it is damaging to discuss your sexual problems with your children, who certainly are not equipped to solve them.

110

The survivor of sexual abuse often has difficulties with disagreements and arguments, because the unresolved shame associated with sexual abuse renders him or her easy to manipulate and can cause him or her to give in prematurely.

INTELLECTUAL ABUSE AND NEGLECT

Intellectual abuse means ridicule or discounting a child's intelligence, convincing the child that the judgments of others are more reliable. The child learns he must mistrust his mind and its conclusions. Report card time is a traumatic experience for the intellectually abused child whose parent focuses his comments on how much better the child should perform, rather than acknowledging the accomplishments. For the intellectually abused child, mistakes are simply not permitted.

Intellectual neglect means failing to provide your children with intellectual stimulation that will nurture their curiosity and creativity. It shouldn't have to be said that despite the fact that education is a responsibility that most parents delegate to the public school officials, the quality and quantity of their children's education remains the responsibility of the parents. Blaming the teachers for your children's problems in school is futile. If you rely on the public schools as your child's only source of learning and commercial television as your child's primary source of entertainment, then surely you'll be disappointed. If you consistently demonstrate an interest in your children's education, they will learn, even under the poorest conditions. If you don't, then there is little that the finest school in the world can teach.

People who have been abused or neglected intellectually have problems with disagreements and arguments because they compulsively mistrust what their mind tells them.

CULTURAL ABUSE AND NEGLECT

Cultural abuse means ridiculing or discounting the child's interest in what is happening in the world around him. It means drawing unreasonably tight boundaries proscribing the flow of information to the child. Worldwide awareness that we are citizens of a global village is increasing. Passing on prejudice about different ethnic or racial groups, their behavior and ways of thinking is cultural abuse. Everyone has a natural curiosity about

111

everything, unless it was stifled as a child. Encourage your children to try many different activities, kinds of food, music and things to read.

Cultural neglect means that the parent does not pay close enough attention to the child to even find out what might interest him.

Culturally abused and neglected people have problems with disagreements and arguments because it will seem to them that the other person has so much more information than they do.

EMOTIONAL ABUSE AND NEGLECT

Emotional abuse means that the child's emotions are ridiculed or shamed. For example, "You shouldn't feel sad about that" or "That is nothing to be afraid of". Instead, make a consistent practice to notice, label and affirm your child's feelings. The labeling part does not mean that you are playing psychotherapist, it simply means that you are acknowledging what you are noticing. For example, "It looks to me that you feel upset and I understand. Would you like to tell me about it?"

Emotional neglect means that the parents are so involved with their own personal dramas that there is no emotional energy left over for their children. In this case, the parents put their energy into controlling their children's behavior and never discuss the emotions that motivate it.

People who were emotionally abused or neglected have difficulties with disagreements and arguments, because most arguments involve emotions and these people either fear being ridiculed for their feelings, their feelings overwhelm them so they can't think logically, or since they have been convinced from childhood that their feelings are not valid, have no idea how to talk about them.

SPIRITUAL ABUSE AND NEGLECT

Much of what passes for organized religion is really spiritual abuse. Any philosophy that is rigid and dogmatic and based on inescapable punishment for violations of arbitrary rules that you had no part in making and didn't agree to keep is bound to be abusive. Any religion that proclaims the benefits of depriving yourself, being ashamed of yourself and constant struggle against the forces of evil is bound to be abusive. The governments and citizens of Latin America have allowed their countries to be devastated from over-population by following the dictates of the Roman Catholic

Church about birth control for centuries. Religious fanatics in the United States are so abusive that they demand the U.S. Government pass laws regulating the reproductive functions of American women by prohibiting abortion. If you are an adult, you probably can apply some mature judgment to these issues and see spiritual abuse for what it is. Children lack this perspective.

For children, parents were their first God. The source of all good things, the arbiters of right and wrong and the original power greater than themselves. It is expecting a lot to think that a child could believe in a loving, forgiving God after having been abused. It's a lot to ask a child to trust an unseen God, when his parents have already proven to be untrustworthy. In some families religion takes the place of spirituality, bringing with it rigid rules about right and wrong which are abusively enforced by an elaborate but unseen system of reward and punishment in the life hereafter, for which no evidence other than scriptural hearsay is presented. This tends to stifle cultivation of one's relationship with God or a higher power.

We think it is spiritually abusive to tell your children that God is to blame for their misfortunes — "God is punishing you" — or to use God to avoid the reality of pain — "It's God's will." Over-controlling your child is spiritually abusive if you demand the right to define your child's identity. Forcing your child to hold you in the position of a higher power through fear or worship is spiritually abusive, too.

The spiritually neglectful parent often suffered abuse from his or her religious experience at some point, and may feel uncomfortable contemplating God or some higher power. The spiritually neglected child misses out on knowing that he can find answers within that are right for him. In this case the spiritual curiosity of the child is stifled and he or she comes to rely on some external condition, like money or his social position, for his well being.

Spiritually abused or neglected people have problems with disagreements or arguments because, lacking an internal method of evaluating what is being said, they rely on their opinion about the status of the person with whom they are arguing. Preserving their veneer of dignity matters more than gaining the understanding that the other person could offer them.

FAMILY DYNAMICS

A family is a dynamic system. The system functions with a complicated arrangement of complimentary patterns and roles which establish boundaries and bonds between members. In a dysfunctional family, loyalty is preserved with an unspoken arrangement of rules and punishment, primarily based on shame. The most destructive of these unspoken rules is "Don't talk about feelings." Especially, "Don't talk about your sexual feelings." When one member decides to no longer follow the rules that he never agreed to, all of the other members either do something to get the rebel back into line or must adjust to the new behavior of the nonconformist. This is good news. This means that you do not have to change your partner to change your relationship. All you must do is change yourself and stick to your decisions. Your partner may act strange with controlling and shaming behavior which you must learn to accept for what it is and leave if abusive behavior persists.

Don't allow people to abuse you. When someone abuses you, ask them to stop. Say, "You're abusing me. Stop immediately. If they continue their abusive behavior, continue to ask them to stop and do everything possible to minimize your contact with them. Anyone who abuses you and is unable to give an honest apology and to change his behavior, not only does not care about you, but needs help to deal with his feelings. Obviously you cannot force anyone to seek help; however you can leave until they do.

12 INTERACTION WITH YOUR LOVER'S PATTERNS

Patterns interact whether you like it or not and whether you know about this or not. In this chapter we will describe how the patterns you may have uncovered in the 40 question quiz interact with other people's patterns. Our patterns are not expressions of our true identity, but rather coping mechanisms that we adopted to deal with the abuse and neglect in our family of origin, which we described in the previous chapter. Thus you can use the techniques in this book to change the patterns that do not serve you.

Homeostasis is a physiological term that refers to the natural tendency of our body to maintain internal stability. This tendency to maintain a balance causes the endocrine, respiratory, circulatory, digestive and elimination systems to respond to changes in temperature, food intake, exercise, blood chemistry and other external conditions for the purpose of maintaining a stable internal environment, thus ensuring our survival and well-being. This homeostatic process causes our body to want things to stay the same. It accounts for the fact that when you change your diet, start exercising, quit smoking or even think about these changes, there are physical and mental reactions that will tend to return you to the status quo. The start is always the most difficult part of any change. If you sharply reduce your amount of food intake, at first your mind will shout at you, about how you are starving yourself, depriving yourself and about how your mother told you to clean up your plate, plus associated body sensations of hunger. After a while, your body adjusts to the reduced intake, which becomes a new condition of stability and your mind tends to quiet down about it.

A dynamic similar to homeostasis occurs in a relationship. The psycho-physiological explanation of habit and addiction also applies to all of our relationships, (tending to maintain the stability of the status quo, even in cases where the current situation is not desirable), because of the interaction between our external conditions and internal emotions. The important issue is to become aware that your patterns interact and learn how to resolve them. Without any skills at resolving patterns, it could be said that your relationship is nothing more than an interaction of patterns that you'd rather not have in the first place. Before you check into your local mental hospital, please understand that all of us have lots of compulsive behaviors. As we mentioned earlier, you wouldn't be normal if you weren't a little strange!

Please be patient, persistent and compassionate with the deeply ingrained patterns. They represent bad habits or automatic responses to childhood conditioning. As such, they are lies about your true identity and not defects in your character. Your ability to accept yourself and your lover with the problems that you have will aid you greatly in solving them, in other words, the context in which you view your problems matter more than the problems themselves.

ALL CONFLICTS ARE BATTLES OF CONTEXT

Many conflicts are battles to see which partner's pattern will rule the relationship. Other times the undesirable, unconscious patterns of both partners mesh together so that each re-inforces the problems of the other, confounding solution. It is impossible to help each other if you don't recognize each other's patterns. This recognition leads to intimacy instead of battles to change each other. When one partner initiates change of any kind, there is an immediate effect on the other, who may consciously or unconsciously strive to prevent a beneficial change from becoming permanent. Your unconscious patterns, even though deeply ingrained, have a dynamic aspect to them. Don't expect them to stay the same. Even in a relationship where patterns remain completely unresolved, all of your patterns will not be evident at first and you can expect new ones to arise. The occurrence of important changes such as moving in together, getting married, having children, career or financial changes, are very likely to bring up previously long suppressed and denied patterns. Honest disclosure about your patterns and the benefits you could have by changing them is important for both partners. This is always a humbling experience. In some cases changes may be perceived as a threat. Nevertheless, you'll be much happier relying on your conscious commitment to keep you together than you will by counting on the unconscious habits left over from your family of origin to do it.

THE TENDENCY TO CRITICIZE

A critic, according to the dictionary, "A person who tends to make trivial or harsh judgments". To be critical means to "be inclined to find fault". Criticism is "The act of faultfinding, judging, or censure".

Nobody likes to be criticized and yet all of us have criticized other people as well as ourselves. Criticism is a covert way of trying to control another person, by making them or something about them wrong and at the same time hoping that they will change. Sometimes criticism is used as a weapon when one partner is feeling hurt by the other and instead of acknowledging that, lashes out in retaliation. Highly critical people are not famous for having what they want or for accomplishing very much. Snob mentality is an extreme example of this kind of thinking. Snob mentality means thinking that the better a person is, the more he or she disapproves of. This is rationalized as discerning taste, despite the fact that thinking this way limits your enjoyment of anything that does not live up to your unreasonably lofty standards. Criticism is one common method of exerting control of people. Others will be described in the next section.

DEALING WITH CONTROL ISSUES

In a relationship, control means exercising your influence to have your partner engage in behavior that he or she would not otherwise do. Almost everyone has the desire to control their partner and wants his mate to make sacrifices for him or for the sake of the relationship. You may find it upsetting to admit this; however, your upset or denial does not alter the truth about it. Everyone wishes that their partner would change and be more like the person that they want them to be. The question is not whether this is true, but whether you are willing to deal with your desire to control your partner.

Couples who are unwilling to acknowledge and address their control patterns discover that the patterns in fact control their love life by establishing the rules for household behavior. It is fine to have rules for behavior; however, it is unlikely that either of you will be satisfied unless the rules are discussed and mutually agreed upon as benefiting both partners. Undiscussed control patterns turn the relationship into a power struggle where each partner struggles for dominance over the control patterns of the other, creating a constant source of arguments and/or resentment. The most enduring control patterns are the ones that are motivated by unconscious fear. These patterns tend to be the most covert, the most denied and the least discussed. In this situation one person is afraid that something bad will happen, if he does not control his mate, but he is not quite sure of what the bad outcome might be. If the person's unconscious mind believes that the undesirable result of not controlling his partner would be that his partner leaves him, then the person may engage in extreme behavior and even tolerate or inflict extreme abuse to keep the partner around.

We can state several examples here.

The man who uses money to control his wife, by
  a. Insisting that he be the only breadwinner, or
  b. Thinking his wife's career is of secondary importance, or
  c. Providing money as a substitute for affection and time, or
  d. Demanding to control the money and withholding it or threatening to do so, when he doesn't get his way, or
  e. Consistently mismanaging money so that his partner feels unable to leave or so that his partner feels that she can't make it without him.

The person who uses his partner's jealousy to exert control by
  a. Excessive flirtation or extramarital affairs, or
  b. Acting the life of the party in social situations, but acting bored and detached at home, or
  c. Making unfavorable comparisons between his partner and other members of the opposite sex.

d. Devoting so much time and energy to his work and other interests that there is little left over for his partner.

The person who uses sex to control his partner by,
  a. Withholding sex or affection, or
  b. Using sex as a relief from tension, or
  c. Unfavorably comparing his partner to previous sexual partners or to the latest Playmate of the Month or the latest rock star, or
  d. Being unwilling to experiment sexually, or
  e. Being unwilling to discuss sex (including the unwillingness to ask for it and to ask for it the way you want it).
  f. Using sex to avoid arguing.
  g. Relying on frequency or technique to provide satisfaction.

The person who uses criticism to control his partner by:
  a. Scoffing at his partner's ability to accomplish goals, plans and dreams, or
  b. Complaining instead of making direct requests, or
  c. Constantly finding fault with his partner and his partner's methods of self-expression and rarely mentioning the extent to which his partner is already the way he most prefers, or
  d. Continually analyzing the cause of his partner's problems and pointing out solutions, or
  e. Demanding that his partner live up to his standards and believing that he is doing his partner a favor by pointing out the extent to which the partner does not measure up.

The person who uses his helplessness to control his partner by:
  a. Denying the problems that his addictions cause him, and preferring to stay helpless about them, instead of seeking the help that will activate associated suppressed feelings, or
  b. Being unwilling to stand up for himself in any argument, or
  c. By allowing his partner to take care of him to such a degree that he feels that he has no power in the relationship, or
  d. Being unwilling to make the desired changes in his life, or
  e. Being unwilling to succeed in work that he loves, resulting a scarcity of money and satisfaction, or
  f. Depending on his partner to make the important decisions and depending on his partner to constantly make up for his emotional shortcomings.

The person whose unresolved shame causes him to use shame to control his partner by:
   a. Referring to the partner in the third person even when the partner is there.
   b. Constantly bringing up old hurts or wrongdoings instead of forgiving, or
   c. Public criticism, blame, ridicule, sarcasm or cynicism, or
   d. Disclosure of tender confidences inappropriately, or
   e. Pointing out how the particular character defects of his partner are the cause of his failures.

In conducting our LSC, we have observed four major unproductive ways in which patterns mesh. We will describe these so you can identify how your own control patterns operate. If honest about your behavior you can see the patterns and may find that you have adopted different roles, depending on the issue at stake. Although your mind may lie about your behavior, your behavior doesn't lie about you. Behavior is motivated in every case by values. Values, whether healthy or not, are contexts that we are unwilling to change.

1. Complainer/People Pleaser
2. Authoritarian/Puppet
3. Withholder/Dependent
4. Guilt Tripper/Guilt Ridden

Recovery Process

COMPLAINER QUIZ.

Based on your behavior in your love life, do you have difficulty stating your desires in the form of requests?
Never ___   Rarely ___   Sometimes ___   Usually ___   Always ___

Based on your behavior in your love life, do you think that there is one right way to do things?

Never ___ Rarely ___ Sometimes ___ Usually ___ Always ___

Based on your behavior in your love life, do you have difficulty acknowledging the good things about your lover?

Never ___ Rarely ___ Sometimes ___ Usually ___ Always ___

Based on your behavior in your love life, do you have difficulty taking no for an answer?

Never ____   Rarely ____   Sometimes ____   Usually ____   Always ____

Based on your behavior in your love life, do you continue to have major sources of dissatisfaction that you have done nothing about except complain?

Never ____   Rarely ____   Sometimes ____   Usually ____   Always ____

PEOPLE PLEASER QUIZ

Based on your behavior in your love life, do you often regret saying yes?

Never ____   Rarely ____   Sometimes ____   Usually ____   Always ____

Based on your behavior in your love life, do you state complaints about your mate to third persons without telling your mate about them?

Never ____   Rarely ____   Sometimes ____   Usually ____   Always ____

Based on your behavior in your love life, do you think that you are responsible for your lover's satisfaction?

Never ____   Rarely ____   Sometimes ____   Usually ____   Always ____

Based on your behavior in your love life, does criticism upset you more than you would like?

Never ____   Rarely ____   Sometimes ____   Usually ____   Always ____

Based on your behavior in your love life, do you change your opinion or desire to accommodate your partner?

Never ____   Rarely ____   Sometimes ____   Usually ____   Always ____

AUTHORITARIAN QUIZ

Based on your behavior in your love life, do you make threats in order to get what you want?

Never ____   Rarely ____   Sometimes ____   Usually ____   Always ____

Based on your behavior in your love life, do you ridicule the ineptitude of others?

Never ____   Rarely ____   Sometimes ____   Usually ____   Always ____

Based on your behavior in your love life, do you find it difficult to lose an argument?

Never ____   Rarely ____   Sometimes ____   Usually ____   Always ____

Based on your behavior in your love life, do you take the initiative in decision making?

Never ___ Rarely ___ Sometimes ___ Usually ___ Always ___

Based on your behavior in your love life, do you have difficulty accepting decisions made by your partner?

Never ___ Rarely ___ Sometimes ___ Usually ___ Always ___

PUPPET QUIZ

Based on your behavior in your love life, do you think you need permission from your partner?

Never ___ Rarely ___ Sometimes ___ Usually ___ Always ___

Based on your behavior in your love life, do you have difficulty in taking decisive action for yourself?

Never ___ Rarely ___ Sometimes ___ Usually ___ Always ___

Based on your behavior in your love life, do you do what your partner approves of?

Never ___ Rarely ___ Sometimes ___ Usually ___ Always ___

Based on your behavior in your love life, do you cave in at the first sign of opposition, even though you have well rehearsed in your mind the points you wanted to make?

Never ___ Rarely ___ Sometimes ___ Usually ___ Always ___

Based on your behavior in your love life, do you give up on an issue after your first failure?

Never ___ Rarely ___ Sometimes ___ Usually ___ Always ___

WITHHOLDER/DEPENDENT PERSON

WITHHOLDER QUIZ

Based on your behavior in your love life, do you more often employ manipulation than direct requests to get what you want?

Never ___ Rarely ___ Sometimes ___ Usually ___ Always ___

Based on your behavior in your love life, do you use your partner's weaknesses to get your way?

Never ____   Rarely ____   Sometimes ____   Usually ____   Always ____

Based on your behavior in your love life, do you have difficulty discussing issues that might be upset your partner?

Never ____   Rarely ____   Sometimes ____   Usually ____   Always ____

Based on your behavior in your love life, do you withhold money or sex?

Never ____   Rarely ____   Sometimes ____   Usually ____   Always ____

Based on your behavior in your love life, do you have difficulty discussing your feelings?

Never ____   Rarely ____   Sometimes ____   Usually ____   Always ____

DEPENDENT PERSON QUIZ

Based on your behavior in your love life, do you have difficulty trusting your own decisions?

Never ____   Rarely ____   Sometimes ____   Usually ____   Always ____

Based on your behavior in your love life, do you need your partner to be happy?

Never ____   Rarely ____   Sometimes ____   Usually ____   Always ____

Based on your behavior in your love life, do you excuse your failures by telling yourself how hard you tried?

Never ____   Rarely ____   Sometimes ____   Usually ____   Always ____

Based on your behavior in your love life, would you have difficulty maintaining your current lifestyle on your own income?

Never ____   Rarely ____   Sometimes ____   Usually ____   Always ____

Based on your behavior in your love life, do you require reassurance from others?

Never ____   Rarely ____   Sometimes ____   Usually ____   Always ____

GUILT TRIPPER/GUILT RIDDEN

GUILT TRIPPER QUIZ

Based on your behavior in your love life, are you often embarrassed by your partner?

Never ____   Rarely ____   Sometimes ____   Usually ____   Always ____

Based on your behavior in your love life, do you think that it is your duty to point out your partner's mistakes?

Never ____   Rarely ____   Sometimes ____   Usually ____   Always ____

Based on your behavior in your love life, do you point out your partner's shortcomings?

Never ____   Rarely ____   Sometimes ____   Usually ____   Always ____

Based on your behavior in your love life, do you think that your partner should do more to improve himself?

Never ____   Rarely ____   Sometimes ____   Usually ____   Always ____

GUILT RIDDEN PERSON QUIZ

Based on your behavior in your love life, do you apologize for things that are not your fault?

Never ____   Rarely ____   Sometimes ____   Usually ____   Always ____

Based on your behavior in your love life, do you have difficulty believing compliments or acknowledgement?

Never ____   Rarely ____   Sometimes ____   Usually ____   Always ____

Based on your behavior in your love life, do you expect or deserve punishment for your shortcomings?

Never ____   Rarely ____   Sometimes ____   Usually ____   Always ____

Based on your behavior in your love life, do you have difficulty saying good things about yourself?

Never ____   Rarely ____   Sometimes ____   Usually ____   Always ____

WHAT HAVE YOU IDENTIFIED THAT YOU WANT TO CHANGE?

Recognition is an essential step in changing patterns. We hope that you have seen that even the patterns which you think control others actually limit your own freedom a whole lot more than they control anyone else. It's OK that you feel ashamed about the pervasive control that your patterns have on your life. See if you can find the courage for open discussion of what you learned with others and ask for their support in changing them.

THE THREE DYNAMIC LAWS OF RELATIONSHIPS

Three Laws of relationships explain how the desire to keep your patterns intact operates (often without your awareness) in your relationships. If you are not aware of the operation of the Laws, they tend to keep the patterns intact. If you are aware of them, you can use them to make conscious changes to your patterns.

They are:
1. Law of Selection
2. Law of Interpretation
3. Law of Transformation

1. **Law of Selection** is that both of you will tend to select and be selected by people with whom your patterns, goals and values are compatible, whether they are consciously developed or unconsciously chosen. Thus, people who like exercise attract each other, people who like the same kind of music attract each other, complainers attract people pleasers, authoritarians attract those who want to be told what to do, rescuers attract those who need help (and vice versa) and so on.

2. **Law of Interpretation** is that both of you tend to interpret the behavior of each other based on the contexts that you have already developed and will continue to do so until you begin to develop different contexts. Thus, the wife of one husband who does his own laundry

appreciates his independence, feels grateful for his helpfulness and is glad she doesn't have to do it herself; while the wife of another husband who does his own laundry laments his unwillingness to let her help him, secretly fears he thinks her incompetent or feels insecure that he doesn't need her.

3. **Law of Transformation** is that both of you try to change each other "for better or worse". What matters here is that this desire to change each other be discussed openly to eliminate covert manipulation and endless arguments. It is fine to have the desire to change your lover. Problems arise when this desire manifests itself in criticism, shaming, complaining, ridicule or guilt tripping. At worst, your lover becomes a project that you take on without their knowledge, consent or co-operation.

The satisfaction that you experience in your love life depends greatly on your ability to use these Three Dynamic Laws of Relationships to your benefit. They are in operation whether you are aware of this or not, so really what matters is how to apply them so that you have what you want.

HOW TO PUT THESE LAWS ON YOUR SIDE.

1. Law of Selection

Become comfortable with saying NO to what you don't want. Become the person that you want to be. Develop a clear idea about what you do want in a relationship and what you have to offer. Practice full disclosure about the values and rights that are important to you. Use the Vivation process to resolve any discomfort associated with receiving what you want.

2. Law of Interpretation

Ask people what they mean by what they say, if you have any doubt. Be willing to change contexts so that you listen and look for the loving intention in the words and behavior of others before jumping to conclusions. Express your mistrust gently and promptly. Ask your partner for what you want, instead of staying stuck in making your partner wrong for not providing it. We all make conclusions about other people based on scanty and often wrong information. Another way to say this is that we live with ourselves for decades without knowing why we do certain things and yet we claim to know everything about someone that we have just met. Using the Law of Interpretation to your benefit requires willingness to challenge long held beliefs.

3. Law of Transformation

Communicate openly with your partner about what you wish to teach him and what you wish to learn from him, so that you agree about this instead of covertly manipulating or complaining about each other. Find out what your partner's goals and aspirations are and ask how you can aid in their accomplishment, so that you grow together instead of apart.

Much of the rest of the book is about how you can use these Three Laws of Relationships to your benefit.

With a highly developed skill at resolving patterns, theoretically you could have a satisfying love life with anyone, if that were all there was to it. There is much more to it, however. We all have patterns and expectations that we are unwilling to change under any condition. These are called our values. You may value politeness and would not abide a lover who was rude, you may value gentleness and refuse to accept brutality from your partner, or you may value fidelity and refuse to accept promiscuity. It is fine that you select a partner that satisfies the consciously chosen values that matter to you and fine that you let your partner know about them.

CHAPTER 13   SEX

There is nothing wrong with sex! Sexual desire is built into your body just like your desire for food, water, sleep and warmth; nevertheless, there is probably no topic on which people have more intensely conflicting emotions and around which there are more firmly established patterns, addictions and compulsions. The well-being of our society and our personal happiness require that we act responsibly about sex and require that we are properly educated. All of this is true of driving an automobile; yet, sex education in high school is a far more emotional and controversial topic than driver education.

All of us are very confused about sex, at best (and neurotic at worst) as a result of the age old conflicting messages about it. One message about sex that is consistently delivered by parents and religion is that it is not OK to talk about sex. This message perpetuates confusion and conflict. For some people, religious training has added the message that it is not OK even to think about sex.

Almost all of us grew up in dysfunctional families regarding sex. By this we mean, sex was not discussed in any useful way, and instead was joked about, denied or hidden. In other words, if your parents were unwilling to talk with you about sex, offer advice and teach you how to be responsible about it, then you will require emotional adjustments to develop attitudes about sex that serve you.

EXPECTATIONS ABOUT SEX

There is an expectation, despite very little education and discussion, that by some magical process, we should grow up to be "good lovers". It is not our desire to impose our sexual values on you. Sex is very personal. What turns you on, may cause another to run screaming from the room. There is no such thing as a normal sex drive, a normal frequency for sex or a normal time, way or place for it, any more than there is a normal desire for egg salad sandwiches. All of this is a function of context. Your parents, religion, advertising, movies and TV, music and peer pressure

impose their conflicting values about sex on you and it is your responsibility to sort all of this out to your satisfaction.

Simply asking for sex when you want it is far more straightforward and far less stressful than the foolish games and rituals of seduction that cause people to feel taken advantage of and which promote emptiness and dissatisfaction. It is surprising we do it at all. No wonder some people fall into bed, turn out the light, crawl under the covers, shut their eyes and don't talk while having sex, hoping that their partner, (who is doing the same thing), is enjoying himself.

Despite all this, making improvements in your sex life is no more difficult than in any other area of your life. You can count on your examination of your sex life to be very emotionally activating. Sex is not an intellectual experience, if its any good. You can be sure that the Vivation process will aid you in making the changes that you want by resolving the uncomfortable feelings, by making discussion and relaxation easier and eliminating the distraction of mental chatter.

Shame is another common destructive context about sex. There is nothing wrong with sex. You can be yourself and have the sex life you want. You have the right to choose your own contexts and values about sex. No matter what they are, you'll enjoy your sex life more if you talk about sex for the very important reason that your partner also is sorting out his or her own set of conflicting messages.

For some, it will come as a surprise to realize that there is a connection between their birth experience and their sex life. People commonly believe that remembering one's birth experience is impossible. However, spontaneous recall of one's birth experience often occurs while engaging in the Vivation process. The analogies between birth and sex are actually quite evident once you think about it. In fact, your sex life began at conception.

1. Birth and sex are both highly emotional experiences.
2. Sex leads to birth, unless their is birth control.
3. Birth and sex both deal with genitals.
4. For the man, sex involves returning the most sensitive part of his body to the birth canal.
5. For the woman, sex activates thoughts about pregnancy and focuses attention on reproductive organs.
6. Sex is how you got here.
7. Your existence is proof that your parents had sex.
8. Sex brings up feelings of being out of control, vulnerability and dependency.

9. Fears about being hurt and hurting someone else are activated.
10. Shame about being a disappointment or the wrong gender or about being wanted at all are activated.
11. The obstetrician and nurse who handled you at birth provided your first experience of being vulnerable in the hands of someone else.

Knowing how sex may relate to your birth experience and integration of the suppressed emotions associated with birth in your Vivation sessions can aid you is resolving some of the sexual difficulties that have plagued you for years.

SEXUAL HISTORY QUIZ

This quiz is designed to recognize patterns about sex and about talking about sex. It's a self-evaluation quiz about your sex life and how you get started with your lovers. This one is more like an essay quiz than the first one which was multiple choice. We ask you to complete this quiz on separate sheets of paper.

WHAT TO DO

STEP 1 Make six lists of the names of people who are in each of the following categories. It is possible that the same person may appear in more than one category.

1. All the people whom you invited to have sex with you and they said yes.

2. All the people whom you invited to have sex with you and they said NO.
3. All the people who invited you to have sex with them and you said YES.
4. All the people who invited you to have sex with them and you said NO.
5. Successful seductions.
6. Failed seductions.

For this quiz, seduction refers to a situation where there was no clear verbal communication about sex beforehand. Some may call it the grope and hope approach to sexuality.

STEP 2.

Go back over your list and write next to the name of each person who, if anyone they remind you of.

STEP 3.

Go back over your list again and write next to each name how you feel about that person appearing on your list. Some examples may be happy, ashamed, longing, betrayed, jealous or angry.

STEP 4

Study what you have written. You have before you extremely useful information about yourself. Does one of your six lists have many more people on it then the others? What does this mean? Do many of your lovers remind you of a family member or of each other? What does this mean? What are the aspects of this list that you want more of in your life and which ones do you want to change? Was there caring in your relationships or were most of them one night stands? There is no end to what you can learn.

RESOLVING CHILDHOOD ABUSE AND SEXUAL ABUSE

Nothing is more destructive to a satisfying sex life than unresolved feelings of childhood sexual abuse. If you were or suspect you were abused sexually as a child, a great deal of effort is required to suppress the fear, shame, rage, mistrust and humiliation associated with this. Sexual abuse covers a wide range of behavior that adults inflict on children including fondling, inappropriate touching, exposure, harassment and intercourse. Even one episode can be very damaging to your sexual enjoyment. Since tremendous effort is expended just to keep the memories suppressed, this tends to close down your feelings, making it difficult to feel sexual desire or arousal, even when you want to have sex. Other victims become pre-occupied with sex, in a desperate search for satisfaction or resolution.

As children, we had a substantial expectation that adults in general and parents in particular would take care of us and treat us gently. In other words we expected them to respect our obvious helplessness. Childhood sexual abuse is a catastrophic violation and often results in doubt or denial that it actually happened, since the act is so vastly contradictory to normal expectations. Often there is suppressed rage toward the family members who were not involved, but who took no action to stop it. It is possible that you were sexually abused as a child, but have suppressed the memory of this.

If you expect that you were, it is ESSENTIAL that you let your partner know and request patience and gentleness. Having sex will cause these memories to flood back at least in the form of body sensations. Struggling to suppress the memories is the cause of most impotency and frigidity. Simply communicating about this will aid you greatly in resolving your shame about it. Being sexually abused means nothing bad about you. The perpetrator is one who ought to feel ashamed.

The primary message associated with childhood sexual abuse is "Don't tell!" or "Don't talk about it!" (because something bad will happen). This can be carried into adult life as a strict rule that says "Don't talk about sex!"

Nevertheless, childhood sexual abuse is receiving greater media and national attention than ever and it has become more socially acceptable to discuss it. People are coming out of denial about sexual abuse. Vivation is an extremely effective method for activating memories and resolving the feelings associated with childhood sexual abuse. This resolution is a very common occurrence among people who attend the LSC. Please refer to Chapter 28 about advanced applications of Vivation for details about this.

14 ATTITUDE BUILDERS FOR YOUR LOVE LIFE
Putting Your Mind to Work

Attitude builders are useful in changing the unconsciously chosen patterns of behavior that you don't like. They are statements that aid your mind in adopting and developing contexts that add to your happiness, well-being or effectiveness. You do not necessarily change your reality directly; instead, you change your attitude or context about your reality, thereby empowering you to take the direct action that WILL change your reality or to CEASE taking the action that prevents the change that you want from occurring.

The methods we will describe for the use of Attitude Builders enable you to put your mind on your side, and enlist its co-operation in telling you the thoughts that contradict your desires and to discover the suppressed feelings that are stopping you from having what you want.

The methods that we describe for the use of Attitude Builders do not rely on endless repetition to get what you want. The human mind is much more like a computer than a piece of sheet metal. If you rely solely on repetition in the use of Attitude Builders, this is like assuming that your mind is a piece of sheet metal and if you could just pound it into the right shape, then it would give you what you want.

Some people have noticed that the appearance of their handwriting changes as they write. Both of us have experienced our penmanship looking like that of an elementary school student, in instances where thoughts and feelings suppressed since childhood were coming to our awareness. Writing your Attitude Builders in your first language (mother tongue) greatly adds to their effectiveness, even if you have not used your first language for decades and have to look up some of the words in a bilingual dictionary.

Choose specific Attitude Builders that produce an emotional reaction in you, in fact, the more intense the better. You want to write the ones that make you feel very wonderful or very awful or cause you to laugh. Writing emotionally neutral statements is a waste of your time. Sometimes changing just one word in an attitude builder makes a big difference in your response. For example, "I deserve lots of loving sex." may produce a very different reaction for you than "I want lots of loving sex." Obviously the techniques we describe in this Chapter about Attitude Builders may be applied to any area of your life, despite the fact that the all examples we use are about sex.

For an attitude builder to produce the results that you want, at least some part of your mind must already agree with the statement. It is fine that your mind contains some conflict about it, but if it is completely convinced that the statement is wrong or untrue or impossible, then you are just wasting your time. One thing you can do in this instance is reword the attitude builder so that it is less absolute. Using the earlier example of "I deserve lots of loving sex", you could change it to "It is OK for me to find out my fears about having lots of loving sex" or "My mind is opening to the possibility of lots of loving sex."

Here is another way, called Proving that its True. Let's say that your mind is producing nothing but resistance to the statement, "I deserve lots of loving sex." For this Attitude Builder to have any effect on your mind, you must shift your context to see the truth in it. After all it is up to you to convince yourself. No one else will do it.

Here's how:

Why it is to my benefit to accept as true "I deserve lots of loving sex".
   1. Sexual frustration distracts me from my work, so I'd be more effective in my job.

136

2. Practice will make me a better lover.
3. Plenty of loving sex will make me happier, benefiting everyone I know and meet.
4. Sex improves my breathing and circulation so it is good for my health.
5. My lover will derive pleasure from it, too.
6. God wants me to have pleasure.
7. If God had wanted me to have sex, then I would have genitals.
8. If I already have lots of loving sex, then I won't need to manipulate or control others to get it.
9. I will be more able to discuss sex with my children.
10. I will be able to help other people with their sexual problems by using what I learn in the process of improving my sex life.

Got the idea?

An important principle regarding Attitude Builders is that the first step is to accept your current reality as it is. In other words, insisting that the situation or other person is wrong will do nothing to aid you in changing it or improving its effect on you. This is because denying that it exists prevents you from dealing with it. Let's say that your lover tells you that he had a one night stand and is now asking for forgiveness. Obviously, anyone would feel distressed in this situation and you may wonder how you could accept this situation. Some of the Attitude Builders that may help you integrate your feelings are:

1. It is OK for me to feel upset about infidelity.
2. It is OK for me to want revenge.
3. I am grateful for my lover's honesty.
4. It is OK for me to express my mistrust.
5. It is OK for me to feel helpless to control the behavior of others.

Attitude builders like those above aid you in accepting the feelings associated with the situation. Without this there will be a tendency to suppress and deny the feelings and perhaps even deny that it happened— we often hear people say, "I can't believe that this happened". Nothing changes until it is real.

Commonly asked questions about Attitude Builders are, "How long should I write them?", "How do I know when I am done?" and "What is the best time for writing them?" We suggest that you write a specific attitude builder until it provides the result that you want. If this does not occur within a week or so, then switch to a different one. Going back to "I deserve lots of loving sex", once you are making tangible progress toward your desire for lots of loving sex (you have improved at discussing sex with your lover or you are attracting more people who are sexually interested in you and vice versa), then it is a good idea to switch to a different attitude builder to re-inforce the progress you have made. Examples could be, "My ability to discuss sex contributes to my having lots of loving sex", or "My sexual attractiveness is a blessing for everyone", or "It is OK and natural for me to have fears about sex." Another way know you are done with a particular attitude builder is to use the sentence in your daily conversation and notice that you feel fine about it.

The best time to write them is mostly a matter of personal preference. Just like physical exercise, establishing a regular time each day or week will make Attitude Builders a habit for you. If you have written some for a while and stopped for some reason, you will probably notice that your mind has gotten flabby and out of shape.

We enjoy writing them together and discussing our progress.

Examples of specific Attitude Builders about your love life.

1. I am grateful I know that my parents were wrong about _____ . (obligation) (sex) (loyalty) (etc.)
2. I am grateful that my love life is this good.
3. I forgive myself for struggling with relationships.
4. I am developing a better sense of humor about my love life.
5. Sex is innocent.
6. It as OK for me to have as few and as many lovers as I want.
7. The lovers I want are attracted to me by my desire for them.
8. I am developing the wisdom, power and ability to have the love life I want.
9. My bedroom is a place for fun.
10. When I mean YES, I say YES; when I mean NO, I say NO.
11. There is nothing wrong with sex.
12. It is OK for me to think about sex.
13. It is OK for me to be interested in sex.
14. It is OK for me to talk about sex with anyone.
15. All my sexual desires are holy.
16. I can take it or leave it.
17. Sex is good.
18. Sex is natural.

19. My sexual desires are approved of by my parents, God and everyone.
20. I forgive myself for my irresponsibility about sex in the past.
21. I am OK whether or not I have sex.
22. My past no longer rules my sex life; my sex life is now ruled by my current desires.
23. It is OK for me to ask for sex.
24. It is OK for me to want to improve as a lover.
25. I am one of the greatest lovers in the world.

We will offer several ways for you to use Attitude Builders as a tool to improve your life, and it is fine for you to invent your own ways. The method that works best for you is a matter of personal preference. In this book, we will focus on Attitude Builders for improving your love life. You can use this tool to improve any area of your life, simply by modifying the content of the Attitude Builders that you use.

Ways to use Attitude Builders

1. Write down the reasons why you do not now have the sex life that you want and then write a statement for each reason in a positive context.
2. Make lists of them.
3. Work them into your conversation.
4. Write them and record your reactions.
5. Write them on signs and place them around your house.
6. Include them in songs or letters that you write.
7. Ask your friends to remind you of them and do the same for them.

Examples of these methods are:

1. Write down the reasons that you do not now have the love life that you want. Start with a clean piece of paper and write at the top: "Twenty reasons that I do not have the love life that I want", then number from

1 to 20 down the left hand margin and write as fast as you can, without considering whether what you are writing is right or whether you believe it. Take an adventurous point of view about learning the content of your mind. Your list may look like this:

Twenty reasons that I do not have the love life that I want
  1. I don't know how.
  2. I don't know what I want.
  3. I'm too old (young).
  4. I'm too busy.
  5. I am afraid of being trapped.
  6. I am afraid I will have to give up too much.
  7. I prefer being alone.
  8. I don't know anyone who has the kind of love life I want.
  9. (Wo)men are all the same.
 10. The (wo)men I want don't want me.
 11. My parents always struggled in their relationship.
 12. There are no (wo)men that I want.
 13. It is impossible.
 14. I am afraid of being hurt.
 15. I will lose control of my life.
 16. I won't like it.
 17. I'd be ashamed to have it better than my friends (family).
 18. Getting what I want would require, or at least risk, upsets.
 19. Having a lover will change me for the worse.
 20. Relationships only stay good for a little while.

If you only go this far, it is possible that you may wish to give up, regretting that you ever started to explore your thinking about your love life. The next step requires some imagination and some willingness to see things differently. Now take another piece of paper and compose an attitude builder to establish a positive context for each of your reasons or excuses.

For example:
  1. I can learn how to have the love life that I want.
  2. I am willing to find out what I want in my love life.
  3. I am the right age to have the love life I want.
  4. The love life I want is worthy of a higher priority.

5. I know how to avoid people who want to control me and I know how to deal with my feelings of being trapped.
6. I am willing to put myself first in my life.
7. Knowing how to enjoy my solitude adds greatly to my enjoyment of my love life.
8. I am excited by the prospect of being a pioneer in having the love life that I want.
9. I am grateful that I have identified what I don't want in a lover.
10. The lover(s) I want are attracted to me by my desire for them.
11. I am grateful for everything I learned from my parents' mistakes.
12. It is fine for me to enjoy my attraction to the opposite sex.
13. I now see the humor of pretending that it is impossible for me to have the love life that I want.
14. I forgive myself for letting my lovers hurt me.
15. It is OK for me to say NO when I mean it.
16. I know how to enjoy my love life and how to maintain it the way I like.
17. My friends and family will be inspired by my love life.
18. I forgive myself for being the compulsive peace maker in the past.
19. I know how to have a love life that contributes to my well-being in every way.
20. I know how to maintain my love life so that it pleases me.

Recovery Process

2. Make lists of them. Making a list of Attitude Builders that would improve your love life is similar to doing the second part of the above exercise on its own.

Start with a clean piece of paper and write at the top: "Twenty Attitude Builders that could improve my love life", then number from 1 to 20 down the left margin and start writing.

3. Work them into your conversation. When talking to a friend say something like: "You know, for a long time I was embarrassed about this, but now I know I deserve lots of loving sex."

4. Write them and record your reactions.

Attitude Builders offer you the opportunity to change your thinking and have peace of mind. Far more important than the intellectual aspects are the emotional issues, for which the Vivation process will aid you.

15   ESTABLISHING AND MAINTAINING HEALTHY RIGHTS AND BOUNDARIES

Most of our parents spent more energy in fostering obedience in us than in fostering self-authority. For this reason, we have a poorly defined sense of our rights the ability to say NO and expect it to mean something. Parents crossed our boundaries to control us and there was nothing we could do about it. This results in either compulsive conformity or compulsive rebellion to anyone asking us to do something, since these were the only choices available to us as children.

Some people stay alone because they are afraid of what they may have to give up in order to have the love life that they want. Other people stay in relationships that provide them little or nothing except avoiding being alone. It is not necessary to give up what matters to you to have and keep a lover in your life. In fact what matters to you most is what you have to offer to a relationship, so giving up your important values to keep a lover around is a mistake that can contribute only to your unhappiness. Defining what your rights are and communicating them to your partner is important because it is all too common for people to sacrifice their important values, beliefs, desires, or emotions in order to preserve their relationship. This most often occurs when there is a disagreement and one partner relinquishes his rights to preserve the peace or the relationship. Some of your rights will be negotiable and some of them are not. This is a very important difference and it is a good idea that both you and your partner discuss and agree on these topics before becoming committed.

It is essential to the equality of a healthy relationship that there be respect for your own values. Closeness does not necessarily result from sameness of values, but rather from respect for differences. By rights we mean to imply those desires that are important enough to you, which, if not met, would cause you to very seriously consider separation.

We have noticed that participants in the LSC Weekend sometimes have difficulties in claiming what their rights are. It is essential that you claim your rights, know what your boundaries are and be able to communicate to your partner, or else there will be no boundaries. Otherwise it is likely that you'll get less than you want and give up more than you want to. If you don't put yourself first, it is foolish to expect someone else to. Serious consideration of what really matters to you is extremely valuable.

Some of the rights that we have reserved as non-negotiable are; the right to discuss any topic, the right to expect honesty, the right to spend our money as we please, time alone, and the right to choose our own friends. We are willing to negotiate about our business policies, our interests, what kinds of food we eat, the amount of time spent together, and sharing household duties etc.

The United States Constitution gives rights to all people and you deserve yours in your love life. Take your time in filling in the blanks above and then share them with your partner. Both you and your partner will be happier in the long run if a sense of equality and independence is maintained, but you'll have to define your rights to yourself first.

BILL OF RIGHTS

I reserve the right to _____
_____ in my relationship.

I reserve the right to _____
_____ in my relationship.

I reserve the right to _____
_____ in my relationship.

I reserve the right to _____
_____ in my relationship.

I reserve the right to _____
_____ in my relationship.

I reserve the right to _____
_____ in my relationship.

I reserve the right to _____
_____ in my relationship.

I reserve the right to _____
_____ in my relationship.

I reserve the right to _____
_____ in my relationship.

I reserve the right to _____
_____ in my relationship.

I reserve the right to _____
_____ in my relationship.

16 THE PURPOSE OF YOUR LOVE LIFE
Mapping out the future

We discussed in the Chapter about patterns, how the unconscious part of your mind creates results in your life that you do not recall asking for. Having what you want means that you have what your conscious mind wants. In other words, you recall asking for what you have. In our LSC, we teach participants how to define the purpose of their love life. You may be surprised that one's love life can actually have purpose and intention. The surprise is likely caused by the hope that we will "fall in love", meaning that we have little or no say about what "happens to us". These expectations leave only blind hope that you will find and marry the right person for you and, then by some undefined process, continue to contribute to each other's dreams and live happily ever after.

Purpose is defined in the dictionary as; "that which a person sets before himself as an object to be reached or accomplished." However, a purpose is not the same thing as a goal, which has a defined beginning, middle and end. Instead, a purpose is something that is continually expressed.

Your relationship has no purpose until you give it one. Without a consciously chosen purpose for your relationship, your love life will be driven by the unconsciously chosen directions dictated by the suppressed conditioning from your family of origin.

Here is a partial list of BENEFITS of defining the purpose of your love life.

You will know why you want a love life and what you want out of it. You will send a message to your unconscious mind about what you want.

You will be able to identify people that you do want (and those you don't want) a lot more quickly, so you won't have to settle for whatever comes along and be disappointed later.

You will feel better talking about yourself to new people that you meet. You will use what you have rather than keep wishing you were different. You will focus your attention on the things that you already like about yourself.

Recovery Process

THE PURPOSE OF YOUR LOVE LIFE

Step 1:

Write a list of 20 personality characteristics that you like about yourself as a lover. By "lover", we mean lover in the broadest sense and not limited to your expression of your sexuality. Express these characteristics as nouns. For example, my gentle touch, my honesty, my compassion, my patience, my sense of humor, my stamina, etc.

Here is some space for your list. (Remember, like most tools, this one won't work for you if you don't use it). Don't quit until you have 20. The faster you write the easier this will be.

1. My _____
2. My _____

3. My _____
4. My _____
5. My _____
6. My _____
7. My _____
8. My _____
9. My _____
10. My _____
11. My _____
12. My _____
13. My _____
14. My _____
15. My _____
16. My _____
17. My _____
18. My _____
19. My _____
20. My _____

Step 2:

Look over the list that you just made and select three to five of your favorite characteristics by circling the numbers.

Write your 3 to 5 favorite characteristics about yourself as a lover in the this blank space _____
_____
_____ .

Step 3:

Then make another list of 20 ways that you enjoy EXPRESSING the 3 to 5 favorite characteristics that you have written. State the items on this list as gerunds. For example; dancing, cooking, making love, buying surprise gifts, going for walks in the moonlight etc.

20 ways I enjoy EXPRESSING my favorite characteristics about myself as a lover:

1._____ ing _____
2._____ ing _____
3._____ ing _____
4._____ ing _____
5._____ ing _____
6._____ ing _____

149

7._____ ing _____
8._____ ing _____
9._____ ing _____
10._____ ing _____
11._____ ing _____
12._____ ing _____
13._____ ing _____
14._____ ing _____
15._____ ing _____
16._____ ing _____
17._____ ing _____
18._____ ing _____
19._____ ing _____
20._____ ing _____

Step 4:

Write a brief description, in 25 words or less, of your personal vision of an ideal love life. Write your statement in the present tense (without any WILL BE, COULD BE) and write your statement in terms of what you do want, rather than by stating what you do NOT want. Make your statement about what you want, and NOT about what you think you can get or how you will get it. Space is provided below.

_____
_____
_____
_____
_____

Step 5:

Return to the list that you made in step 3, and select the three to five items from that list that will contribute the MOST to your ideal love life as you have it stated in step 4.

Step 6:

The final step is where we put it all together into one sentence that is a statement of the purpose of your love life.

The Purpose of my love life is to use my _____
_____

by _____
_____

so that _____

_____

_____ .

The sentence contains three blank spaces. In the first blank space (after the word "my"), write in the three to five items that you selected from the list in step 1. In the second blank space (after the word "by"), write in your three to five favorite ways of expressing yourself as a lover that you chose in step 5. In the third blank space (after the words "so that", write in your statement of your ideal love life that you made in step 4.

You may find it useful to do this process several times refining the statement until you have it exactly the way that you want it. We suggest that you redefine the purpose of your love life once a year, to account for any change in desires, values or progress in your own self-development.

You know you have the statement written exactly the way you want it reading it stimulates enthusiasm and inspiration. Once you have done this, put it somewhere you can refer to it frequently: a 3×5 card in your wallet, posted on your refrigerator or framed and hung on the wall. In the LSC, there is often spontaneous applause and cheers in response to participants reading their statement of purpose.

TEACHING THE PURPOSE PROCESS TO PROSPECTIVE LOVERS

Teaching this process to someone else is a very effective way to get to know them quickly. This is because you will find out what is important to them, and what they want from their love life. It is very easy to say something like, "I just finished reading a wonderful book called Love, Sex and Communication For Everyone. In it the authors showed me how to define the purpose of my love life, would you like to hear my purpose? Would you like to define your own? It's very simple and alot of fun." Now, this maybe a very new idea for them to consider and they may even be suspicious at first. However, even if the other person runs for the door, you will have gained some very useful information about them.

In this section we have covered understanding your emotions, the effect of your family of origin, resolving patterns, sex, Attitude Builders, defining your boundaries and the purpose of your love life, which help you to make the most of being single.

151

17 HOW TO ENJOY BEING SINGLE
Putting Yourself First

Being single is not the same for everyone. The difference is your context or attitude about your singleness. This largely depends on your ability to enjoy your own company. Some people shudder at the thought of being alone, and rush to fill up the void while agonizing over the hunt for their ideal mate, while others enjoy the solitude, thriving on their self-reliance while pursuing their studies or career. For others, their singleness is a compulsive struggle to avoid commitment. You have probably discovered that your feelings about being single change from time to time. The key to enjoying being single is resolving feelings of loneliness (and sometimes associated rejection). If it is not OK to feel lonely, then you may be are compulsively driven to associate with others and won't enjoy their company very much when you are with them, because of the worry about doing something that may drive them away, leaving you lonely again. Shame about your loneliness may also keep you by yourself. Learning Self-Vivation is the best way that we know to resolve feelings of loneliness and to enjoy your own company.

Both of us were single for many years before we were married. Sometimes we enjoyed it and sometimes we didn't. In this section we will tell you about some of the ideas that added greatly to our enjoyment and peace of mind. We are not advocating being single or being committed, you can choose to live happily ever after alone or with someone else. Being happy or unhappy is a matter of context and the context in which you hold your life at this moment determines whether you enjoy yourself or not.

1. Do not constantly make yourself wrong for not having the lover of your dreams. Many people make the mistake of thinking that their loneliness proves there is something wrong with them. They begin to focus only on the loneliness they feel to the point of hating the opposite sex and themselves, until this is projected on to everyone they meet. Work, money and activities can never take the place of someone who loves you. Loneliness does not prove there is something wrong with you. Sometimes the best thing to do is to relax, forgive yourself and continue to work on yourself. Another way to say this is instead of searching for the the perfect mate, become that perfect mate. The ability to do Vivation on your own helps immensely with this. If you insist that you need another person to make you happy, most likely you will be miserable with yourself until he or she shows up. Another problem with this is that you put the responsibility for your happiness on someone else, giving them all the power, leaving you feeling helpless.

2. There is nothing wrong with being alone and your aloneness means nothing about you. If you need a partner to feel good, then you'll always worry that they might leave you and worry whenever they are away.

3. The happier you are with yourself the more attractive you will be to others, unless you are interested in attracting someone who will take on the job of cheering you up or who will accept the challenge of thinking that their love will fix you.

4. Focus on what you have to offer to a relationship and learn how to improve this instead of only focusing on what you want to get. It is perverse that people think they can love someone else more then they love themselves.

5. It is a good idea to develop friendships with people of the opposite sex, so that you develop the ability to have relationships with an aspect of equality and without sexual attraction.

6. Use your singleness as an opportunity to develop your financial independence, if you haven't already done this.

SUPPORTING YOUR FRIENDS IN THEIR LOVE LIFE AND RECEIVING SUPPORT FROM THEM

ALLOWING YOUR FRIENDS TO SUPPORT YOU

DO

Moaning and complaining is OK, but has limited value.
Let your friends know about the good things in your love life, otherwise they will have a distorted picture, if you only tell them about the problems.
The emotional support and compassion of your friends, in most cases, is far more valuable than their advice.
Ask for confidentiality if you want it
Tell your friends what kind of support you want. You can ask them to just listen, hold you, as you cry or help you figure out what to do next.

DO NOT

Use your discussion with your friends to avoid discussing the topic with your mate.
Provide ammunition for gossip.

AIDING YOUR FRIENDS WITH THEIR PROBLEMS

DO

Ask what kind of help they want. Sometimes simply listening is of great value.
Help them to integrate the feelings that they are making wrong, so they can think more clearly
Remind them that the aid that you can provide is limited and that is essential that they discuss the problem with their partner.
Confront your friends who just want to complain

DO NOT

Agree to confidentiality if you don't want to
Take sides
Point out the shortcomings of people not present.

155

Be so quick to give advice that you don't hear them.
Say things like "People don't change" or "All (wo)men are like that".

REJECTION

We all reject people all the time. Rejection is a manifestation of our ability to make choices about what or whom we want. Everyone would agree that rejection does not feel good. We don't like rejecting others because it makes us feel guilty and it also reminds us of the feelings we experienced when we were rejected. If you are going to reject someone, perhaps someone has just asked you out on a date, be gentle, direct and honest, "Thank you for asking me, but no thank you." will ease the rejection. Remember to be compassionate and thank the other person for taking a risk.

When someone rejects us, the pain associated with the feeling of inferiority may cause us to give up, without asking why, or it can make us unwilling to take another risk. Our context or attitude about the rejection governs our future behavior about taking the initiative. Some people are so afraid of rejection that they reject the other person first; thereby avoiding the experience of even possible rejection. Some people feel so guilty about rejecting others that, rather than take steps to end an unwanted relationship, they engage in behavior that they think will motivate their partner to leave or just stay and suffer.

Our point here is that rejection is almost always uncomfortable for both people concerned. Vivation will help you integrate the uncomfortable feelings associated with rejection. Resolving this discomfort doesn't prevent you from being rejected; however, it does prevent you from having your behavior motivated by avoiding rejection.

It is possible that, even with Vivation, you may never completely resolve your fear of rejection. It is not necessary to wait until you feel OK about the possibility of rejection before you make the first move.

THE MAGIC OF MAKING THE FIRST MOVE (FOR MEN)

Some women disapprove of men who make the first move and some women disapprove of men who are afraid to make the first move. Therefore it is possible that the woman who attracts you will disapprove of your behavior no matter what you do. Additionally, some women appreciate

156

the man who is willing to make the first move, while others appreciate the opportunity to do it themselves. Once again, it is possible that the woman who attracts you will appreciate whatever you do.

For these reasons, you are better off if you go ahead and take the initiative, unless you want to waste a lot of time struggling to figure out this puzzle.

It is always uncomfortable to risk rejection and let a woman know that she is attractive to you. It is always fine to let her know that you feel uncomfortable about it. (She'll probably notice your discomfort, whether you mention it or not, unless you are a good actor) It is always OK to say, "I am interested in you." and then talk about your nervousness.

THE MAGIC OF MAKING THE FIRST MOVE (FOR WOMEN)

Most women have been conditioned to let the man make the first move in social situations. We have been told that the man will think you are too forward or pushy if you make the initial approach. We have been told that the way to meet a man is to sit back and look vulnerable and pretty, using body language and a shy flirtatious looks to let the man know of our interest. Clearly this method is effective in many instances; but if it is the only method available to you, you have put yourself in the helpless position of being a permanent contestant in the undeclared beauty contest.

Some women refuse to take any initiative and expect men to make the first move. Then they make the men wrong if their approach does not live up to our uncommunicated, pre-conceived standards of how we think they should act. If they come on too strong we don't like it and reject them as cocky or too fast, or if they are not forward enough we reject them too.

GIVING THE OTHER PERSON THE BENEFIT OF THE DOUBT

When you first meet a person give them a chance to relax and get to know you. It is foolish to brush someone off after the initial contact just because you didn't like their opening line. Some women are far too hard on men expecting him to sweep her off her feet, be aggressive, (but not too aggressive), and make love just they way she prefers even with no responsibility on her part to discuss what she likes.

Sometimes men do a similar thing by expecting a women to be forward, (but not too forward) or having the perfect figure and refusing or not refusing to have sex on the first date. We all have bad days sometimes and most people are at least a little nervous on their first date with a new person, so being too much of a perfectionist may cause you to overlook someone wonderful.

Most people have had the experience of meeting someone and not being very impressed at first. Then, when you find out more about them, or see them in a different context or situation, you are shocked by how different they are and you realize that your first impression was mistaken. You may meet a man in a bar who is a little drunk brush him off as rowdy, at first. Your opinions may change when you see him at the park playing with his young nephew. You may hear a woman conducting a business meeting, where she seems tough and cold hearted, then you meet her at a party and notice her captivating sense of humor. When you are getting to know someone else, it is important that you don't take your initial context or first impression too seriously.

IDENTIFYING THE LOVER THAT YOU WANT

The next important question is: " What do you want?" Most of us know what we don't want. Dwelling on this only leads to frustration. It is good to know what is that you don't prefer and where your boundaries are. Once that is established, then you want to fill your mind with the thoughts of what you do want. Another way to say this is "How will you recognize your ideal lover when they show up if you don't know what you want?"

Recovery
Process

Make a list of at least 100 characteristics of your ideal lover. Be sure to think in detail. It is fine to write down those preferences that seem shallow or unrealistic. For Phil it was important to have a woman that was close

158

to his height of 6'4", that she was self-employed, and that she was interested in Vivation.

For Jeanne, it was important to have a man that was interested in service to mankind, had good relationships with his family, and had work that he loved. If it is important that your ideal mate love gardening or baseball or reads murder mysteries, write it down. Make sure you include that they are available and want you also. Do you want children? Do you want to get married? or have a different lover every day of the week? Do you want a lover 3000 miles away or do you want them to live with you? This is your own personal wish list. It will change as you do, so it is important to keep it up to date.

A benefit of knowing exactly what you want is that it gives you great peace of mind. It is likely that your mind will have thoughts like: "I don't know", "I'll never get this", "Maybe I'm not supposed to have a lover", It's not worth it", etc., etc. Use the occurrence of thoughts like these as a useful cue that Attitude Builders about having what you want would serve you.

Make a list of at least 100 characteristics that you have to offer to a relationship. Once again, be sure to think in detail.

If you don't take the time to notice what is good about you, then it's possible that you'll suspect the people who give you compliments of trying to manipulate you or you'll just shrug them off, without letting them in. Everyone has thousands of things to offer.

WHERE TO LOOK

Once you have made your list, do not sit at home and expect the phone to magically start ringing. It is fine if this happens, but now is the time to DO something. It is our opinion that singles bars are among the worst places to meet people. They are dark and noisy and everyone is either on edge or drunk, depending how long they have been there. We suggest that you go places and do the things that you enjoy doing for their own sake. There are several advantages to this. One is if you don't meet someone, you enjoyed yourself anyway. Another is that you will meet people with interests similar to yours. Ask yourself, "Where do people who are interested in congregate?"

DEALING WITH SHYNESS

The first thing to realize about shyness is that EVERYONE is shy. Some people allow their shyness to rule their social life and others don't. Shyness is a tyrannical and complex mixture of emotions relating to fear of rejection, fear of making a mistake, fear of not measuring up, fear of attention and shame to mention a few. Shyness is an obvious example of an irrational fear. The next time your stomach is in knots and you don't know what to say, ask yourself, "Where is the danger here?" The ability to use Vivation is the single most helpful aid we know of to empower people to get free of the tyranny of shyness. Let yourself feel the feelings in your body completely, take a deep breath and GO FOR IT.

Opening lines—what to say?

You are at a party, meeting or social function and suddenly you notice someone attractive. Perhaps you already have someone in mind whom you see from time to time and have not had the courage to strike up a conversation or to ask for a date. Clearly, there is no single statement that will work in every case; in fact what you say is of far less importance than THAT you say SOMETHING. It is important to remember that the other person may have the same anxiety that you do, or may be pre-occupied by whatever they are doing or thinking about. It is even possible that they will not hear your opening statement. Many books have been written about "How to Pick up Women" or "How to Pick up Men", the best approach is to state the truth. State the truth about your attraction to the other person and state the truth about your nervousness. You don't have to be cool, hip and slick unless you are interested in attracting someone who insists that you are. A bit of honesty, gentleness and kindness will take you a long way. Isn't that what you want? Remember that you are beginning the process of getting to know someone, so ask the questions that are most important to you.

160

18 COMMUNICATION SKILLS FOR SINGLES

Knowing and asking for what you want, saying yes and saying no

In the preceding chapters we discussed the importance of KNOWING what you want. KNOWING is good, but not enough. This chapter is about ASKING.

All of us have desires. It is unreasonable and foolish, as well, to expect that other people are invested with psychic powers that enable them to know what you want, without your speaking up. As a pre-verbal infant, it may have seemed that your mother knew what you wanted without your asking. This may have been true as a child. However, now that we are grown up, we can manifest our ability to get what we want in a far more effective and reliable way by speaking up. Once we learned to talk and to verbalize our desires, it became necessary to deal with our parents' responses to our requests. Most children learn to talk long before they realize that their parents do not possess the financial resources to buy everything they see.

An important principle in asking for what you want as an adult is to ensure that the person that you are asking has it to give. Sometimes asking is the only way to find this out. However, you are wasting your time repeatedly asking the same person who has already demonstrated that he doesn't have what you want. The anguish of the woman who dates a married man for an extended period, hoping he will divorce his wife and marry her, only to find out that he can't seem to leave his family is a common theme. This is an example of wanting something from someone who does not have it to give. Another example is marrying someone who says they don't want to have children, when you do, and hoping somehow that your love for them will change their mind. Asking another person for what you want does not necessarily mean that you will get it, however it is the best chance you have.

COMMON EXCUSES FOR FAILING TO ASK FOR WHAT YOU WANT

"Asking for what I want reminds me of what I don't have."
This is a self-fulfilling prophesy which works to deny you what you want.

"Asking for what you want makes you vulnerable". This is the fear that once the other person knows what you want, then they can use your desire to manipulate you by withholding it or bargaining with you.

"Asking for what you want is impolite" This is common for those who were admonished and called selfish or ungrateful by parents and others when they asked for things. They believe that they should be grateful for what they have and that asking for more, is a sign of ingratitude or greed.

"If you ask for something you will just be disappointed" or "It is not worth the effort." This is obviously self fulfilling, too. The person has already decided that they can't get what they want and that manifesting their desires is impossible. Their fear of disappointment is stronger than their desire, so instead of risking more disappointment they prefer to give up at the first hint that they might hear NO.

"I have already asked for that and I didn't get it." If you insist on getting what you want the first time you ask, and insist on giving up the first time you fail, it is unlikely that you'll ever get much in life. It is possible that the other person forgot, or didn't hear you or didn't give it to you for a reason that no longer exists. It is also possible that you did not ask in a clear straightforward way.

162

"It is more blessed to give than receive." If this is true then it is blessed to give your partner the opportunity to give. There is no one keeping score. If you think that people will start giving to you just because you give to them then you are banking on obligation and hope. Or if you think that if you just give "enough", then you will surely be worthy of receiving. The problem with this kind of thinking is that there is no one to tell when is enough is enough.

"I don't know what I want." You are the only one who DOES know. Probably you know what you DON'T want; so it is reasonable (although not always accurate) to conclude that what you want is the opposite of what you don't. Also experimentation can aid you greatly. Even a date that turns out to be a disaster provides you with information about what you don't want. If you allow your mind to persist with "I don't know what I want", then you'll never find out.

In asking for what you want it is a good idea to make a request rather than a demand. Some people are so uncomfortable in asking for what they want they become somewhat nasty. Nasty to armor themselves from the rejection they anticipate, nasty to scare the other into saying yes or nasty because they have avoided asking for what they want for a long time. Sometimes when you ask another person for something they will become defensive and present a long list of seemingly irrelevant reasons and justifications for saying NO. Some people interpret any request as a complaint. This often happens when couples are discussing their sex life. It is to your benefit to know what your partner wants. It is also to your benefit to give your partner what he or she wants, if it does not hurt you.

Ask for what you want in a clear straightforward manner. If you feel guilty or afraid or embarrassed, it possible that you will not be clear in your request. Be clear about details, like when, how, what and how much. Also ask any questions necessary for you to be certain you are understood. It is a good idea, but not essential, to formulate in advance ideas for dealing with your partner's objections and considerations. This will make it easier for you to show your partner how both of you will gain from what you are asking for.

WHAT YOUR LIFE MAY BE LIKE IF YOU DON'T ASK FOR WHAT YOU WANT

For women who don't ask for what they want, life can become a never ending beauty contest in which they rely on their attractive appearance alone to give them what they want. It's fine to want to look your best and to take steps to do so. A glance at the headlines of the tabloids at your supermarket check out stand will convince you that conventional beauty alone is not enough to ensure happiness in your love life. Relying on your appearance alone creates a covert, competitive struggle with other women that costs lots of time and money. Although you may attract men, the struggle does nothing to ensure that you attract the men that you want. Even if your appearance does bring you the man that you want, anxiety about the constant threat of younger, more beautiful women will rob you of your happiness.

For men who don't ask for what they want, life becomes a perpetual achievement test. In this model of behavior the skilled automobile mechanic can increase his attractiveness by owning the garage and the garage owner can increase his by owning a chain of five garages. It is fine to want to improve your financial situation, but men (and women too) who rely on this method to attract members of the opposite sex often discover that the people they attract are helpless to provide for themselves and have a never-ending list of demands, relying on material objects for proof of love. The person who is attracted primarily by financial security often complains that the provider is a workaholic who has difficulty with intimacy.

An aspect of maturity is realizing that there are things that no one can give you. No one can give you self-respect, a feeling of accomplishment or make up for the love and care that you did not receive from your parents. No one else can heal your wounds of past abuse. These are all things that you must do for yourself. Maturity is accepting what is given with gratitude and knowing when to give up asking one person and ask someone else. Maturity then is accepting responsibility for your own self-development.

SAYING "NO" AND SAYING "YES"

We probably all have had an experience of saying one thing when we wanted to say something else. Saying "yes" when you mean "no" creates resentment. Sometimes it is OK to give in to your partner's request to please them on an issue that is of minor importance to you, but of great importance to them. Our feeling is that if your lover wants something and it is not going to hurt you then at least have some willingness to say YES. However, if you are motivated to say YES, because of thoughts like "If I don't do this they will get angry, or leave me", or "I don't trust them without me", then you are just asking to be upset, and even though you give your partner what was requested, you'll miss the joy of giving it and lose a certain amount of self-respect, as well.

Saying "No" when you mean "Yes" may be a covert way of controlling the other person or of protecting yourself. If saying "NO" when you mean "YES" becomes predominant in the relationship, much energy will be wasted thinking up socially acceptable methods of retaliation for past hurts. "You didn't want me when I wanted you, so now that you want me, too bad" or "You didn't give me what I wanted, so now that you want something, too bad for you." This is keeping score. Our minds get lost in thinking "Am I giving too much?" or "Am I getting enough in return?"

DEALING WITH CRITICISM:

Why defending yourself doesn't (hasn't and won't) work

The criticism we are discussing here is unsolicited criticism. If you ask someone, "How do I look?" and you receive criticism in response, you could hardly call the criticism unsolicited. The partner who attacks you REPEATEDLY with verbal abuse, name-calling and unsolicited criticism is simply projecting his or her shame and insecurity upon you. The partner who is insecure about his or her weaknesses is often equally intolerant of weaknesses in others. It is important that you know this, because this knowledge will enable you to have compassion for your critical partner and at the same time assert boundaries about how you want to be treated.

It is important to remember that the truth is a matter of context and as we mentioned earlier, all battles are battles of context. There is no right and wrong in the absolute sense. For example, if your partner says, "You are a lazy bum," perhaps what they really mean is "I think you are a lazy bum and I don't like it." If you respond by 1. making excuses for your inactivity, or 2. rapidly listing your recent accomplishments, hoping to disprove their statement, then what YOU are saying in response to the criticism is, "You're right. I think I am a lazy bum, too. And I don't like it either." Defending yourself adds validity to the criticism. Most likely an unresolvable argument will occur, involving the proper definition of a lazy bum.

Regardless of whether you think you have been lazy lately, you are far better off saying, "I understand how you feel. I could work harder." This doesn't mean that you will or even that you should. Isn't it also true that, no matter how industrious you are, you could in fact work harder? Surely there is someone on earth who works harder than you.

CHAPTER 19

THE DATING GAME
Look Before You Love

Since time began men and women have sought each out for companionship, procreation, and preservation. Men literally hunted women; as the traditional prey in this game, women's tactics have generally been more subtle, but no less intentional.

Today desire is the same. The methods of the mating game are a bit gentler than in pre-historic times, and adherence to so-called rules and manners is less common than say thirty years ago.

The purpose of dating, other than the obvious one of enjoying yourself and the company of others, is to get to know another person. Dating can be a wonderful recreational activity, regardless of your age or interests. There is an almost brutal aspect of dating in that it is similar to deciding which car to buy. You take them for test rides and and questions about different models to gain as much information as possible before making an important decision about the possibilities for the relationship. If you don't inquire to find out the information that you want, then it is like buying a car simply based on liking the color.

As teenagers, we got our first (often confusing, inept and under a great deal of peer pressure) experiences with dating. As an adult, you have a chance to manage your dating experience in the way that you most prefer. We suggest that almost any single person can benefit from additional experience at dating. Therefore we suggest that you have lots and lots of dates. If you modify your views about dating, there is no reason you cannot have ten dates per week.

PRACTICAL SUGGESTIONS ABOUT DATING

1. Dates do not have to be time consuming. A half hour spent sharing a snack with someone can qualify as a date.
2. Take the initiative in inviting others on dates.
3. Relax your standards about whom you date. Remember that when you first meet someone, you have very little information about them (often nothing more than their appearance). A date is not forever. Clearly, inviting someone to share a snack with you does not imply any sort of commitment. Make a list of everyone you know and invite them for a snack with you, unless you have a reason NOT to.
4. Go on double dates. This reduces the pressure.
5. Engage in some ACTIVITY that you both enjoy on your dates, so that you don't feel responsible for entertaining each other.

There are really no rules of conduct that will guarantee that you will enjoy dating; however we can make some suggestions. To a large extent, what you talk about depends on your intention for the date.

1. **Take the initiative about introducing sensitive topics.** There is no one to say what is OK on the first date, second date and so forth. We suggest that you treat the other person with gentleness and respect, remembering that your date is probably nervous, too. Oftentimes if you open up first with frank conversation, it will make it easier for them. If the topics that you are willing to address are determined only by your desire to please the other person and continue dating them and you repeatedly make excuses for postponing discussion about what is important to you, it is difficult to imagine that you'll be happy. The "right time" to discuss uncomfortable topics will never show up by itself; it is up to you to make the time. We have heard questions like, "If I talk about marriage (sex) (children) (other lovers) on the first date, won't I scare them off?"

168

That is always a possibility, but it is worth the risk. If you don't find out what the other person wants and state what you want as quickly as possible; then you will find out later, perhaps after you have been going out for several months and perhaps after you are sexually involved. There is no excuse for resenting the other person for leading you on, when you could have found out for yourself, by asking the uncomfortable questions. The problem with trying to please and impress others is that you have to keep doing it. After a while, you'll probably get tired of it; so a common complaint is, "You weren't like this when I first met you"

2. **Find out if what you want from the other person is something that they have or are willing to give.** The only way to find this out is to talk about your desires clearly. For example; if you want to be married and raise six children and you begin dating a divorced man with grown children, for example, it is unwise to assume that he will want to give you what you want simply because he loves you. This type of thinking is based on HOPE and the idea that "My love will change him". The sooner you learn about your date's goals and plans, the better off you will be.

3. **Tell your lovers about each other.** It is fine if you want more than one lover. It is foolish to expect disclosure about other lovers from your partner if you don't bring it up. We discovered that lying and deceit are not worth it. And wouldn't you want to know? It may be uncomfortable for you and they might even leave. However, your peace of mind is much more important. It is not necessary to go into explicit details unless you want to. In short, treat people the way you want to be treated.

4. **For single people, having sexual relationships with married people is almost always less than satisfying.** You can analyze forever the reasons that motivate you to attract married people (wanting Mommy or Daddy, addiction to excitement and intrigue, fear of commitment). And you can analyze forever the reasons that you stay in a relationship with someone who is married to someone else, (it is better than nothing, I feel needed, they plan to leave the marriage, the quality of our love does not require commitment). Sexual relationships with people married to someone else may offer an opportunity to activate and resolve feelings of guilt and jealousy, but there are other ways to do this. Regardless of your moral convictions about fidelity, having a relationship with someone who is married to someone else is unwise just from a practical point of view, for several reasons:

a. Rarely does the married person leave his marriage, so it is very unlikely that you'll have a partner who is committed to you.
b. You lie to your friends.
c. Your partner lies to his spouse.
d. There is constant struggle to suppress guilt.
e. You have little to say about when and where you see each other.
f. You must delude yourself into believing that it is enough.

GETTING TO KNOW YOUR DATE

A LIST OF IMPORTANT ISSUES THAT COULD BE DISCUSSED WITH YOUR DATE.

It is possible that your date will want to head for the hills when you bring up personal topics. It is OK to say, "Would you really rather talk about something besides yourself? I wouldn't. I am interested in you. I know this is a personal subject, but I am tired of discussing movies, sports and music." If you can persuade the other person to open up and be real, your relationship has definite possibilities to contribute to you; and if not then you haven't really lost very much.

Here is a list of topics that may be important to you, depending on your situation and how you feel about your date.

The purpose of your love life.
Sex
Future plans, goals and careers
Religion

Money
Self-improvement
Family background

The purpose of your love life. This is the fastest way to get to know someone, simply because it makes the conversation REAL right from the beginning and sets a tone of gentle disclosure. It is the fastest way we know of for you to find out if you are compatible with the other person. Discussion about this prompts you to talk about what really matters. If your partner, exhibits extreme unwillingness to talk about what he or she wants at the outset of your relationship, it may be unwise for you to rely solely on your spending more time together to dissolve this unwillingness. We suggest that you show your partner how to do the Purpose of Your Love Life Process that we described in Chapter 16 and discuss the statement of purpose that you have made.

Sex For many people, sex is an uncomfortable topic. Most parents were not comfortable talking about sex with us so we concluded that it is a difficult subject to discuss. You may discover that your date will be delighted and relieved when you are willing to bring up sex for discussion. Possibly your date has never discussed sex on a date before. It may be a good idea to point out that just because you talk about sex, neither of you is obligated to do anything about it.

WHAT COULD YOU FIND OUT ABOUT SEX ON THE FIRST DATE?

Do you have many lovers?
Have you had many lovers in the past?
What do you like about sex?
What do you not like about sex?
Do you want a lot of lovers?
Do you have important religious beliefs about sex?
How do you feel about birth control and sexual diseases?
Questions about any other issues that have been a source of upset for you in past relationships.

If you wish to be monogamous, then it is good to say so. If you wish to continue having sex with existing lovers or to find new ones, then it is good to say this, too. Peace of mind is the major benefit, simply because

172

lying and sneaking and worrying about being found out are so anxiety producing. Regardless of your intentions, if your lover plans to continue having sex with other people, it is better for you to know this at the beginning rather than to be shocked and angry when you find out later. Monogamy is a very important. Demanding and expecting your lover to be monogamous could be a desire to control the other person so that you can avoid feeling your own jealousy. Most people do not like being threatened and told what to do, although some seem willing to tolerate it. If you want to have a sexually exclusive relationship we suggest that you offer to be monogamous and ask for it in return. If their answer is "no" then you can decide whether or not you want to continue the relationship. If the answer is "Yes", then congratulations on asking for what you want and getting it! You will always enjoy sex more if you talk about it before doing it.

There are no hard and fast rules about when and with whom to have sex. Most problems about sex relate to uncommunicated expectations. Just because you spent a small fortune on your date, does not obligate him or her to go to bed with you. It is fine to ask for sex and we suggest that you do it in a gentle straightforward way. Everyone likes to know that they are sexually desirable. Saying "Yes" out of guilt, obligation or fear that they won't ask you out again is a poor reason to have sex. Saying "No" out of fear or as a weapon to exert control or "playing hard to get" is unlikely to give you what you want, either.

Don't act dumb about sex. If you think that your date's invitation to go parking or to see his etchings is in fact an invitation to have sex, then ASK.

Future plans, goals and careers

When you meet someone that you're interested in, don't wait until you are head over heels in love before you find out about their plans and goals. If they are planning a job change, have a long term educational goal, or long to live far away or join a commune, then you want to know that. Don't necessarily expect your date to tell you about himself or herself if you don't ask. This also applies to the desire to have children, be married, or retire at an early age. Discussing these topics as early as possible can eliminate surprises and disappointments.

Religion

For some people religion is a lot more important than it is to others. We do not think it is necessary for two partners to have the same religious beliefs to get along; however, religion may have a lot more significance to you, to your date or to the respective families. A frank discussion about the religious beliefs and practices of both people right at the beginning can save a lot of upsets later.

Money

Historically men pay for dates. It is fine for men to pay and it is fine for women to pay. The method we like best and still use for our dates with each other is: He who asks pays, unless agreed otherwise. It is a good idea to discuss this in advance. We think it is more important to find out your date's attitudes about money, than the size of their bank account. Often people are very covert in gathering information about money, relying on external indicators like make of car, profession, or restaurant selected to categorize the other person's financial situation. These are highly unreliable indicators, simply because there are broke and financially irresponsible people in every profession, and with every type of car. You and your date can enjoy yourselves at a five star restaurant and at the local hamburger stand; however, the enjoyment depends far more on the quality of the conversation than on the amount of money spent.

Self-improvement

Since we are in the self-improvement business and travel extensively conducting our LSC, we often notice that many couples face the problem of one person having a driving interest in becoming all he can be, while the other could care less about this. This may never be an issue for you, although if you are reading and using this book, it is safe to say that you have some interest in becoming all that you can be. Anyone who has used any effective self-improvement method accepts responsibility for the conditions in his life. This creates a very different outlook than the attitude that one's emotions, happiness and lot in life depend on external circumstances. The person who is interested in self-improvement is usually more willing to talk about anything, including upsetting emotions and their resolution.

It is not necessary for both of you to be committed to the same method, because different methods work better for different people. Besides, the results matter far more than the method. We have discovered that unless each of you has some on-going method for personal growth, then unnecessary limitations are placed on the degree of intimacy, closeness and contribution to each other.

Family background

It is always interesting to find out the details of someone else's background. Most people like talking about themselves and many TV talk shows are based on this. Although the facts are interesting, they are insignificant compared to how they influence the person now. It may be interesting to find out that your date's father is a self-made millionaire or a complete financial failure; but is more important to know how this affected your date. Are they compulsively driven to exceed this accomplishment, do they feel helpless about measuring up while waiting for the inheritance, do they remain financially dependent or do they use their father as a positive role model for their own success?

It may be interesting to know that your date is an only child or has lots of brothers and sisters. However how this effects him is far more important. Does he compare all women to his mother, is his mother's opinion and approval still of major importance, does he plan on taking care of his mother in her old age, or does he hate his mother and hasn't spoken with her for years?

It may be interesting to know that your date's parents were stern authoritarians with her. What matters more is her present attitude about this treatment. Does she compulsively rebel against any sort of authority, does she rely on others to tell her what to do, or does she interpret instructions as possibly useful suggestions to be considered on their own merits. It is important to ask about these topics because you can be certain that patterns of behavior adopted from their family will be acted out in your relationship.

In summary, we think you'll enjoy dating a whole lot more with these suggestions:

Talk about what matters to you, even when you feel embarrassed about bringing up the subject.

Be straightforward and prompt in discussing your intentions regarding sex, commitment and the future of your relationship.

Don't make the mistake of seeing someone you are not really interested in just to avoid being alone.

Don't believe that the way to get over a painful breakup is to begin to date someone new, it's harder to attract a new person in your life if your heart is still hurting or you are still angry or desperate.

Most people need practice at dating. Give yourself lots of practice by having frequent short dates. An early evening snack or a brief cup of coffee can qualify as a date and give you an opportunity to get to know someone if you don't waste your time discussing the weather.

THE GROWTH OF A HEALTHY RELATIONSHIP

A committed relationship that works for you does not occur by accident. It must be built. Start from the beginning and take your time. SLOW DOWN. It is our opinion that many people rush these stages, resulting in having sex with or married to people that they do not know very well. We were friends for four years before we were lovers. Sex with strangers is pretty hollow, (could be dangerous, too). Our advice is only have sex with your friends.

STAGES OF RELATIONSHIPS

Casual Contact or Friendship
Courtship
Romance and Sexuality
Commitment and Monogamy
Many people have relationships where there has been movement in both directions on this list. People who have been lovers in the past can continue as friends after the sexual relationship has ended. One stage of relationship is not necessarily better than any other, and in some cases the dividing lines between stages may be less than precise.

Discussion about what stage your relationship is essential, despite the inevitable nervousness. Without this, possibilities for disappointment, betrayal and abnadonment abound. It is usual that one person is more willing to discuss sensitive issues than the other. Be gentle and take your time. Take the initiative in discussing the development of your relationship, thereby eliminating deception, delusion and unrealisitc expectations. Don't wait for the other person to do it.

CASUAL CONTACT OR FRIENDSHIP

Meeting members of the opposite sex. Casual dating is included in this. Double dates are a good idea. Making friends with people of similar interest and meeting people whom you can laugh with. Plan your dates around activities that you enjoy.

COURTSHIP

Courtship implies that you have singled someone out that you want to spend time with. You spend more time together alone. Courtship is not necessarily exclusive. Be honest about this. You do things for each other. Men may bring flowers, women may bake cookies, although the other way around is fine, too! Sexual desires are on the rise. Sexual boundaries must be agreed to. Take your time to enjoy the excitement. Honest discussion about the possibilities of intercourse is essential.

ROMANCE AND SEXUALITY

Couples are more together than apart. Some people choose to live together during this period. The honeymoon stage. There is a euphoric sense of bliss. Many decisions are based on the presence of the other person in your life.

COMMITMENT AND MONOGAMY

The hunt is over forever. You have made a decision and feel peaceful, solid and trustful about this. You are willing to make your partner the most important person in your life after yourself and before other friends, family or associates. Your relationship has top priority. You begin to grow together, you make significant contributions to each other's personal growth, there is nothing that cannot be discussed. Maintenance of your love life becomes important because of the inevitable activation of family patterns caused by commitment.

20 GETTING SERIOUS

Most people fall in love with someone that they don't know very well. Although it may be impossible to find out everything that you want to know before making a commitment to someone else, we will discuss in this chapter some of the issues that are essential to be discussed before making any kind of commitment. This will aid you in avoiding the heartbreaking experience of "If only I had known that about him (her) beforehand, I sure wouldn't have gotten so serious."

All humans seem to have conflicting desires regarding commitment. These are the desires to be free and the desire to be committed, the desire for independence and the desire for union, the desire to be married and the desire to be single. Resolving these conflicting desires is different for everyone. We can offer some pointers by discussing various contexts about commitment for your consideration. It is also a good idea to remember that commitment is not logical. When a couple agrees to monogamy, for example, they agree to pass up future sexual partners many of whom they have not met yet. We are not necessarily selling commitment. It may not be for everyone, despite the fact that it seems that most singles are looking for Mr. or Ms. Right.

Commitment activates fear for most people (so does lack of commitment). This fear is valid and irrational. Clearly marriage commitments can be used to repress women, and to restrict freedom, growth and self-expression. Some argue that monogamy is monotony and contrary to human nature. Commitment at its worst means that you give up what is important to you in order to keep the other person around. The fear of commitment regarding relationships is primarily about fear of making an irreconcilable mistake. An examination of human behavior, however, indicates intense and lasting desire for committed relationships since the beginning of recorded history and before.

DESIRES FOR FREEDOM AND UNION

Any relationship is only as strong as the commitment. This is VERY important to remember during arguments and disagreements. By commitment, we mean that you consciously offer another person a special place in your life, involving trust, honesty and closeness beyond what you offer to others. Commitment involves an offer to love, serve, protect and maintain sexual fidelity with another person. It involves giving our word. Going steady, maintaining sexual fidelity, engagement and marriage are the most common forms of committed relationships. The conflict between our desires for freedom and our desires for union can be resolved, but for many people this resolution requires the destruction of romantic notions about relationships. The primary romantic notion is that love can come from outside of us, from Cupid or from another person. This misconception is the result of our suppressed grief about the love our parents did not give us.

Love is not something that happens to us. Quite to the contrary, a loving relationship that lasts is a matter of conscious volition. A matter of intention. Since it is impossible to make someone love us, then a lasting relationship becomes largely a matter of willingness. Your commitment to your relationship and your willingness to have it serve both of you is not a one time event. To have a relationship where both partners actually contribute to each other requires a conscious renewal of commitment every day. It is our belief that commitment happens one day at a time. For this reason, commitment is far better offered than demanded. Commitment is an uncomfortable topic to discuss (because of the fears of entrapment and abandonment); however, avoiding discussion is FAR more uncomfortable. Despite frequent parental objections about the behavior of their teenage offspring, going steady can be thought of as people's natural desire to get some practice at having a committed relationship. Commitment will not necessarily put an end to the doubts that you may have about the other person, nor will commitment put an end to your attraction to members of the opposite sex; however, commitment fosters a sense of intimacy, unavailable in casual relationships. We value and honor the commitment that we have to each other. It provides us benefits that nothing else could. Despite all this, there is nothing wrong with you, if freedom is more important to you than commitment.

Many of the conflicts that couples experience are the result of unresolved loyalty issues left over from their family conditioning. This can be especially true if your parents were divorced and you chose sides. To have a committed relationship that works for you, it is necessary to have your priorities straight. Put yourself first. Next comes your partner and then everyone else. This means that your partner comes before your friends, your work, your family and your children. If you are not willing to put your partner first after yourself, you are not really committed and are asking for endless, futile conflicts. In a marriage you in fact become a member of your spouse's family. Sometimes people act as if they are married to their children. Sometimes a man or woman continues to consult their parents or friends about decisions that are really between the two of them. This does not mean you don't talk things over with others, but it does mean continuing to live by their rules and standards is likely to cause upset. It is fine if you are not willing to put your partner first after yourself. If that is the case, we suggest that you remain uncommitted.

ENGAGEMENT

An engagement is a mutual agreement to marry. When you become engaged you can expect that all of your reservations about marriage and all of your reservations about marriage to your fiance in particular will come to your awareness in a very strong way. These doubts are natural. They do not mean that you are not ready nor that you have necessarily chosen the wrong person. If your fiance discounts your doubts as foolish to the point where they are unwilling to listen, THEN there is a likelihood that you did choose the wrong person, because their inability to discuss emotional will cause you lots of problems later.

We found it very useful to discuss all of our fears before the wedding. We found that gentleness and a sense of humor aided us in being able to talk about our doubts and hear those of the other.

WHAT DOES IT TAKE TO MAINTAIN COMMITMENT?

If you have ever read romantic fairy tales, they are usually about the hunt, and they often end with: "And they lived happily ever after". What they don't report is HOW they accomplished this. Our analogy is; if you went to a store and bought the finest Persian carpet, took it home and never vacuumed it, in six months it would look no better than the cheapest rug available. Yet, this is the way many people conduct their love life. We

may think we can go out and find the perfect mate, settle down, and never do anything to insure us of long lasting happiness together.

It is common that when two people set up housekeeping, the suppressed memories and patterns about their parent's relationship begin to surface. If you are unwilling to acknowledge their presence, it is likely that your once blissful relationship will be headed for trouble. In extreme cases it looks to us that two peoples patterns are having a relationship. A common retort is "You act just like my Father (Mother)" or " You treat me like a child!"

For all of these reasons, maintenance must be made a priority if you wish to have a lasting, loving relationship. As Jeanne likes to say in our seminars, "Don't put your love life on the back burner and expect it to stay hot!"

Listen to your partner, especially when it is uncomfortable. Many extra-marital affairs are motivated by the desire to have someone listen. Participants often say, "She understands how I feel" or "I can say anything to him and he really listens"or "It feels so good to be able to talk about what I feel without getting lectured".

An important topic for committed couples, is to establish agreements for issues concerning their love life together. These issues could include how much time is spent together, how the money is spent, personal privacy, etc. It is also necessary to agree on limits or boundary lines for arguments and speak up when someone has crossed that line. For example, if you are unwilling to argue in a restaurant full of other people and your lover starts an argument then it is up to you to remind them of your agreement. Clearly the preferences of both partners regarding these issues will change over time. The communication methods that we will describe in Chapter 24 will enable you to keep up to date with each other.

21

LEAVING
How Long Should a Relationship Last?

We leave people all the time. If you never left anyone, then everyone you ever met would still be following you around. A separation or divorce does not mean that anyone failed, or that anyone is at fault; it means that one or both partners changed, sometimes for the better. A marriage that began when the couple were in their twenties is expected to last sixty, eighty years or more. By then both people are very different than at the wedding. Although the techniques in this book are designed to help you grow together instead of apart, this doesn't always happen. You are the only one who makes the decision whether you prefer to accept the difficulties of your current situation and integrate them by changing contexts about the feelings, whether to ask for something different, whether to seek outside help or whether to leave.

Staying in a relationship longer than you want is usually caused by the uncomfortable feelings about saying good-by. You know how it feels to be rejected and you don't want to play the villain. Most likely the other person will be hurt or angry, therefore making you the object of their wrath. Sometimes people are covert about their desire to leave and hope by withholding love, sex or intimacy, the other person will leave first.

Leaving too soon is usually caused by the unwillingness to communicate about the uncomfortable issues that arise in every relationship. If you think that upsets prove that you chose the wrong person, there will be a tendency to leave rather than work out the difficulties.

You are the only one who can decide whether it is time to leave and under what circumstances do you give up trying to make it work. Even though it's likely you'll feel sad, ashamed and guilty about considering a divorce, it does not necessarily mean that you are a bad person or that you did anything wrong.

IS IT TIME TO CONSIDER A DIVORCE?

Knowing whether to give up or to stay is an entirely subjective decision that you will have to make. We can offer some guidelines for your consideration. Although a divorce is not the end of the world, it is a very permanent decision that will affect the entire rest of your life. Divorce is always somewhat unpleasant. If you think that getting a divorce is no bigger deal than getting a new address, then you are in for a tremendous shock. This decision is worthy of very careful consideration and discussion. In most states in the United States, if your partner really wants a divorce, he or she can get one no matter how hard you fight it. Besides, it is doubtful that you would want to stay remain married to someone who didn't want you, except to feed unconscious patterns.

Additionally, staying in a marriage just because of the children is a lame idea. One of the most valuable things that parents can offer their children is a working model of two people in love. If you stay with your spouse only because of the children, the resulting resentment prevents you from providing the model they need.

Make sure that you take the time to explain the divorce to your children. It is important that the children know the truth about the reasons for the divorce, or they will make their own conclusions about it, in order to explain it to themselves and their friends. Make sure that your children understand that you are getting divorced from each other and not from them. Expect your children to be upset about the divorce and invite them to share their feelings.

Social research about the effect of divorce on children is somewhat sketchy. How children fare after a divorce seems to depend greatly on the attitudes of their parents toward each other. If one or both parents has nothing but criticism for the other, the children are forced to take sides (or at least pretend to take sides). In some cases, the divorce marks the end of hostilities; but in others, the divorce frees the partners from their obligation to be nice to each other, allowing freer expression of the previously suppressed hostility. In a divorce it is important to acknowledge responsibility for your hostile feelings, rather than trying to convince your children about what is wrong with their other parent. Share your feelings with your children and let them know that they are not to blame. Don't expect your children to serve as your therapist. Children have a right to a say about custody and visitation issues. Discuss this thoroughly before making any final decisions. Divorce does not have to be harmful to the children involved and may in fact be a substantial improvement over the constant tension and conflict. Your children notice a lot more about your love life than just what you tell them. If you are staying together just for them, then it is highly likely that they will feel guilty and/or resentful about this, as well as model your behavior by sacrificing their happiness for their children when they grow up or by concluding, "I saw my parents go through a nasty divorce, so I'll never get married."

Staying in a marriage, because you cannot make it on your own is equally lame. Economic and emotional self-reliance can be learned by anyone, whether or not you learned it from your parents. We suggest that you give careful consideration to these questions when considering a divorce.

Would you like to be married to yourself?
Does your partner constantly violate rights that are important to you?
Have the two of you made a real effort at seeking and using the information in this book and professional help?
Is there violence or abuse?
How do you know that divorce will be better?
A brief explanation about each of these questions follows:

Would you like to be married to yourself? If you do get a divorce, you will be alone. It is somewhat like being married to yourself. If you are not a person that you would like to be married to, then it is likely that the only benefit you could gain from divorce is removing yourself from the undesirable characteristics of your partner. Use the techniques in this book and any other self-help methods that appeal to you to become the person that you want to be. If you are considering a divorce, you will tend to notice all of the things that are wrong with your partner in order to justify your decision. It is also prudent to consider improvements to your character or behavior that you could make to maintain the marriage. (It is likely that some of these are represented by your partner's complaints about you.) A divorce is rarely just one person's doing.

Does your partner constantly violate rights that are important to you? If your partner has endless justifications and rationalizations for criticizing you, or for ignoring rights that are important to you at some point you will consider giving up on the relationship, because there is little you can do to force someone to respect you.

Have you made a real effort at seeking and using professional help? Professional counselling can aid you greatly. Your willingness to ask for help is a sign of your strength. If your partner is unwilling to participate in professional help with you, your chances are slim. High quality marriage counselling can help you learn to talk to each other more gently. Do everything you can think of to encourage your partner to participate. Even counselling that provides you only with an amicable divorce is very valuable.

Is there violence? Compulsive wife-beaters (husband beaters, too, just to be fair about it) do not change by themselves. Domestic violence seems to operate in a three stage cycle. First, tension builds up perhaps characterized by loud verbal fights, criticism and blaming. In the second stage the actual battering occurs. In the third stage there is apology and honeymoon stage, which lasts until the tension builds up once more and it starts over. Both of these people need and require help. Unless you are willing to be a punching bag for the rest of your life, you had better pack up. "Hit me once, then shame on you; hit me twice, then shame on me" is an excellent guide for thinking about this. If you are the victim of domestic violence, it is likely that your mind is filled with rationalizations and delusions about how things will change. If you have doubts about leaving, we suggest that you visit any battered women's shelter and discuss the situation with one of the victime there.

How do you know that divorce will be better? Divorce might be better and it might not. It is a risk. It is doubtful that it will be any better if your mind remains mired in resentment and shame left over from your failed marriage. For this reason, unless you are leaving in a rush to avoid violence, it is extremely valuable to tell your partner ALL the communications that you have withheld during your marriage. Don't let your mind get away with telling you that you have told him or her everything. If the two of you had been communicating openly, you probably wouldn't be getting the divorce.

Some people find out from their divorce that their former spouse was not in fact the cause of their problems; but rather that the same problems crop up in their lives after the divorce. If you have been divorced for a while and find that you have many of the same problems that you had in your marriage, it is highly likely that these problems are caused by your unwillingness to communicate. This is good news! Take some time to communicate to your former spouse all of the communications that you withheld during your marriage and you'll be delighted with how quickly things clear up.

MAKING THE SEPARATION FINAL

From time to time, we meet people who have been legally separated from their spouse for five years or more and have not obtained a final divorce, despite having no intention or inclination to return. When asked why they haven't made the divorce final, they most often respond with outlandish excuses that make no sense whatever. In almost every case these people have major problems in their current love life and yet they insistently deny that the undissolved marriage has any effect on their current situation.

Unwillingness to obtain a divorce makes it virtually impossible to find someone else to marry. Additionally, anyone who would stay with you for an extended time while you are still married to someone else most certainly has conflicting views about marriage. Even though you FEEL that a long separation is the same as a divorce, there is part of your mind that knows you are still married and must therefore struggle to deny the truth, despite your conscious claims that legal papers don't mean anything to you.

Even if you have gotten a divorce, no separation can be final if you are clinging to souvenirs from the ended relationship. It is impossible to make space in your heart for someone new, if your wallet, scrapbook and closet are filled with photos and mementos from the relationship. Included in this are gifts that you received from your former partner. To make space in your heart, make space in your house by returning, discarding or selling all of these souvenirs.

III TAKING ACTION WITH YOUR PARTNER

wherein we answer the question "I have a lover. How can we contribute to each other more?"

The majority of what we have to say about taking action together is about honest communication. We do not mean honest in the courtroom sense where you tell the truth, the whole truth and nothing but the truth, in response to questions. In your love life, honest communication means much more than that. It means the willingness to come forward and talk about and the willingness to listen to your partner talk about those topics that are uncomfortable or painful, topics that make you feel confused, afraid or ashamed. Essentially by honest communication we mean the willingness to talk about your feelings. Without this willingness, the contributions that you and your partner can make to each other are severely limited by your desire to hide certain parts of yourselves from the other. We have learned that talking about our feelings together is scary, exciting and therapeutic. Neither of us grew up in families where feelings were OK. The honesty we give each other makes each of us stronger as individuals and strengthens our marriage, as well. We are becoming better friends and better lovers and know that living happily ever after is solely up to us and primarily a result of our willingness to be honest in talking about our feelings.

INTIMACY

Intimacy is the result of talking about the things in your life that are not OK with you, without fear of retribution by the listener and without defensiveness on the part of the speaker. You can contribute to your partner by accepting the validity of their feelings even if you don't understand them by just listening. This is where you learn to grow together instead of apart. A relationship based on deception and withholding the truth is an impossible struggle to maintain. If, like most of us, you grew up in a family where feelings were discounted, dismissed and rarely discussed, then some practice will be required for you to learn to discuss feelings in a productive way.

The most productive way is simply to notice, label and affirm your feelings and those of your partner. The purpose here is NOT to become each other's unsolicited psycho-therapist, but rather to create intimacy and compassion. The feelings that plague you will not change with your continued unwillingness to feel them. Hoping your feelings will change, before you talk about them will never work. NOTHING CHANGES UNTIL IT BECOMES REAL. Once you and your partner become skilled in emotional resolution, the existence of problems and associated feelings are treated with respect and welcomed as opportunities for you and your partner to grow as well as deepen the love between you.

There is magic about telling the truth and your relationship is as sick as the secrets you keep from each other. Everyone wants and needs to be heard. You provide a valuable service for each other just by listening and allowing all the crazy thoughts and confused contexts to be discussed. Often you will find that you have differing values. These do not have to destroy a relationship.

Perhaps there are some things that you are afraid to tell your partner, because you think they may become upset, or worse, leave if you do. Clearly you are not required to tell your partner anything. Your relationship works as well as it does now and probably will continue to do so, even if you are unwilling to open up. The discomfort of saying the things you have withheld is temporary compared to the eternal effort of withholding them. Being open with each other is easy when it becomes a habit. Each

192

of you encourages the other to do so by his own example. It only takes one of you to get started.

In this section, Taking Action Together, we make several important assumptions about your relationship. We assume that you have a partner whom you love and whom you wish to stay with. We assume that you want your love to deepen and grow. We assume you know that it is uncomfortable and foolish to pretend or demand that you or anyone else is perfect and always right. We assume that you know it is uncomfortable and sometimes painful to find out that your relationship could improve. We know that it is sometimes difficult to maintain the love in a relationship, but we can guarantee you that it is not impossible.

WHY YOU MUST COME FIRST

The first step is to put yourself first in your life. The previous section Taking Action by Yourself was designed to help you with that. Your partner must be the second most important person in your life. Some couples attend the LSC who have spent the last 20 or 30 years of their marriage raising children, building a business and a secure retirement. These projects can be distractions from the maintenance necessary to keep their love life growing. With their children away at college or married, they are shocked to see the issues between them that have been neglected for decades while they gave their love and attention to matters that seemed more important at the time. Children grow up and leave, friends, addresses and careers may change but your partner will be there much longer, barring divorce or tragedy.

Other couples are devoted to each other and want to continue their marriage, but their inability to talk about almost everything without having a fight creates a maddening, sullen silence. No matter if you have been together two weeks or twenty years, you can learn the skills that we teach in this section that you need so that you and your partner contribute to each other. Effective use of these skills require willingness and very little else. We can show you how to do it. You must supply your own willingness. Expect this to be weird. Think of it as an adventure. Humor and patience are essential.

CHAPTER 22

ARGUMENTS
Learning to Argue Can Improve Your Love Life

It is to your benefit to learn how to argue, and it is to your benefit to have a partner who is willing to argue. If you don't learn how to argue together, it is very unlikely that you will ever resolve any disagreements. We suggest some method of resolving the inevitable disagreements be established at the outset of the relationship. Discussion of the reservations and fears you may have about arguing is extremely important. Without a method of resolving disagreements, one partner has all the control, while the other is manipulated, leading to resentment on both sides. If it is not OK to discuss your feelings openly, then couples begin to covertly express their anger. For women a common way is to withhold sex and affection. For men a common response is to work long hours away from home and be preoccupied. Sometimes one or both partners engage in the "cold shoulder" or "silent treatment" tactic. Often this continues until it becomes unbearable for one partner who then gives in and breaks the silence to restore a facade of harmony without discussion of the disagreement which started it all. In these instances, you can be reasonably sure that the same disagreement will come up again.

The communication processes that we describe in the following chapters are designed to promote discussion about vitally important and highly sensitive topics. You will discover that these topics may stimulate disagreement and arguments and even bring back old memories. Although it is far better to have these uncomfortable topics out in the open, rather than lurking in the closet, you will have more success in actually resolving disagreements if you learn how to argue first. It is likely that you expect (or hope) that when two people are in love and committed to each other that there will never be an intensely uncomfortable disagreement or argument that could threaten your relationship. We haven't met every couple, so it is possible that some couples may, in fact, never have any disagreements. Some of the couples who attend the LSC say they never argue. In the seminar, they actually discuss the topics in this book and often discover how denying their disagreements had limited their intimacy. To the extent that intense arguments clash with your expectations about how it SHOULD be to be in love, you will tend to believe that any disagreement is an unfavorable verdict about your relationship or proof that you (or your partner) is a bad person.

THE PURPOSE OF AN ARGUMENT IS TO RESOLVE A CONFLICT OR A DISAGREEMENT. Resolving conflict increases co-operation. Increasing co-operation leads to living happily ever after. When an argument is over and a disagreement is resolved, both parties win. An animal is limited to fight or flight as possible behaviors in the face of disagreement. As humans, a successful argument, represents a far more attractive alternative. An argument then is different from a fight; the purpose of a fight is to destroy your opponent. **LEARNING HOW TO ARGUE SUCCESSFULLY CAN SAVE A MARRIAGE.** Failing this, it is difficult and virtually impossible to resolve disagreements. An argument is different from a fight. The purpose of a fight is to hurt and control the other person. When a fight is over there is only one winner. Arguments are intense discussion of thoughts and feelings.

What your relationship may be like if you do not learn to argue effectively.

1. You will seek other people for support on the issues that you cannot discuss with your partner.
2. There will be a painful sense of isolation, even when you are together.
3. One partner lives in fear, while the other disrepects the ability of his partner to stand up for himself.

4. People who do not learn to argue with each other sometimes end up hiring lawyers to do their arguing for them in divorce court.

5. There is a tendency to hurt each other covertly, thus acting out the hostility that is suppressed by never arguing. Your marriage begins to resemble the Cold War.

Jeanne's story. When Phil and I were first married it was not long before our first argument occurred. I had come from a family tradition where arguing was not OK, and arguments often led to someone being punished. It was not often that I won an argument with my parents, and being the youngest of five, it seemed that my siblings always won merely because they were older. Arguing scared me and usually left me feeling alone, invalidated, and unloved. Because I wanted my family to love and approve of me, I vowed to become the peace maker and to avoid upsets whenever possible. This often resulted in my pouting in silence and often becoming impossible to console. I slowly began to believe that I couldn't get what I wanted and was too afraid to try.

In Phil's family arguing and debate were encouraged as a means of family discussion, and being the oldest child as well as smart, he often won arguments with both his parents and sister. As you can imagine, our different ways of handling arguments did not blend very well at all, in fact, the first year of our marriage we were arguing alot and rarely resolving any of them. I began to think that our arguing meant that there was something wrong with our relationship, and began to worry that I might have married the wrong man! The more I resisted arguing, the more Phil wanted to argue; the more Phil argued, the more I resisted. Soon we were upset a lot of the time. The turning point came when one night Phil pointed out that, no matter what it seemed we were arguing about, we were really arguing about whether or not it was OK to argue. So we agreed to argue about that. As I remember that took us until about 3:00 AM. before he convinced me of the benefits of having and resolving an argument. It was the best argument I ever lost.

Soon thereafter, I won my first argument with Phil and it felt like the first time I had ever stood up for myself. I realized that arguing with Phil didn't mean we didn't love each other or that we were unsuited for marriage, nor would the willingness to argue lead to a constant stream of upsets. We began to resolve the disagreements that we had suppressed in our frustration, and we were both delighted to notice that we were arguing less than ever (actually, I was shocked). When we did have upsets we both felt committed to resolving them as quickly as possible, and move on. We still have arguments of course, but I now have a completely different context about them. I will always be grateful to Phil for teaching me to stand up for myself and argue.

Phil's story. When I was about eight years old, I became interested in current events and geography and I read the newspaper daily. My father was far more interested in these topics than my contemporaries, so he and I often engaged in lively debates at the dinner table about topics like the benefits of labor unions, the containment of Communism, and various aspects of American foreign policy. Despite the fact that our discussions were sometimes heated, my father listened to my newly formed opinions and treated them with respect. Both of us learned from our arguments and I learned that disagreement was OK and that disagreement did not necessarily mean disrespect or disapproval. I will always be grateful to my father for that lesson.

Althouth I learned from this that it was OK for me to argue, I unconsciously adopted a pattern of being somewhat compulsive about arguments. Characteristic of unconscious behavior patterns, it had escaped my attention, until I resolved it with Jeanne's help. My mother and paternal grandmother, who lived with my parents from before I was born and until long after I had left and was on my own, engaged in a constant and mostly covert battle, about my grandmother's presence in the house, which my mother deeply resented. It was impossible for them to argue with each other, because the feelings were far too intense for them, so each of them secretly and constantly pleaded their case to my father, who either could not or would not make the arrangements for his mother to live elsewhere. When my mother and grandmother observed at the dinner table that I could win arguments with my father, both of them began to plead their case to me, telling me what they wanted me to tell my father. As an eight year old, all of this turmoil and suppressed tensions was pretty anxiety producing. I didn't tell my father anything about whay they told me, but I concluded that I should have and felt guilty that I didn't. I had concluded from this that I SHOULD argue or that I was supposed to argue, and this conclusion led me to be more compulsive than was necessary or useful in my arguments with Jeanne. By doing the Recovery Process that comes next about describing your family's arguments, we were thankfully able to resolve this.

Recovery Process

DESCRIBE YOUR FAMILY'S ARGUMENTS

PART 1

A says to B: "Please describe your family's arguments." B talks without interruption until he or she "runs out of gas", then A says: "Thank you. Please describe your family's arguments." Then B talks again without interruption. Keep doing this for five minutes.

PART 2

A says to B: "Please tell me how you argue with me like your family argued." B talks without interruption until he or she "runs out of gas", then A says: "Thank you. Please tell me how you argue with me like your family argued." Then B talks again without interruption. Keep doing this for five minutes. And then switch and go back to the beginning of Part 1.

CHILDHOOD CONDITIONING ABOUT ARGUMENTS

A question we ask in our seminars is: How many of you ever won arguments with your parents? Rarely do we meet people who did win with any regularity. Our parents often ended arguments with statements like: "Because I said so" or "Because I'm your mother" or "I said no and I don't want to hear any more about it!" These responses left us feeling angry and helpless with no choice but to suppress our feelings. We may have concluded that it was impossible for us to get what we wanted by arguing, and that our desires did not matter. Many children develop devious methods of getting what they want without arguing, having given up on arguing because it led to punishment or separation. Many children are brought up to believe that "children are to be seen and not heard". This is often due to the parents' desire for peace and quiet at home and to have their children appear and act socially acceptable, especially in public.

Oftentimes the only recourse we had as children was to have a temper tantrum. If we screamed, kicked and behaved badly enough, our parents gave in to our demands just to stop our behavior. This type of tactic for getting what you want is still practiced by some adults. Often children learn to get what they want by withdrawing into sullen silence until the parents' guilt forces them to give in.

Some parents are so uncomfortable with arguments that they always let their children have their own way. As adults, these people think they must have everything they want.

For all these reasons and others we haven't thought of, people seem to have difficulties with arguing.

ANGER AND VIOLENCE ARE DIFFERENT

In instances where child abuse occurred, anger is often thought to be the cause of violence. Although you may have reason to believe differently, it is not anger that leads to violence. **SUPPRESSED** anger is what leads to violence. Have you ever noticed that when a serial murderer or a perpetrator of a senseless machine gun massacre is caught, and when reporters interview his neighbors; the neighbors very often say how shocked they are that such a "nice, quiet guy" could do such a terrible thing? In almost every case, the person who abuses his children is acting out his own still suppressed anger from the treatment he received from his parents. Clearly, there are exceptions. There are families where debate and often loud debate were accepted and encouraged and where no abuse occurred.

We can almost guarantee that sooner or later you will feel angry at your lover, even if you thought you never would. Often the first time that anger comes up, is the most devastating. Some couples never get past this and are still hurting from their first argument. The question is not whether anger will come up in your relationship, but rather what to do about it.

200

If you never argue about anything, it is highly likely that you are compulsively avoiding the uncomfortable feelings associated with arguing, usually anger or fear. When two people agree on everything, you can be certain that only one of them is doing all the thinking. If you compulsively argue about everything, it is highly likely that you are avoiding feelings of helplessness and are terrified about being hurt, controlled or manipulated by your mate. Equanimity occurs when it is OK to argue about what is important enough to you and you are willing not to argue about what doesn't matter enough.

There are many ways to deal with the disagreements that arise. It is quite possible that you have already tried several of these. One popular method is to avoid disagreements at all costs. You don't have to know someone for very long before you become aware of the subjects that you disagree about. Even with casual acquaintances, you probably know which topics are sure to create an argument: sex, politics, religion, local police policy, abortion or whatever. With this knowledge, it is a simple matter to carefully avoid these topics and avoid arguments. This is probably a fine thing to do with casual acquaintances. We doubt that you want your life to be a constant argument (although some lawyers seems to enjoy this, and even create a good income from it). Although it is probably OK to maintain a degree of social politeness among your casual acquaintances and avoid highly sensitive or personal topics, if you do this in a committed relationship, the results are disastrous.

HOW BOREDOM SETS IN

As time passes, more and more subjects are avoided and communication becomes more and more restricted to the subjects that are known to be safe. If your conversation is primarily limited to the events of the day, the weather, the neighbors, sports, then we are talking about you. In a marriage like this, communication is as superficial as between strangers at a cocktail party. We observe couples like this at restaurants from time to time. They speak only to the server and barely look at each other. The effort to suppress the discomfort associated with the things they withhold from each other becomes greater with each passing year.

Another ineffective method of dealing with disagreements is to pretend that nothing matters enough to be worth the trouble of an argument. Others are to threaten to leave unless your partner gives in to your desires, or do nothing and just feel silently hurt. Some people even wait until they are certain that they are right, that they have caught their partner at something that both agree is wrong. Then the pent up anger pours forth. The sense of righteousness overcomes his everyday suppression resulting in an explosive outburst that includes complaints that have been unsaid but not forgotten. By this time, usually the list of complaints is too long, the emotion too intense and out of character for the recipient of the tirade to do anything else than experience their shock that this had not been communicated earlier and try to defend himself.

Winners are people who take responsibility for their lives, for their desires and for what happens to them. Losers look for someone else or something else to blame. In a marriage, if your partner loses, so do you. Therefore, love and happiness in a marriage depend greatly on whether you are willing and able to find or develop a win/win method of settling disputes and disagreements.

It is necessary to agree upon some rules for conducting arguments. We are going to describe the rules that we have developed, and you can adopt them as your own, if you like. If not, we invite you to create your own rules. That you have agreed upon rules is far more important than that you adopt the same rules that we have. The purpose of rules for arguing is to facilitate any argument toward resolution of a disagreement. It is essential to agree upon the rules BEFORE an argument starts.

Without rules about how arguments are conducted, you may have discovered that the winner is the person more verbally abusive and the loser is the person who wants peace at any price. It is essential to respect each other all the time, even when having an argument. There is no set of rules that will resolve every disagreement. There will be instances where, after you have heard each other out, you can only agree to disagree about the topic discussed. However, it is greatly to your benefit to learn to argue effectively and it is greatly to your benefit for your partner to learn to argue effectively.

A FOURTEEN POINT PLAN FOR SUCCESSFUL ARGUMENTS

The original Fourteen Point Plan was proposed by American President Woodrow Wilson after World War I as a plan to prevent international war. Despite the fact that President Wilsons' Fourteen Points and his proposed League of Nations failed ratification by the isolationist U.S. Senate in 1919, resulting in Wilson's complete despair during the last few months of his administration, we have adopted the title of Fourteen Points for our plan for preventing domestic war.

14 POINT PLAN FOR PREVENTING DOMESTIC WAR

RULES FOR ARGUING

1. Be willing to argue about what is important to you and willing not to argue about what doesn't matter.
2. Be willing to distinguish between these.
3. Be willing to be a gracious winner.
4. Be willing to acknowledge when the other person convinced you. (In other words, you are willing to admit when you are wrong.)
5. Be willing to state clearly what you are arguing about.
6. Be willing to discuss one subject at a time and acknowledge when you change the subject.
7. Be willing to acknowledge when you are being abusive and willing to respond to your partner's request that you stop it.
8. Be willing to give your partner their say without interruption.
9. Be willing to ask for or to agree to a break when the intensity becomes uncomfortable.
10. Be willing to refrain from making threats or manipulation by guilt or shame as a method of arguing.
11. Be willing to agree to disagree.
12. Be willing to refrain from arguing in the dark, on the phone, in the car or in public.
13. Be willing to refrain from playing "therapist" unless your partner requests it.
14. Be willing to apologize and forgive each other when either of you breaks the rules.

A beautiful, 8½″ by 11″ printed poster of this Fourteen Point Plan for Preventing Domestic War, suitable for framing or posting on your refrigerator is available for $ US 2.00 postpaid. Send your name, address and phone number to:

Miller/Laut Trainings
PO Box 8269
Cincinnati, OH 45208 USA

Rules for successful arguments — explained.

1. Be willing to argue about what is important to you and willing not to argue about what doesn't matter. You are the only one who can decide what is important enough to argue about. If your partner doesn't agree that your topic is important enough to argue about, then it is your responsibility to convince him or her that it is.

If you seem to have the same argument over and over without any resolution, it is possible that you are not discussing what the argument is truly about. Many arguments between couples fail to address the real issue. Sometimes discussion is necessary just to define the issue. It is good to keep saying, "Please tell me exactly what you are upset about" until you understand. At this point, you'll be able to argue about the real issue. For example, the arguments between parents and children are actually about control vs. freedom, although the words may be about something different.

2. Be willing to distinguish between these. Someone who is afraid to argue and who compulsively avoids arguments at any cost may find it difficult to know what matters to him. Be suspicious if nothing ever matters enough to argue about. This "peace at any price" strategy will allow suppressed resentment to build up until a minor disagreement causes a major blow up. Additionally, those people who find it necessary to argue about everything are often terrified of being controlled by their partner.

3. Be willing to be a gracious winner. Statements like, "I told you so", or "You know I'm always right", will only damage the love and respect between you, shame your partner and make future arguments harder.

4. Be willing to acknowledge when the other person convinced you. (In other words, you are willing to admit when you are wrong.) Simply say, "You won, you convinced me" If you demand to be right about everything, you will only be happy living with a person who has virtually no regard for his or her own opinion. By demanding to be right in every case, you are cheating yourself of what the other person has to teach you. It is important to remember that if your partner convinced you, then you have actually won, because you have now adopted a better point of view than you had before. Resentment and distance is created when one partner gives up out of frustration or helplessness. For this reason, it is essential that you agree to continue the argument until both of you feel like you have won (either in the sense of winning the argument or winning a better point of view). You can expect to feel angry sometimes during arguments. This does not mean anything bad about you, despite the fact that you may have received strong parental messages to the contrary. It is far better to feel angry during an argument than to hold a grudge.

5. Be willing to state clearly what you are arguing about. If you and your partner are arguing about different topics, there is no way to resolve the disagreement, no matter how skilled you may become at arguing. Some examples of this are: One partner is arguing about which car to buy and the other is arguing about how to pay for it, or one partner is arguing about the tone of voice being used and the other is arguing about the content of what is being said, or one partner is arguing

about when to pay the bills that already exist and the other is arguing about the best priorities to manage their budget.

A related example occurs when one partner is arguing about something other than what they are upset about. The husband who usually fixes his own breakfast may start an argument about his wife not cooking breakfast, because he is too embarrassed to acknowledge that he is upset about the fact that she wanted to sleep when he wanted sex, the night before. Check out with your partner what the topic of the argument is, by asking something like, " Are you really upset about breakfast or is it something else?"

6. Be willing to discuss one subject at a time and acknowledge when you change the subject. A common argument tactic is to change the subject without saying so, at the point where it looks like you are about to lose. This tactic may prevent you from having to acknowledge that your partner convinced you; however, it does not lead to resolution. It is OK to change the topic and it is OK to reserve the new topic for future discussion. Ask something like, "You just changed the subject, do you want to argue about _____or _____?"

7. Be willing to acknowledge when you are being abusive and willing to respond to your partner's request that you stop it. Abuse means different things to different people. You have the right to define your own standards about this. We consider name-calling, ridicule, shaming and violence to be abuse. Name-calling means that you are verbally attacking your partner, rather than attacking your partner's points. There is a big difference.

Domestic violence began receiving increased national attention during the 1980's. The key message that many people received about domestic violence is "Don't tell". For this reason, you can expect this to be an uncomfortable topic to discuss. Additionally there is painful shame and humiliation that you have tolerated their violence to keep the relationship or that you hurt your lover, depending on your role.

Nevertheless, discussing it is far more comfortable than experiencing it. Regarding abuse we recommend that you decide carefully what your boundaries are and discuss these with your partner. It should be evident that most men could win a fist fight with most women. When this is accepted as a given, then it is not necessary for the man to prove himself by physically abusing his partner. If your partner becomes violent, we suggest that the best strategy is to leave the house as soon as possible and decline all offers to return until the issue is discussed to resolution with a professional. Another suggestion is to call a neighbor to come to get you if your partner becomes violent. Domestic violence is the cause of almost half of the police calls in most major cities. There is nothing wrong with asking for protection when you need it, that is what the police department is paid for. Until fairly recently, law enforcement authorities could not prosecute domestic violence unless the victim swore out a complaint. This is not the case any more and physical abusers can now be arrested and prosecuted just like any other petty criminal. We realize that calling the police may seem like drastic action to you. It is drastic action. It is so drastic that it may ruin your marriage or save it. However, it is a better alternative than being a punching bag for the rest of your life.

8. Be willing to give your partner their say without interruption. You serve your partner and yourself by listening to each other. On one occasion, we conducted a consultation to aid a couple in learning to argue. He interrupted her every other sentence to correct her grammar! Sometimes people are upset when they argue and they don't say what they mean very clearly. Sometimes they are not logical and make no sense at all, even to the point of contradicting themselves. None of these are good enough reasons to interrupt. Just listen. This offers your partner the opportunity to convince you. You can learn a lot just by finding out why the issue under discussion is so activating to your partner.

9. Be willing to ask for or to agree to a break when the intensity becomes uncomfortable. We mentioned earlier that even the best of communication techniques will never take the place of being able to resolve uncomfortable and conflicting feelings within yourself. Taking a break for a Vivation session or just a walk around the block can prevent both partners from saying things that they will later regret. Even in a heavy-weight boxing match, there are breaks between rounds. We surely hope that your arguments are not as violent as a boxing match, however arranging for breaks is a good idea. For people with uncomfortable memories of childhood arguments simply having an argument will tend to activate discomfort that is in no way associated with the issue at hand. This makes taking breaks even more important. Before the start of the break, we suggest that you agree that the argument is not over and agree on a time to continue.

TAKING A BREAK It is not necessary to have your partner's permission to give yourself a break. If your partner is nasty or abusive, you can say, "We are getting nowhere with this. I am taking a walk around the block." After all everyone has a right to call time out. Additionally, it is a good idea to acknowledge that you are afraid of being hurt or of hurting your partner.

Related to the idea of taking breaks when required is the issue of choosing an appropriate time and place for an argument. If you are compulsively afraid of arguing, it will seem that there is never an appropriate time for it. If you are waiting for the "right" time or until your partner is in a better mood, it will never come along. Clearly, there are some times that are far more appropriate than others, but generally it is better to resolve disagreements sooner than later. While your partner is busily engaged in an important project or on the way out the door to an appointment, it is best to say something like, "I am feeling upset about. I want to talk about it. When is a good time for you?"

10. Be willing to refrain from making threats or manipulation by guilt or shame as a method of arguing. A threat is an attempt to use your partner's fear to manipulate him or her. Threats are often caused by desperate fear of losing the argument or, worse losing the partner. There are lots of disadvantages to making threats. One is the threatened person may actually say, "Fine. Go ahead and DO what you threaten." Another problem with threats is that, if the threatened partner complies with the demand, he or she will resent being controlled. It is impossible to have an equal relationship on these terms, not to mention a joyous sex life.

The problem of giving in to threats is like negotiating with a terrorist. Once your partner knows that he or she can get what they want by making threats, it is likely that soon you are making concessions for the hostages that the terrorists is threatening to take or execute during the next decade. As applied to relationships an example of this strategy could be continually making concessions so that your partner won't leave you for someone else.

A better way to deal with threats is to say something like, "I prefer that you don't do what you just threatened; however, there is really nothing I can do to stop you (unless I threaten you with something worse). I refuse to have my life run by your threats. Please stop threatening me."

Most of us grew accustomed to our parents using guilt and shame to manipulate us into behaving as they wanted. This tactic is almost certain to create hurt and resentment for your partner. Statements like, "If you loved me, you'd _____," or "It's your fault that _____" or "When will you ever change?" Using shame or guilt to manipulate may be effective in the short run, but it is disastrous to your love life. If you find yourself doing this apologize immediately.

11. Be willing to agree to disagree. It is not necessary for you and your partner to agree on everything in order to have a satisfying love life, simply because many issues are not important enough. It is foolish to expect or demand that your partner agree with you on everything and it is foolish to continue arguing about topics of minor importance. Even if you have difficulty respecting your partner's opinions about politics, music, or art (for example), you could have respect for their right to their opinion. It is important to remember that closeness does not require sameness, so you can disagree and still be close.

12. Be willing to refrain from arguing in the dark, on the phone, in the car or in public. Many studies about human communication have revealed that the WORDS themselves are way less than half of the information that is communicated when someone speaks. Body position, tone of voice, facial expression and eye movements also say a lot about what we are saying. Arguing in the dark or on the phone cuts off communication on these visual channels. Additionally, arguments in the dark most often occur in bed. When an argument starts in bed, you will be much better off to get up and continue the argument anywhere else. Don't argue while one of you is driving, simply because the driver cannot safely give his partner much visual attention.

People have different degrees of comfort about arguing in public. It is fine to do it if it is OK with both of you and your friends don't mind. We have discovered that we can resolve our disagreements more quickly when we are by ourselves, than in a restaurant, for example.

13. Be willing to refrain from playing "therapist" unless your partner requests it. Statements like "You are just like your mother", or "Just because your father rejected you, doesn't mean you have to take it out on me", or "This is your case about sibling rivalry" or "Your problem is that you compare everyone to your mother" can quickly destroy the love and respect in any relationship. When you get close to someone, you quickly discover what their personal unresolved issues and tender spots. Clearly you have freedom of speech and can say whatever you want;

however, pushing on these spots without permission will most likely cause hurt and resentment and reduce the intimacy because your partner will close down, if you insist on using them as weapons.

14. You are willing to apologize and forgive each other if either of you breaks the rules. Despite the best intentions of you and your partner, you are only human and not perfect. For this reason, it is virtually inevitable that, from time to time, both of you will break the rules. An apology is the most and the least that you can expect when this happens. Patience is required in learning to argue. Every resolved disagreement is a victory for both of you!

HOW TO ARGUE WITH SOMEONE WHO IS UNWILLING TO ARGUE OR UNWILLING TO ABIDE BY ANY RULES

It is exasperating to argue with someone who is completely unwilling to follow any rules. In this situation, any argument has the potential of developing into a fight. When this happens, knowing when to give up (to preserve your peace of mind or personal safety) becomes more important than the validity of your point. Other times, arguing with someone who is unwilling to follow any rules is more upsetting than any argument could be because the other person constantly changes the subject, diverts your attention or laughs it off.

Feeding Back (don't be rational when your partner is acting crazy) If your partner begins to use threats or constantly changes the subject and does not acknowledge that they are doing it, it is useless to try to reason with them. We suggest that you stop trying to persuade them to your point and instead listen to them. When they seem to have "run out of gas", then restate what they have said. You might say things like, "I want to be certain that I understand you. What you're saying is if I do _____, then you will do _____. Is that what you are saying?" or

"Do you mean that you think that _____ could be solved by _____? "Is this what you mean?" or

"Exactly what do you want from me?"

With some people, you will discover that it is necessary to ask this same question many times before you get an answer, despite their getting upset. If they don't answer your question, say, "I understand, but what I asked was _____" and repeat your question. It is OK if you sound like a broken record.

This method provides the evasive or abusive person with another opportunity to consider whether he really means what he is saying. Sometimes if you are just quiet, relaxing your body and facial expression will enable the abusive person to realize that there is no one fighting with him. After you have repeated back to them what they said you might ask the abusive person, "How can this help (our problem)? What about if ____ happens?" The purpose of questions like this is to get you past the desire to avoid being yelled at to discover whether there may in fact be some practical wisdom in what the abusive person is saying. Sometimes this is very difficult to do. Take time to hear how the other person thinks. Often when a person is being irrational, just hearing their thoughts said back to them allows them to hear the problems with how they have justified their opinions.

If your partner is unwilling to argue, using excuses like "I don't have time" or "It doesn't matter"or "Leave me alone", then it is most likely that he does not know how to deal with the feelings associated with arguing. He is uncomfortable with his feelings about arguing to the degree that he prefers to invalidate your feelings about what is important to you, rather than deal with his own. (This is an emotionally abusive tactic.)

You may find it necessary to sell your partner on the benefits of the two of you learning to argue successfully. Many couples attend our LSC to learn how to argue. A good marriage counselor can help you with this, too.

HOW TO TELL WHEN AN ARGUMENT IS OVER

It is important to be willing to continue the argument until it is resolved. Incomplete arguments often leave one or both partners holding a grudge. When an argument is resolved, there is peace and your body feels relaxed and emotionally stable. If you still hold a grudge or feel resentful, the argument is not over and do not say so. If one person is still hurting, then the upset has not been fully integrated. Don't say everything is OK, if it's not! If one or both partners wish to prolong an argument for a covert reason like wanting to control the other or fear of acknowledging that they lost, then you'll spend a lot of time upset with each other when you could be in love.

The major benefits of learning to argue effectively are:

1. You will no longer behave as though an argument could be caused by something wrong in your relationship.

211

2. You will be able to stand up for yourself and not say "yes" when you mean "no" and get more of what you want instead of settling for crumbs and hoping for improvement.
3. Successful arguing promotes a sense of equality and partnership in a relationship.
4. An argument leads to greater intimacy resulting from each person's willingness to show the other parts of his personality that may not be all right with him.
5. Resolving disagreements leads to greater co-operation. co-operation contributes to living happily ever after.

AN ARGUMENT IS OVER WHEN . . . .

You both feel good in your body.
You are both back in love with each other.
You are not secretly resentful or holding a grudge.
You both kiss and hug and mean it.
You both laugh about it.
You are both grateful for the benefits of what you learned.
Your relationship is strengthened by your ability to get over the rough spots.

A RECIPE FOR COMPLETE ARGUMENTS

The first few times you made chocolate cake, you most likely followed the instructions given in a recipe from a cook book. After the third or fourth time, the recipe became no longer necessary, although you may glance at it from time to time to ensure you have the right measurements.

The recipe we will be providing for communicating when you feel upset is like that. At first you may feel a little foolish following the recipe, because it may seem that you are not really communicating, instead you are reading from a book. (It's a good idea to get an additional copy of the book for your partner, so both of you can do this). This recipe is similar. After a little practice, it will become second nature. Once you learn how to follow our recipe, we doubt you will wish to use other methods of communicating when upset, such as pouting, yelling, kicking things, stormy silences or raging out of control.

Like all recipes, this one has steps to follow:

STEP 1: Remember to refer to this recipe.

STEP 2: Take a minute to review any counter productive behavior you may have used in the past during arguments. Acknowledge to yourself the feelings that are bound to be activated. Let yourself be willing to listen to your partner and to keep going until the argument is over.

STEP 3: Review the recipe and take a minute to think about what you want to say and what you are really upset about. (This is like gathering the ingredients to make a cake). Prepare yourself to listen to your partner. In other words, don't dump your upset on them and storm out.

What to Say

STEP 4: Identify the issue. What I am upset about is _____.

STEP 5: What I think is _____.

STEP 6: What I feel is _____.

STEP 7: What I feel like doing about this is _____.

STEP 8: What is motivating me is _____.

Listener feeds back, paraphrasing what was heard, remembering to acknowledge, affirm and validate his partner's feelings.

Then original listener (now the speaker) follows steps 4 through 8. First speaker feeds back, paraphrasing what was heard, remembering to acknowledge, affirm and validate his partner's feelings.

STEP 9: Closure, requests for different treatment and what was learned, said by both people.

STEPS 7 through 9 require some explanation.

STEP 7: What I feel like doing about this is _____.
State what your urges are. What I feel like doing about this is never talking to you again, asking you to leave, taking away your credit cards, never letting you use my car again, etc.

STEP 8: What is motivating me is _____.
When you are intensely upset, you will inevitably be able to make connections from your personal history. What is motivating me is that I always got blamed for everything my sister did, my father never paid attention to me, my parents never kept their word to me, etc.

STEP 9: Closure, check to see if there is any upset left, requests for different treatment and what was learned, said by both people. What I learned from this argument is that you want to be more involved in the state of our finances, etc. The different behavior that I want from you is that we have a regularly scheduled meeting each month about finances, etc.

23 HAVING YOUR SEX LIFE EXACTLY THE WAY YOU WANT IT

Sexual problems seem difficult to solve primarily because they are uncomfortable to discuss. The most important advice we can offer you is: **DO NOT WAIT UNTIL YOU HAVE A PROBLEM WITH SEX BEFORE YOU START USING THE SUGGESTIONS IN THIS SECTION.**

People who attend the LSC have a wide variety of ways of expressing the problems they have with sex. The vast majority of them boil down to the complaint that they are disappointed with sex. In other words, their sex life does not live up to their hopes and dreams. When they compare their sex life to the imaginary standards that they have about it, their sexual experience comes up short and then they make sex wrong, or they make themselves wrong, or they make their partner wrong. As we mentioned earlier, making anything wrong creates an uncomfortable pattern of energy in your body, which we then tend to suppress. Make wrong always involves comparison; comparison to how it should be, could be, might be, etc. There is no way you can enjoy anything no matter how inherently pleasurable, when comparing it to an imaginary standard of something better. Since sex is in essence about enjoying the feelings in your body, comparisons are ruinous to your enjoyment. If you were cuddled in God's lap, listening to angels sing, you could probably imagine a softer lap and better music. Enjoying sex is a matter of personal responsibility and willingness.

Talking about sex is difficult for almost everyone for two reasons: 1. In most cases, our parents were uncomfortable talking about sex with us, so we copy their example and find it uncomfortable, too and 2. It is a tender topic, involving, for some people, their self-worth and fear of loss of their partner. No matter how uncomfortable it may be for you to talk about sex, it is far, far more uncomfortable NOT to talk about it. We suggest that you expect talking about sex to be uncomfortable and go ahead anyway. Vivation will aid you greatly in resolving the uncomfortable feelings.

An important advantage of a committed monogamous relationship is that the closeness and the time that you spend together provide you with an opportunity to have your sex life be exactly the way that you want it. A monogamous long term relationship only provides the opportunity. Whether you can turn this opportunity into reality is up to you. It is our desire here to help you with this.

ESSENTIAL IDEAS AND SUBJECTS FOR DISCUSSION ABOUT HAVING SEX EXACTLY HOW YOU WANT IT.

1. Love is the best aphrodisiac. Get close to your lover first. Sexual excitement has virtually nothing to do with technique. Due to personal preferences, the ideal technique for one person may be a turn off for someone else. Sex will not fix your love life. Some people seem to be willing to settle for sex without love, even on a long term basis.

2. Sex will not take the place of an apology when one is due. Sex will not take the place of affection and respect if they are lacking.

3. Honest communication can solve the vast majority of sexual problems.

4. If either of you have been sexually abused, then it is imperative that you tell each other about it.

5. It is your responsibility to teach your partner how to make love to you, otherwise how will they know what you want?

6. It is the responsibility of both partners to initiate sex and to have their own orgasm.

7. There is no normal sex drive.

8. Sex creates relaxation and intimacy. However, if sex is the only method you have to get close or to relax, this puts an undue burden on your sex life and tends to objectify your lover. We suggest that you avoid using sex and orgasms to reduce your stress or to medicate or suppress your feelings.

9. If you have sexual fantasies, tell your lover about them. Focus on the sensations in your body while making love. Any real lover is better than a fake one.

10. Don't have sex if you don't want to. Since it is obviously to the benefit of both of you to be sexually satisfied, it is wise to give your partner an opportunity to warm you up.

11. Thank and acknowledge your partner for wanting you and for being your lover. Repeat more often than possible!

12. A good sex life alone will not hold a marriage together, but a consistently dissatisfying sex life can break up a marriage. There is more to marriage than sex; however, sex is an important part.

13. If your sex life cools down a bit after you have been together for a while, this may just mean that your body's need for sex is temporarily satisfied. Although it may seem otherwise, your sexual desire does not have to decrease when you get married. Supporting a family, raising children, or keeping a beautiful home will never take the place of a satisfying sex life, no matter how much you struggle to delude yourself about this.

Honest communication can solve the vast majority of sexual problems. We suggest that you be creative in finding ways in addition to sex to experience closeness; holding each other, doing Vivation together, bathing together, massage or anything else that you enjoy doing together. Very

MAKING THE FIRST MOVE IS UP TO BOTH OF YOU!!

few sexual problems are medically caused. It may not be a bad idea to consult a physician for help with impotence or frigidity; however, it is likely that you'll discover that lack of communication is the root of the problem.

LEARNING TO TALK ABOUT SEX
How to improve your sex life tonight

Almost everyone received, sometimes brutally enforced, parental messages that it was definitely not OK to talk about sex. In this section, we provide you with several structured communication processes to get you started. After all, by doing these processes, you are violating what may have been a strict parental or religious prohibition about talking about sex. If you have avoided talking about sex in the past, the first few conversations may be awkward for both you. However they will be fruitful, if you acknowledge that the topic is difficult and if you refrain from yelling, blaming or complaining.

How to do these processes.

In the LSC, we establish for participants the following conditions that greatly aid the emotional processes. They will be an intense experience for you that has tremendously good results. Sit facing each other. Maintain eye contact, looking at each other the whole time. Breathe and relax your body. Establish conditions so that you won't be interrupted. Acknowledge that it's intense and let yourself enjoy the excitement.

STRUCTURED COMMUNICATION PROCESSES TO
IMPROVE YOUR SEX LIFE

If you have been having sexual problems, do these processes once or more per week. There will be some awkwardness at first until you get used to talking like this. With a little practice, the resulting ease in talking about sex will make it a normal topic of your conversation.

1. **Your family's sex life** (A structured communication process to get you started talking about sex and sexual conditioning)

One person starts and says, "Please describe your family's sex life."

The other person talks with interruption until he runs out of things to say, then the first person says, "Thank you. Please describe your family's sex life." Keep doing this until ten minutes have elapsed and then switch roles. In this process, it does not matter whether your memory is accurate, what matters is anything that you remember about what your parents, siblings or other family members did, said or didn't say or didn't do related to sex.

2. **Fears about sex** (A structured communication process) It is highly likely that many of your fears will be foolish, but say them anyway.

One person starts and says:

"A fear I have about having sex with you is _____."

and the other person responds with:

"Thank you."

and without discussion.

Then the first person continues with:

"A fear I have about having sex with you is _____."

"Thank you."

and so on for two minutes.

Then switch parts.

3. Finding out what your partner likes (A structured communication process)

We suggest that you take responsibility for finding out what your partner wants. Without this, you are forced to rely on your often inaccurate interpretation of your partner's moans and groans. Unless what your partner wants will hurt you, then it is a good idea to give it. After all it is to your benefit to have a happy partner. We suggest that you use the following process that we invented on our honeymoon and have been using ever since to our great delight. Ask your lover,

"Please tell me a way that I could improve as a lover."

The temptation to be distracted into chit-chat or into arguments about what happened in the past may be strong when you do this. For this reason, we suggest that you continue the conversation for at least five minutes without discussing anything else.

For example:
A: "Please tell me a way I could improve as a lover."
B: "Well, you could initiate more often."
A: "Thank you. "Please tell me a way I could improve as a lover."
B: "You could make love in the mornings like we used to."
etc. . . . .
Then invite your partner to ask you the same question.
Enjoy yourselves more than possible!
If both of you are willing to ask and answer this question about improving as a lover and actually do what the other person requests some of the time, there is no reason that your sex life can't get better and better regularly.

This question and answer process is one of the optional Saturday night homework assignments for people who attend our Love, Sex and Communication Weekend Seminar. They return Sunday morning with delighted grins and exclamations of surprise about what they learned about their partner and themselves. We do this process with each other once per month or so and it has always resulted in a greater appreciation of our sex life together. Both of us feel that the other is the best lover we have ever had by a huge margin. Our willingness to improve at lovemaking is an essential contributor to this.

4. Disclosure about using sex for control (A structured communication process)

"Please tell me how you use sex to control me". To a certain extent, everyone attempts to use sex to control his or her partner. Sex is so pleasurable that it is a convenient bargaining chip. The question is not so much whether you use sex to control your partner sometimes (because you probably do); but instead whether you can discuss the issue and be above board about it. When we started discussing how we used sex to control the other person, both of us experienced fears that an argument would start and that we would lose some of our ability to get what we wanted from the other. Obviously parts of our minds thought that the methods we had used to control the other needed to be covert in order to be effective. Instead, both of us have discovered that we are willing to fulfill each other's desires in response to a simple, straightforward request. This resulted in a greater sense of closeness between us and we both realized that the covert control patterns hadn't given us any satisfaction any way.

Common answers to "How Do You Use Sex to Control Me" could be:

I refuse to have sex with you when I am mad at you;

When you don't give me what I want, I flirt with someone else to activate your jealousy;

I play hard to get;

I act seductive;

I use sex to "make up" instead of resolving an argument by talking about it.

After softening you up with great sex, then I ask for something that I want.

I pretend that sex doesn't matter to me.

I purposely give you conflicting messages about my interest in sex.

It is to your benefit to be willing to experiment. Clearly you have the right to say no to any request. If your lover suggests something that seems too unusual or scary to you, it may be to your benefit to relax your standards about what is OK. In general, we think that, if it is safe, then it is worth trying once. You might like it. Experimentation ALONE will not create a happy sex life; however, if your sex is the same year after year without any variation, it will surely become boring, even if it is what you want. Strawberry may be your favorite flavor of ice cream, but you can still enjoy butter pecan once in a while as a change of pace.

Other topics that you may wish to discuss with your partner to aid you in having the most outrageous sex life that you can imagine are: Your Parents' Sex Life, Religious Messages about Sex, Masturbation, Teenage Messages about Sex, Your Most Embarrassing Sexual Moment, Pregnancies, Birth Control, Abortions, Sexual Abuse, Greatest Fears about Sex. Also refer to sexual history process in Chapter 13.

EXTRA-MARITAL AFFAIRS

Regardless of one's moral view, affairs cause more problems than they solve. It seems unreasonable to conclude that anyone would get married and plan to have extra-marital affairs. Also it seems reasonable to conclude that an extra-marital affair is a sign of unresolved problems. Whatever drives the person to have affairs is surely some issue that is very difficult for him to discuss, or he could talk about it and would not have to act out. People may be driven to affairs by unresolved patterns of childhood sexual abuse, abandonment as a child, imitation of one parent who always maintained the upper hand over the other parent by having affairs, by revenge against their partner for withholding sex or some other perceived wrong doing. Honest communication with your partner can prevent affairs. One way to describe an affair is that one partner is using his or her sexual organs to say something that they are unwilling to communicate with their vocal organs. The communication is much more comfortable to hear if made with the vocal organs.

Affairs occur when accumulated resentment from undelivered communication builds to the point where it seems impossible to do anything about it. Having an affair is rarely a solution to this problem as all that it does is add a layer of shame and deceit to the already existing resentment. Having a affair adds greatly to the stress in your life. Just as a benefit of telling the truth is that you don't have to remember what you said, the major disadvantage of lying is that you must put constant attention to what you have said in the past and to the excuses that you have made.

Affairs are often motivated by the suppressed desire for Mommy or for Daddy who were sexually unattainable by us as children. Incest or sexual abuse, prolonged absences of one parent, the desire to participate in the love that the child saw the parents giving to each other or the desire to fulfill the adolescent desire of "getting away with something naughty" can all be motivating factors.

Open marriage rarely solves marital problems. Couples who are clear enough with each other so that an open marriage will provide both partners with satisfaction usually find that they do not want an open marriage. Conversely, the couples who want an open marriage are rarely clear enough with each other to make it work to their individual and mutual benefit.

24 COMMUNICATION SKILLS FOR COUPLES
How to Say What You Mean in a Loving Way

Communicate about your feelings. Do not shame your partner for talking about his or her feelings or for having feelings. LOVE IS A FEELING. You'll never stay in love for very long if one or both of you is unwilling to talk about feelings. How could you care about someone who never lets you know how he feels? How can you expect someone to care about you if you never let him know how you feel? Practice voluntary emotional self-disclosure. Sure, it's difficult at times, but it's far easier than compulsively suppressing your feelings and pretending that everything is OK, when it's not.

Make your communication direct, honest, loving and gentle. Just because you are discussing intensely emotional topics does not require that you be sheepish, nasty or insulting about it. Conversely, just because your partner is talking about issues that are upsetting to you does not necessarily mean they are out to get you, nor is it necessary for you to be defensive. Use the techniques in this book so you can claim responsibility for your feelings and simply listen, rather than defending yourself. Do not take it personally if your partner becomes emotionally activated. We are not suggesting that

225

you go out of your way to activate your partner; however, if in every case your partner's serenity is more important to you than your own desires, then it is very unlikely you'll enjoy your love life at all.

You can learn to communicate better, even if you have decades long history of withholding from each other.

Do not keep secrets from your partner. We have discovered that a policy of full disclosure works best. Often there is risk about revealing the truth. This risk is momentary compared to the eternal struggle to avoid it. Secrets do not improve with age, so it is to your benefit to be more open and honest starting right now. Take responsibility for your fear about communication by telling your partner something like, "I have something to tell you and I'm afraid you will want to leave me when I do" or "I have a topic to discuss that is difficult for me, so I want you to just listen until I'm done, then I want to hear what you have to say".

Acknowledge that you have had difficulty discussing this issue in the past. If you want to discuss your financial situation with your partner and previous discussions about money have led to an unresolved argument, it is a good idea to start with something like, "I know we have had difficulty discussing money before, but it is an important issue, so I'd like to learn to discuss our finances with you in a way that serves us both", or "It is important for us to discuss money and in the past it's always led to a fight. How can I discuss money with you so we don't fight about it?" It is important to realize that two people are required for there to be communication problems. For this reason, arguing about who is to blame for communication problems is a waste of time. Both of you are to blame and both of you must make steps to improve. Couples who attend our LSC often express their thanks for the practice that the Weekend offers them in discussing difficult topics gently and effectively.

MANIPULATION AND DOMINATION

It may be frustrating for some to discover that we do not have control over other people. We do, however, have the power to persuade and influence others. For some, their life is a constant hopeless struggle to establish and maintain control of their partner by manipulation or domination.

We will discuss three ways to motivate others and discuss why some work more effectively than others.

FEAR AND PUNISHMENT

One method of motivating people could be called the fear and punishment approach. This methods aims at causing people to engage in certain behavior or to avoid certain behavior by threatening and/or actually delivering harm or punishment. Almost all of us have been subjected to this method of motivation. For example, "If you do that again, you'll be sent to your room.", "If you don't clean up your room, you'll go to bed without dinner", "Talk back to me one more time and I'll show you who is boss". Using motivation by fear and punishment tends to produce consistently undesirable results in a sexual relationship because it leads to a power struggle that neither partner wins. In some instances, people have become so accustomed to motivation by fear and punishment as children, that the same pattern carries over into their adult relationships without their awareness. If you feel obligated to ask permission of your mate, even regarding minor decisions, it is likely that you are allowing yourself to be motivated by fear and punishment. Conversely, if your partner asks permission, even on minor issues, then it is highly likely that you are using fear and punishment to motivate your partner. The same is true if your partner complains or nags or engages in the "silent treatment" or continues to act upset about your behavior and keeps it up until you do something different.

REWARD AND INCENTIVE

Another method of motivating people is the reward and incentive method. Certain goodies and privileges are awarded for certain kinds of behavior and then withheld for failures to produce the desired behavior. Most of us are familiar with this kind of motivation. "No TV until your homework is done.", "No dessert until you eat your lima beans." Most business concerns use the reward and incentive method to motivate their employees with varying degrees of success. This method tends to work best in an organization, where members are willing to participate in an established hierarchy. The reward and incentive method is poorly suited to a marriage or other sexual relationship because there is no legitimate authority. Use of reward and incentive motivation means that one member has a bigger supply of the goodies and must maintain this imbalance of supply in order to keep the game going. A sense of equality is impossible. This method of motivation in a marriage also results in a power struggle just as ruinous, but often more covert, than what results from motivation by fear and punishment.

Motivation by reward and incentive most commonly occurs when men use money to control women and women use sex to control men. The resulting power struggle requires constant attention and produces constant anxiety. The man, for example, must constantly evaluate the situation so that he withholds money often enough to keep her under control, but that he gives her enough money so that she will not leave to find a better provider. The same dilemma confronts the woman who uses sex to manipulate her partner.

Persuasion and Influence

Persuasion can be considered the art of convincing other people that certain behavior is to their benefit because it is harmonious with values that are already important to them. For example, if you want to move to the country, you can persuade your spouse by convincing him or her that such a move is already harmonious with his or her values of peace and quiet, fresh air and love of nature, for example. Clearly this method does not guarantee that you will succeed, but the manipulative approaches do not offer this guarantee either.

TEACHING AND LEARNING FROM EACH OTHER

We live on a planet with five billion other humans. Each of them has things to teach and things to learn. Obviously, not everyone perceives others this way all the time. Some people perceive others as adversaries, competitors, people who want to control them, people to be controlled, or as superiors or inferiors in a hierarchy of some sort. Clearly there are some people whom you prefer not to have as friends or lovers, however the ability to see others as teachers and students will aid you in creating a context of equality and respect in your relationships.

As we explained earlier, there is no legitimate authority in a romantic relationship. The closeness of a sexual relationship can be enhanced by you and your lover agreeing about what you are teaching and learning from each other.

Discussion about what you are teaching each other will answer the question, "What can we contribute to each other?"

By teaching we mean teaching in the broadest sense, so that in some cases, it may be very different from classroom instruction and be more like providing emotional support for the other person to learn.

HOW TO IDENTIFY THE MOST LIKELY TOPICS FOR TEACHING AND LEARNING FROM EACH OTHER

(Some of the examples are items that we have already taught each other or are in the process)

1. Unconscious patterns, the resolution of which would aid your partner's personal development. For example, fears about arguing, sex, improving as a lover, resolving shyness, fears or procrastination about accomplishing certain goals, resolution of childhood conditioning or abuse.

2. Qualities or skills that you see in your partner which you wish to develop for yourself. For example, effective money management, enjoying exercise, learning to ask for what you want, how to use a computer, how to enjoy free time more.

3. Topics that you constantly argue about and have not yet resolved. Almost any example would satisfy this category.

4. Topics that you complain to third persons about regarding your mate. Examples are: eating habits, how to drive, personal hygiene, household duties or communication skills.

By agreeing on the subjects that you wish to teach and learn from each other, you can actually turn your desire to control each other into a desire to contribute to each other. By doing this, you can have your love life contribute to your personal growth.

WHAT ARE YOU TEACHING AND LEARNING FROM EACH OTHER?

Take 2 minutes to list 20 or more things that you would like to support your lover in learning.

229

Take 2 minutes to list 20 or more things that you wish to receive support in learning.

Now that you have written your lists we suggest that you take time to discuss your desires. Consider the ways you could apply them now and in the future together. You may discover things you had no idea were of importance to your partner. Also you may feel upset about what your partner wants you to learn. It is also possible that your lover doesn't know how to teach you some of the things that you wish to learn; however, they can aid you greatly by encouraging you and offering emotional support.

GUIDELINES FOR TEACHING AND LEARNING FROM EACH OTHER

Learning new things is a tender process. Infantile feelings of helplessness are often experienced by the learner, not to mention sensations related to fear, shame and ignorance. Since you are no longer a schoolchild, you have the right to ask for teaching and support to be delivered in ways that will best serve you.

FOR LEARNERS

1. Identify what you want to learn.
2. State all of the problems that not having learned it earlier has caused for you.
3. Why do you want to learn it and what benefits do you expect?
4. Notice the progress that you have already made towards learning it or the degree to which you already know how to do it.
5. Specific ways that your partner could support you.
6. State all of your reservations and considerations about your ability to learn this.
7. State your fears about your partner teaching you.

FOR TEACHERS

1. Ask the learner to be specific and to give examples about what he or she wants to learn.
2. Ask the learner to identify specifically what problems they have because they haven't learned this.
3. Ask the learner what they hope to gain by learning this.
4. Acknowledge the progress that the learner has made already. Just speaking up and indicating a desire to learn is an important step.

5. Ask the learner how they want to be taught, how they want you to intervene and how they want you to offer correction.
6. Ask the learner to state all of his fears about learning this. Do not take these seriously, simply listen.
7. Be patient and compassionate. Gentle humor helps a lot; mocking doesn't. Encouraging the learner to resolve the sensations that the learning process activates is often more important than presenting information in the best way. Be generous with your praise and stingy with your criticism.

Learning new skills represents change and impending changes tend to activate fear. It's tougher for anyone to learn when they are struggling to suppress their fear.

Learner: A fear I have about learning to _____ is _____.

Teacher: OK or Thank you.

Continue for two minutes or until complete.

GROWING TOGETHER

THE PURPOSE OF OUR RELATIONSHIP

Please refer to the writing process described in Chapter 16 for defining the Purpose of your Love Life.

Read the purpose of your love life to each other and choose the personality characteristics and the ways of expressing them that you think are most important to your relationship. Together, write a vision of the ideal love life that would satisfy you both. Then write your statement in the following format:

The purpose of our marriage (or relationship) is to use our

_____

_____

by _____

_____

_____

so that, _____

_____

_____

_____

_____.

Your written statement of purpose serves as a map for choosing future goals and in making important decisions. As well as a source of inspiration. You know that your done writing it when each of you feel delightfully challenged by it and you feel in harmony with your partner. Frame and post it in a prominent place in your home, discuss it and revise it, if desired. Every anniversary is a good time for revisions to accommodate for changes in your personal values, changes in the size of your family or changes in location, finances or employment.

The Purpose of Jeanne and Phil's Marriage

The purpose of our marriage is to use our honesty, our willingness to discuss any topic, our passion and compassion, our desire to serve people, our playful spirit, and willingness to learn by telling the truth and listening, kissing and making love, and by doing work that we love, including writing and teaching, by helping to end suffering, by enjoying our bodies, so that we contribute to world peace and a pure environment, we are a beneficial presence to all the world, and we have and enjoy increasing love for God and each other, sexual pleasure, health, wealth, happiness and service to others now and forever.

PRAYERS

Daily Communication

A major highlight of our LSC is a daily communication process that

232

enables participants to stay up to date with their partner and having honest communication daily. We receive frequent reports from graduates that this process has added enormously to their happiness. They often tell us that once they start to experience the benefits of the process, and then for some reason get out of the habit, they quickly notice that the feelings associated with what is not being communicated begin to weigh heavily in relating to each other. Some even report that the daily process saved their marriage. The process solves the problem of not having anything to talk about. By tradition, we refer to the daily communication method that we are going to describe here as prayers. If your religion has a method of prayer that you use, which is different from what we describe, then you may wish to refer to them by a different name. If you were traumatized by your childhood (or later) religious experience and prefer not to call them prayers, that is fine, too. The purpose of daily prayers as we describe

them are to provide a positive context for honest communication in which each person brings himself up to date with the other. Both members of a couple change with time. Daily prayers provide space for talking to each other and enable you to stay up to date with each other so that you grow together instead of apart.

Complaining about your partner is of little benefit to anyone. Assuming you were in love, when you got together and you are upset with your partner now, then it is wise to ask yourself, "Who changed?" Often people who complain about there partner tell us, "We just don't talk like we used to" or "He'll never change". Obviously people change. And obviously a relationship is a dynamic entity, changing all the time. It is up to you to ensure that it changes for the better.

Another benefit of prayers is that you become accustomed to discussing your relationship regularly. Without this opportunity for frequent discussion, things that are not said tend to accumulate, making it difficult to be close. The harder it is to be close, the harder it is to talk about it. This tends to go on until one person says, often in an ominous tone, "It is time for us to have a TALK."

In restaurants, we often see couples who look as though they have been together for some years, and yet stare off into space. They speak more to the server than to each other. They may rationalize that they have nothing to say to each other; however, it is much more likely that they have so much to say to each other that they don't know where to begin.

If you are not accustomed to talking with your partner in a straightforward way, then you may discover that, at first there is an overwhelming amount of material to discuss. The best thing to do about this is to start. Prayers is an expandable and contractable process which does not require a lot of time. Once you get started, you'll discover how good it feels to be honest and to have a partner that is your friend, lover, and confidant.

Say: "Let's do prayers."

If your partner says: "What's that?", then please show this book to him or her.

If your partner says: "No", then ask, "When?" and make an appointment. Clearly, you cannot force your partner to do this, any more than you can force him to do anything else. Solutions others have used to the problem of a partner that is unwilling to participate in prayers are:

1. Say them to your mate, who just listens and doesn't talk.
2. Write them down and give to your mate.
3. Do them with your children or a friend.

234

Recovery Process

FORMAT FOR PRAYERS

GRATITUDE
ACKNOWLEDGEMENTS
FORGIVENESS
REQUESTS

It works like this:

GRATITUDE

One person begins expressing his gratitude about anything. No matter how bad your day was, no matter how bad your life is; you can find something to be grateful for. For example: "I am grateful that my boss can't yell any louder than he can." "I am grateful that I am with you." "I am grateful for my health." For some, the temptation to chit chat or converse is very strong. Especially, until you get accustomed to the process, it is best to refrain from chit chat and respond to your partner's statements just by saying "Thank you for telling me that" or "Good". When the first person is done, the other person expresses his gratitude.

ACKNOWLEDGEMENTS

The first person says: "Something I acknowledge you for is _____" and the other says "Thank you." When the first person is done, the other person makes his acknowledgements.

235

FORGIVENESS

The person who went first then proceeds with forgiveness about anything or anyone. Examples: "I forgive myself for forgetting our anniversary." "Please forgive me for being late to dinner." "I forgive you for ignoring me at the party." "I forgive my boss for making unreasonable demands." When the first person is done with forgiveness, it is the other person's turn.

Clearly, it is possible that arguments could come out of the forgiveness section unless you communicate responsibly. There is a substantial difference between: "I forgive you for being a $*&@#@" and "I forgive myself for thinking you were a $*&@#;@". If an argument does arise, it is best to finish prayers first and argue later.

REQUESTS

A request is a statement of a desire that you have. "I request that we are more and more in love all the time." "I request that the mechanic tell me that there is nothing seriously wrong with my car." "I request that I do what it takes to improve my health." When the first person is done, the other person makes his requests.

Questions about prayers
How long should they last?
Until you feel like you are done. This will be obvious to you. If you are not obviously done, then keep going. Prayers will probably take longer at first if you have a great deal of undelivered communication to catch up on. Once you're up to date, staying up to date takes less time. Our favorite time to do them is at dinner.
When is the best time to do them?
Any time is far better than none. A regular time each day works well. When you feel upset with your partner. When you think your partner is upset with you. The best time is when you are alone together. When you first wake up, first go to bed, in the car, even on the phone.
Do I have to tell my partner everything?
Of course not. It is best to focus on the important issues, on the items that you feel uncomfortable about mentioning to your partner or at all. It is greatly to your benefit to be willing to tell your partner everything.

Any communication that requires conscious intention for you to withhold from your partner will necessarily limit the flow of love between you.

FOR VIETNAM VETERANS AND THOSE WHO LOVE THEM

For Veterans

For many of the more than five million Americans who served in the Vietnam War, unresolved memories and feelings continue to have undesired and unnoticed effects, despite the fact that American involvement ended there many years ago. Time alone will not heal the wounds. Phil survived the War, spending a year in Vietnam in 1967, and Jeanne's high school boyfriend also survived, but both of us were adversely affected and took steps to recover from the War's devastating consequences. We know that millions of you lost friends, or family members or are married to people who did. We know that unresolved feelings from the War are as intense as any feelings from unresolved abuse and can result in just as irregular behaviors as adaptive mechanisms to keep the feelings suppressed.

War is insane. Anyone who spent a year fighting for his life every day and claims to have emerged from this experience completely sane about it must have been crazy to begin with. For this reason, if you are a Veteran you can and should expect to be affected by your experience. For Phil, the biggest shock of my War experience was finding out how easy it is to kill someone who represents a mortal threat. The self-preservation instinct is a very intense emotional paradox: it is terrifying to experience and gratifying to possess.

For Jeanne, the biggest shock was dealing with the loss of her relationship with her boyfriend due to the trauma he endured. She could see he was suffering, but had no idea then how to help.

At the time of the writing of this book, some Veterans have recently returned to visit Vietnam to aid in the resolution of their War experience. You may do this too, but it is not necessary. It IS necessary to take some action for resolution. The feelings are with you all the time. You are alone with your unresolved feelings, until you can talk about them. Find someone who will listen to you as soon as possible. De-briefing about the War is an essential part of resolving your feelings about it. Your War experience cannot be resolved simply in your mind. This is because your mind naturally will seek reasons and justification.

237

There are none good enough. The suppressed feelings are what must be resolved, or they will continue to haunt you. Nevertheless, there is much of value that can be learned from the War. We learned that we don't want to see another one. By working for peace, we can make ours the last generation of Veterans. America may finally be ready for this.

The bad news is that the wounds from the War may never heal. The good news is that it is not necessary for you to be adversely affected by your experience forever. Clearly we lost friends, suffered in a losing cause and received condemnation for it. The important question at this point is: "Are you going to let this ruin your life?" Almost every Veteran suffers from survivor's guilt to some degree. Survivor's guilt always involves the mistaken conclusion that there is a cause and effect relationship between your being alive and the death of someone else. It is OK for you to be glad that you are alive; sad that they are dead and know that these two conditions have nothing to do with each other.

Visit The Wall in Washington, DC. Just sit on the ground in the park there and engage in the Five Elements of Vivation, as will be described later. It is OK to let the feelings activated by the thought "Never Again!" rage through your body. It is OK to feel upset at The Wall. We have done this several times and plan to continue the practice as long as it provides excellent therapeutic value for resolution of rage and grief. We have been surprised and delighted at how quickly we can resolve long-suppressed feelings and know you can do it too. Self Vivation while watching "Platoon" or any of the other movies about the War has produced similar beneficial results for us.

For Those Who Love Them

It is likely that your Veteran will always act a bit weird when you ask him to tell you about the War or when he does talk about the War, or when he sees movies or TV shows about it or even when a helicopter flies over. Would you really want the kind of man who pretended to be unaffected by such an experience? Knowing that your Veteran has many suppressed feelings from the War will help you understand why he may become upset by the normal screams of children at play or experiences nightmares or rages at the newspaper headlines or isolates himself.

Your Veteran has a lot of suppressed rage about having to kill people. The struggle to come home and try to make sense of the insane act of war may seem impossible to him. He may be tough and demanding and out of touch with his body. The fear, rage and guilt the Veteran has

238

suppressed is vast. As with any suppressed feeling, there may be periods of activation, followed by shame and withdrawal. He may exhibit a kind of hypervigilance, never able to relax without constantly monitoring his surroundings for danger that has long since gone. Be compassionate, patient and supportive. As women who love them we can support them best by reminding them that they do not have to feel ashamed for fighting our war, but instead thank them for fighting it (doing their "duty") for us and tell them often, how glad we are they they made it home alive. *In fact tell that to every Veteran you meet!*

War hurts people. War hurts everyone associated with it. The major difference about Vietnam Veterans is that, for the first time in human history, it has become OK for Veterans to acknowledge this hurt. Finally, we Americans, in defeat, have let ourselves become more human.

If your Veteran tells you that he just worked in some rear area and so has no feelings about the War, he is most likely deluding himself and you too. In Vietnam, everywhere was the front line. Every Veteran suffers from Post Traumatic Stress. All Veterans experience the symptoms, some

suppress them and others get help to resolve them. For many, coming home was the biggest disappointment.

For some, our comments about Vietnam may seem extreme. However, it is generally agreed that survivors of airline crashes require therapy and counselling to recover from the trauma of their experience. For most Veterans that we have met, the War was far more terrifying.

Your Veteran will not turn into a berserk Rambo, when he begins to talk about the War. Sylvester Stallone has less right than most people to misrepresent the behavior of Vietnam Veterans. Every Veteran with any sensitivity deeply resents his exploitation of our suffering.

If you have children, please don't buy them war toys unless you get them a body bag to go with them.

We know the World Peace begins at home. Resolving your own feelings about the War and aiding others in doing the same is something that anyone can do for World Peace.

25 COUPLES AND MONEY
The Effect of Your Career and Your Attitudes about Money on Your Relationship with each other.

Before we were married, each of us had had our own income for more than fifteen years. Since we each had developed the ability to provide for ourselves, we knew that it was essential to agree about how we would handle our money in a way that would retain the aspects of personal independence which we valued and enable both of us to contribute to the prosperity of the other. Additionally, at the time of our marriage, we agreed to work together in conducting seminars and in writing this book. We knew that in addition to acquiring a marriage partner, each of us had acquired a business partner as well.

That each of us knew how to provide for ourselves was an element in our attraction to each other. We wanted to maintain that independence and at the same time learn how to contribute to each other and to share our good fortunes and setbacks, too.

One of the first things that we discussed was how to divide the income and expenses in a way that we both liked. Perhaps, this was easier for us because each of us knew that we could provide for ourselves. We had several setbacks in the early days and one intense argument, but we kept modifying our method of handling our money until we arrived at one that suited us both. We are very grateful that we did this. Now our financial discussions are focused on how to serve more people better by expanding our business and how we can contribute more to each other in accomplishing our individual and mutual financial goals.

It is possible that making a workable agreement will be more difficult for you, simply because you haven't considered this before and because the model that your parents gave you about money was so unworkable. You should expect that discussing money will activate intense feelings, because of conflicting values related to survival, self-worth, greed and providing for your family. When discussing money, it is essential that you remember that there is no right and wrong here, that all conflicts are battles of context.

We are grateful that we knew and agreed that our happiness does not depend on the balance in our bank account, that in fact the best things in life are free, that being in love with each other matters more than money, that a shopping trip to the mall will not solve emotional problems and that enjoying the work that we do contributes far more to our happiness than money. The paradox here is realizing that we could be happy with a little or happy with a lot freed from many compulsions about earning money, leaving us free to engage in projects that we love to do and which add to our income as well. In summary, it is essential to use the methods we will describe in this chapter to achieve harmonious alignment about your finances.

In our Money Is My Friend Weekend Seminar, we cover all aspects of financial success. In this book, we present the parts related to dealing with money with your partner.

Like it or not, that men provide financially for women and children has been a predominant social tradition for many centuries. This is changing. A very small percentage of women live in a household where their husband is the only income producer. It is no wonder that the methods our parents and those before them used for dealing with money are disastrous today. Since the pre-conceptions that most of us have about money were unconsciously gained by observing our parents, conscious discussion of family finances is a necessity.

Describe your family's financial life (A structured communication process for revealing unconscious conditioning about money.)

One person starts and says, "Describe your family's financial life." The other person talks without interruption until they are done and then the first person says. "Thank you. Please describe your family's financial life." Continue for five minutes and then switch roles. In this process describe who made the money, who made the decisions about its use, how you got money, how your family felt about their work and financial situation, what your family told you about money, their arguments about it and their opinions about rich people and poor people and anything else you can think of about money.

After you have both done this, discuss with your partner which aspects of your conditioning about money aids you in having what you want and which parts still function as obstacles to your financial success.

AN EXCERPT FROM MONEY IS MY FRIEND

Phil wrote and published his first book in 1979, entitled "Money is My Friend." In the section about money and relationships, it says,

The safety that we feel in intimate relationships frequently allows thoughts and feelings about money to come to the surface that we are not in touch with in other relationships. I am not going to tell you what what the best financial arrangements are for your household; but I can tell you how to arrive at the financial arrangement that will be the most harmonious for you. The way to do this is to experiment. Most people handle money in their relationships the way that their parents did. Unless your parents' financial life together was totally harmonious, then it might be worthwhile to experiment a little. Parental arguments about money frequently give people the idea that money is not a socially acceptable topic of conversation because of the upsets that are caused by discussing it.

Here are a couple of mind expanding ideas about money in relationships. If the woman is the one who stays home and takes care of the house (A recent Government survey tells me that only 34% of American adult females are in this category) and the man is the only income producer; then it is reasonable for her to receive a salary for the household managerial services she provides. If he objects, then she can suggest that he look in the local newspaper to find out how much live-in maids cost these days. Conversely, if the man is the only income producer and pays the rent or mortgage payments; then there is no reason that the woman should not pay rent. I always recommend that both parties in an intimate relationship have their own checking and savings accounts. Joint checking accounts usually turn into a race - a race to see who can spend the money first or a race to see who can be the most martyrous by not spending it.

Successful negotiation can be accomplished by having a financial discussion with your partner at regularly scheduled intervals (the beginning of the month seems to be a good time). At this discussion you make agreements about who will pay how much of each of the expenses. This is a reasonably risk free way to do it, even if both of you are afraid about negotiating, because the agreement lasts only for a month. At the beginning of the next month you will have had a month's experience with the agreement you made and an opportunity to make a different one or just change parts of it, if you want to.

Being clear about money with your partner will the reduce the upset and confusion in your relationship and will add to the joy and freedom of being together.

THE SIGNIFICANCE OF YOUR CAREER

There are 168 hours in a week. If you spend 40 hours per week working and 8 hours per week getting to work and coming back home, and if you spend 56 hours per week sleeping, then you have 64 hours per week left over for everything else, including spending time with your partner. For most people the "everything else" that they do in the approximately 64 waking hours when they are not working or commuting are filled with a wide variety of activities, leaving work as the waking activity that uses most of your time. This means that if you do not like your work, then you are likely to make unreasonable demands on the rest of your life, (your love life, for example) to provide you the satisfaction that you are missing at work. Everyone has a bad day from time to time; however, if you repeatedly come home from work stressed out and expect your spouse to take care of you, this puts the relationship out of balance. If both partners come home from work repeatedly stressed out, then they have little left over to give each other. Even if both of you have work that you love, it may be useful to have some time between work life and home life to "shift gears".

In the worst context, your job is simply a statement of how much you need money and the things that money will buy. Making a lot of money doing something that does not satisfy you is a bad deal, no matter how much money you make. Today, national surveys report that Americans are less satisfied with their work and their income than in the past.

Due to conditioned fear of failure, fear of change or fear of having what they really want, many people pick careers and stay in jobs that are far less than full expressions of themselves simply for the illusion of security. It is likely that the purpose of some of this delusion is to suppress the resentment about HAVING TO work. Unless you have already acquired a large personal fortune, then it may be true that you have to work, but that does not necessarily mean that you have to hate it. Among humans and animals alike, a primary difference between the adults and the young is that the adults provide for themselves and the young and the young are provided for. The ability to create an income for yourself and your family is a sign of your responsibility and maturity. The ability to create an income for yourself and your family doing work that you love is a sign of your willingness to give yourself what you want.

It is unreasonable to demand that your job be a delightful experience every moment. It is reasonable to expect that your work provide you with a sense of accomplishment, with satisfaction that you are making the world a better place and with the peace of mind that comes from expressing your purpose in life. If this is not the case for you, please obtain a copy of "Money Is My Friend" by Phil Laut and use it as an action guide to career satisfaction.

Money is consistently named as the leading cause of divorce. It is doubtful that too much money would drive a couple apart. Too little money may cause depression and disappointment, but not necessarily a divorce. The inability to discuss money without fighting and the inability to contribute to each other's financial well being is what causes most problems.

If you find it impossible to discuss money with your romantic partner, then important financial decisions and spending behavior will be determined by your momentary emotions and unconscious thinking patterns rather than by the effective alignment of your decisions and behavior with your financial goals. It is essential to manage your finances in a businesslike way if you desire to serve humanity, achieve more and accumulate more.

Successful negotiation can be accomplished by having a financial discussion with your partner at regularly scheduled intervals (the beginning of the month is usually a good time). At this discussion, make agreements about who will pay how much of each of the expenses. This is a reasonably risk free way to do it, even if both of you are afraid of negotiating, because the agreement only lasts for a month. At the beginning of the next month you will have had a month's experience with the agreement you made and an opportunity to make a different one or just change parts of it.

Many couples find it difficult to discuss money issues in a straightforward and honest way. A comment we frequently hear is "Talking about money always leads to a fight." It is essential that you practice the following suggestions so that you and your partner can learn to discuss your finances without criticizing each other and yelling at each other. If you don't, then you won't get much more money than you already have. In other words, as long as you believe that money leads to fights, you may conclude: if we have more money, then we'll have more fights. This conclusion can result in unconscious sabotage of even the best made plans to accumulate wealth. You won't manage your money very well if you don't talk about it.

It is inevitable that you and your partner will have disagreements from time to time about money and about other issues as well. If two people agree on everything, you can be sure that one of them is doing all the thinking. The purpose of the methods described in this chapter is to enable you to reduce conflict about finances, resolve quickly the conflicts that do occur and to enable you to contribute to each other in defining and accomplishing your goals. Defining the purpose of your relationship as described in Chapter 24 makes it much easier to select goals.

If the financial values of your spouse are vastly different from yours then you are bound to have problems unless you can reconcile the differences. To state an extreme example, if one partner insists on saving every spare penny to buy a house and the other insists on spending every spare penny gambling at the local race track, then resolution of these differing values is an essential pre-requisite to financial harmony and co-operation. That two people with such greatly different financial values would marry each other or stay married for very long is unlikely.

Most couples already have substantial agreement about financial values and some differences. Learning to contribute to each other's financial success involves identification of similar values and minimization of the conflict caused by differing values. Keeping all of your money in joint accounts makes each and every expenditure a source of potential conflict. If each partner has separate money of his own that he or she can spend, save or invest without justification or explanation, then the potential for conflict is greatly reduced. Keeping all the money in joint accounts is most often a sign that a couple is not effectively discussing their finances. Many couples who keep all of their money in joint accounts do so simply because their parents did and have not considered alternatives. If your parents had a less harmonious relationship regarding money issues than you would like to have, surely it is time for you to consider alternatives.

Recovery Process

COUPLES QUIZ ABOUT FINANCIAL VALUES

Please pick the answer that most applies. Your behavior is what matters here and you may discover that it is upsetting to notice that your behavior in some cases is in opposition to your mentally held values.

1. YES __ NO __ Based on your behavior, do you value spending money more than saving money?
2. YES __ NO __ Based on your behavior, do you value procrastinating paying your bills more than paying your bills on time?
3. YES __ NO __ Based on your behavior, do you value personally managing your finances more than leaving it up to someone else?
4. YES __ NO __ Based on your behavior, do you admire the values of the poor more than the values of the rich?

5. YES__ NO__ Based on your behavior, do you value privacy from your partner about your money more than complete disclosure about it?

6. YES__ NO__ Based on your behavior, do you value your own ideals about money more than your parents' ideals about money?

7. YES__ NO__ Based on your behavior, do you value ensuring your financial success more than ensuring the success of your relationships?

8. YES__ NO__ Based on your behavior, do you value taking risks to make money more than earning money with predictable methods?

9. YES__ NO__ Based on your behavior, do you value budgeting and planning more than carefree money management?

10. YES__ NO__ Based on your behavior, do you value work time more than time off?

11. YES__ NO__ Based on your behavior, do you value keeping track of the money you spend more than being unaware of where and how your money is spent?

12. YES__ NO__ Based on your behavior, do you value paying taxes honestly and legally more than lying and cheating on taxes (even a little)?

13. YES__ NO__ Based on your behavior, do you value taking direct action to increase your income more than waiting and hoping your income will increase?

14. YES__ NO__ Based on your behavior, do you value going into debt to get what you want more than living within your means?

15. YES__ NO__ Based on your behavior, do you value the satisfaction of the money you earn more than the satisfaction of your work?

Clearly, these 15 questions won't cover every issue in your financial life together. However, they will provide a very useful basis for discussion, as well as providing an opportunity for greater alignment of your behavior with your consciously held values.

MANAGING YOUR MONEY IN A BUSINESSLIKE WAY

A successful business endeavors to increase its profits by finding new and better ways to serve new and existing customers with the products and services that it offers by finding ways to deliver its products in a low cost, high quality way and by developing new and improved products and services to contribute to increased income in the future. Regarding your personal finances, effective co-ordination of these activities and making the best trade offs to define and accomplish your goals requires frequent discussion with your partner, just as business people require frequent meetings to co-ordinate their activities. The essential difference in a romantic relationship is that there is no legitimate authority. A romantic relationship is a partnership of equals and therefore functions best by agreement. Businesses are invariably structured as hierarchies where some people have authority over others. Financial harmony and co-ordination in a romantic relationship therefore requires even more communication than in a business. Both people must have a say in how the money is managed.

SCHEDULE AND HOLD MONTHLY FINANCIAL COMMITTEE MEETINGS WITH YOUR MATE

You'll probably require an hour or so for each meeting. Discuss only financial matters at your committee meetings. Prepare and agree upon agenda topics beforehand. If topics unrelated to your financial situation come up during the meeting, postpone them for future discussion. At the first meeting, start with full disclosure about your financial situation, if you have not already done so with your mate. Discovering that your mate has $50,000 stashed in an undisclosed bank account is likely to be just as upsetting as finding out that there is a $50,000 undisclosed debt.

If you do not have a complete and up to date statement of assets, liabilities, income and expenses, then agreeing on who will prepare this and when must be a topic at your first meeting. If your finances are complicated, you may wish to hire an accountant or bookkeeper to help you with this.

There must be clear agreement on job assignments—who deals with the stock broker, the creditors and the bank accounts. Full disclosure is an important element.

Secrecy about money has no place in intimate relationships. Secrecy is an aspect of conditioning learned from parents who didn't know how to discuss money openly. Parental conditioning even pervades major companies who insist on keeping secret the salaries of their employees.

Social conditioning contributes to making money an unacceptable conversation topic. One could argue that people are more uptight about money than about sex; surely, there are fewer jokes about money. Clearly it is neither necessary nor advisable to discuss your money situation with everyone you meet; the point is that if talking about money with your partner makes you uncomfortable, then you are reducing your chances of getting more of it.

Effective money management is not a luxury only for the wealthy. Conversely the less money you have, the more good management is required. If you wait until you are rich to begin to manage your money wisely, it is unlikely that you'll get rich. Even if you do, the cost of your sloppy money management habits will increase with your wealth.

ACKNOWLEDGE YOUR FEARS ABOUT GETTING RICH

You may be a whole lot more aware of your fears about going broke than of your fears of getting rich. Almost everyone fears change, because it is unknown—even changes for the better. Often women are afraid that their husband will leave them or be too busy for them once he gets rich. Some men are afraid that they will lose control of their wife once she experiences the independence of succeeding on her own. Take a moment to consider your fears about having an immediate and permanent hundredfold increase in your income and discuss these with your partner.

(Two Structured communication processes)

Spend two minutes repeating to your partner, "A fear I have about getting rich is _____" and ask your partner to respond to each repetition simply with "Thank you" and no additional comment. Complete the sentence by filling in the blank with whatever comes to your mind without rehearsal. Ask your partner to do the same with you.

One person starts and says, "How would our relationship change if we were suddenly wealthy?" The other person talks without interruption until done and then the first person says, "Please tell me how our relationship would change if we were suddenly wealthy?" Continue for five minutes and then switch roles.

FIND WORK THAT YOU LOVE

It is impossible to enjoy your life very much with the "Thank God It's Friday" attitude. Unless your work is a source of satisfaction, an outlet for your creativity and an expression of your important values, you are making unreasonable demands on the rest of your life to satisfy you. If you are like most people, you spend more time working than any other activity except sleeping. At worst, your job is an expression of how much you need money. Having work that you do not like places undue stress on your family relationships.

Some people complain that they are tired after a week at the office, where they lift nothing heavier than a telephone. Yet after three sets of tennis on Saturday, they claim they feel wonderful. Thus, it is not the work that makes them tired, instead it's the constant effort to suppress their feelings about being there that does it.

MEN AND MONEY

Most men have been sold a self-defeating bill of goods regarding financial success. This is the idea that if we have expensive possessions (fine car and fine clothes), then more women will be attracted. This myth works to some extent (as most myths do); however, most men sooner or later discover that a relationship with a woman for whom the possessions are a major attractive factor lacks emotional content and simply serves to reinforce habits about struggle. Regrettably, some men never discover this.

WOMEN AND MONEY

For women, financial success in a business that you love will make it very clear that you don't need men to provide material goods for you. Although this may sound delightful to female readers, those women who have relied on their helplessness to attract men are likely to feel threatened by the prospect of their own personal financial independence. Additionally, women readers who have used the willingness of their male partner to provide financial support as a measure of judging the loyalty or suitability of a sexual partner will find that new ways of thinking and choosing will have to be developed. This we believe is good news for women, who can select their partners more of the basis of personal preference without regard to finances.

PRENUPTIAL AGREEMENTS

A prenuptial agreement is a legal contract that attempts to define the division of individual assets in the event of divorce. Without a prenuptial agreement, the division of assets in the event of divorce is likely to be determined by the laws of your State as interpreted by a divorce court; in other words, you may have little to say about the outcome. The idea of a prenuptial agreement may threaten dearly held romantic illusions.

Many lawyers contend that prenuptial agreements rarely hold up in court. Nevertheless, the process of negotiating a prenuptial agreement is more important than the agreement itself. If you find that it is impossible to even TALK with your prospective marriage partner about a possible prenuptial agreement, then it is unlikely that the two of you will have much success in discussing money once you are married.

We know that you will not solve your financial problems or decide your financial future overnight, however talking about this will get you moving toward solutions and plans.

TOPICS FOR YOUR MONTHLY FINANCIAL COMMITTEE MEETINGS:

1. Current financial situation
2. Income this month
3. Expenses this month and unexpected bills
4. Amounts that were saved.
5. Progress toward financial goals
6. Discussion of new goals
7. Your feelings about your work or anything else about money.
8. Anything either of you want to change about how you manage your money.
9. Future prospects for increasing your income
10. Any and all of the structured communication processes in this chapter.

26 BUILDING A FUNCTIONAL FAMILY

EFFECTIVE PARENTING

Raising children is a lot of work, even if you do an ineffective job of it. Doing a good job is at most slightly more difficult and in fact you may discover that doing a good job of it is a whole lot easier. The essential characteristic of unhealthy, dysfunctional families is that feelings are not discussed, feelings are not OK to have or to talk about and feelings are discounted and invalidated.

A functional family is one that operates to the benefit of all members. Each member knows what his needs are, can communicate them to the others and is supported in having his needs met. There is respect for individual needs. Feelings are expressed without abusing each other. How many times did you see your father cry? We are not claiming to have the answer to every question about parenting; however, we can offer some useful guidelines. Many parents seem to invest the majority of their energy regarding their children into encouraging them to conform to prescribed standards of behavior rather than encouraging their creativity and self-esteem. This results in trying to use threats, ignoring, defensiveness or retaliation as methods of exercising control. "Do as I say; not as I do" is the message that is unintentionally delivered, and which naturally produces rebellion. Instead, use communication methods such as, setting a good example, listening, compromise, discussion and negotiation to get what you want.

There are widely varying views about discipline. Some would say "Spare the rod and spoil the child", but to us it is obvious that much of what passes for discipline and punishment is thinly veiled child abuse caused by the parents' unresolved feelings from their own childhood. Frequently children raised under tight controls run wild after leaving home, since they have never developed self-discipline, which is best taught by example.

As the parent, it is up to you to take the initiative by talking about your own feelings, thereby providing the rest of your family with proof that feelings are OK to have and to talk about. Since parenthood is emotionally activating it is essential that you discuss your feelings. Do not expect to have perpetual peace and harmony in your family. This expectation can lead to denial about the problems in your family that are obvious to any impartial, outside observer. Acting out by stealing, drugs, failing grades or other serious behavior is a sign that your child is crying out for attention about something he is afraid to communicate. Let your children have their anger against you (or any other strong emotions). This doesn't mean you let them abuse you or manipulate you; it means you let them have their feelings. "I know you are angry about my decision about the skateboard and I know you hate me for it. I can understand that you feel that way."

If you try to define their identity (by telling them what they should be, feel, think and say), the resulting lack of development of their own sense of Self or identity is likely to cause lots of problems—problems which parents often blame on peer pressure on their children. Peer pressure causes them to want to look the same as their friends. Teenage pregnancy, alcoholism, drug abuse and suicide are not caused by peer pressure, they are caused by lack of identity.

Do not ignore serious changes in behavior. Take action that is reasonable. Drastic action or intense upset on the part of the parent can lead to further alienation of the child. Professional help is readily available today. Help from counselors and psychologists can improve family communication, manage anger and resolve conflicts. Seeking help when needed is a sign of your good judgment and does not mean you are a failure.

Since there in no one right way to raise children, you and your mate are bound to have disagreements on this subject. Discuss values, behavior, rewards and punishment with your mate and reach workable compromises can you both can live with. Do not tolerate your mate abusing your children. Children deserve the same gentle treatment that you would want for yourself. If the course of action you agreed on, doesn't work, then figure what went wrong and take corrective action. Don't blame your spouse if his ideas didn't work and don't argue about this in the presence of your children. Don't let your children play you one off against the other. If you complain about your mate, don't do it to your children. Don't use your children to deliver your personal communications to your mate, under any circumstances.

Don't expect to be a perfect parent. Acknowledge your mistakes to your children and apologize for them. Don't make rules that you are unable or unwilling to enforce. Your children will feel safer with consistent and clearly defined boundaries. Don't allow your children to tyrannize the household by monopolizing the phone, stereo or TV. These are privileges. Negotiate a system fair to all.

LABEL, AFFIRM AND VALIDATE FEELINGS

Parental example of willingness to discuss feelings creates an atmosphere where it is safe for the children to discuss their feelings and problems. Listen. Let them have their say. Let them propose their own solutions by keeping your ideas to yourself until they have proposed their own solution. This will add to their self-reliance. Label, affirm and validate their feelings, whether you agree with them or not. Say "I understand that you are angry about this." Reward and acknowledge them for telling you the truth, even when the truth is upsetting or seems foolish to you, by listening and saying something supportive. You can make sure they know you understand by re-phrasing what they have said. Become the parent you wish you had had by giving the gift of understanding.

As your children grow, you will naturally lose power over them. If your relationship with them is a fight to retain as much power as possible for as long as possible, they will fight back against this. Allow them to learn by making their own mistakes. Let it be OK for your children to say NO to you. If you demand absolute obedience from your children, it is foolish to expect them to be able to say NO to sex or drugs.

We are privileged to serve in the building of functional families with our LSC Weekend. Children age 18 and under can attend free of charge with their parent(s) and are encouraged to do so. It is always a beautiful moment and it brings tears to all our eyes to watch the so called generation gap dissolve between family members. The structure of the communication and emotional resolution processes in the seminar provide an environment where family members begin gently telling the truth to each other and long repressed feelings are resolved.

256

TEACHING YOUR CHILDREN ABOUT MONEY

In human and in animal societies, full grown individuals accept the task of caring for the young. The instincts that motivate creatures to the accomplishment of this task are built into the genes of any reasonably complicated species that survives longer than one generation. The ability to provide for oneself distinguishes between adults from children. Children lack money, power and skills. The task of a parent is to assist and guide the development of a helpless, inept and financially poor infant into a healthy, happy, productive, independent and prosperous adult.

The majority of important lessons that children learn are learned from the example that their parents provide about how to be an adult. Actions speak louder than words. Parental love and caring is far more valuable to children than anything that money can buy for them. It is not your job as a parent to deprive yourself of the things that you want so that your children can have what they want. If you do this, you will provide your children with the example that the way to be an adult is to sacrifice for your children. Your children, in this instance, will not want to grow up and will probably be asking you for money long after they have reached maturity.

Teach your children how to manage their own money. Let them experiment with a wide variety of jobs and businesses before they become concerned with building a stable resume. Give them the opportunity to learn from their mistakes about spending and saving. Children have a natural knack for selling, before it is repressed, usually by the stifling conformity of teenage peer pressure. Encourage your children in their financial ventures and in the enjoyment of the rewards that they receive.

Teach your children to have a reasonable perspective about money. Teaching them to have an open heart, to practice self-discipline and responsibility and how to solve their own problems will do a lot more for the world than encouraging them to become a thermonuclear scientist, doctor or lawyer.

TEACHING YOUR CHILDREN ABOUT SEX

Expect it to be uncomfortable to discuss sex with your children. However, not discussing it can be catastrophic. If you don't take this responsibility yourself, then your children will learn about sex somewhere else and you'll have nothing to say about it. It is abusive (foolish, too) to neglect your children's education about sex. Planned Parenthood can help with coun-selling and sexuality education for parents and their children of all ages. You can find them in your telephone White Pages or reach the national office at 212-603-4600. It seems that each generation grows up more quickly than the one before. For this reason, give your children as much information as they ask for and let them know that they can ask for more. Don't lie to them or tell them fairy tales about where they came from. Tell them the truth. If you act upset, ashamed or embarrassed about their questions, they are likely to conclude that there is something wrong with sex.

It is natural for children to curious about each other's bodies and about sex. If you find out about this, it is important not to shame them about it. Instead give them a chance to talk about it if they want to. THERE IS NOTHING WRONG WITH SEX. There are, however, inappropriate expres-sions of it. It is necessary to modify your behavior as your children grow to maintain appropriate boundaries. Bathing your children, letting them see you naked or curling up in bed with them may be fine when they are age three; but at thirteen these are inappropriate and cause undue stress for the child.

At the onset of puberty, sex drive increases and masturbation is almost universal. Risks of unwanted pregnancy and venereal disease must be discussed. If your teenager is incapable of managing these risks, clearly they are not ready for sexual intercourse. Counselling, listening and educating (rather than lecturing) about birth control and self-discipline will add reason to their passion. It's abusive to be overly suspicious about their sexual behavior and interrogate them about it on their return from dates. Any teenager is sensitive about his sexuality. Embarrassing him about it will not help. This will increase their motivation to hide it from you.

This is not a manual for effective parenting. In fact we think that the most effective thing you can do for your children is to resolve your own childhood, so that you do not pass along the same destructive patterns that you received. In the LSC, parents often tell us, "I said I'd never treat my children like my parents did, but I find myself doing the exact same thing." Talk about your feelings with your children in a responsible way, thereby offering them permission and an example to do the same. Stop taking things so seriously. The best thing you can do for them is provide them a good example of someone who takes care of himself and offer them a model of a couple in love.

Anyone who has had a child will always be a parent; however, there is a time to let go of ACTING as their parent. Sometimes grown people in our LSC complain that their parents still treat them like children, imposing their values and opinions about their lifestyle and decisions that they are now making as adults. We remind them that it may be a good idea to invite your parents to retire from their parental responsibilities and instead become a close friend who has known them since birth.

PART IV

APPLYING EMOTIONAL RESOLUTION TO YOUR LOVE LIFE

27   VIVATION

Vivation is a skill of emotional integration or resolution. Like most skills, you will improve with practice and probably will require a trained instructor at first, but you can do it with your family or anyone or on your own. Vivation is completely internal and personal, it can be done anywhere, although at first it is usually done lying down in a relaxed position with a Vivation Professional in dedicated sessions lasting 1 to 2 hours. The result of learning Vivation is the ability to manage what your emotions mean to you, so that the effort to suppress them no longer limits your freedom, happiness and effectiveness. You accept your feelings as they are and can relax and think more clearly. We call this resolution, "Integration." Integration is an ability that all of us already possess, but oftentimes people think of it depends on luck or an ability that only few people have. The ability to integrate is a skill that can be easily developed regardless of your age, gender, life situation, or how long any problem has existed.

As a natural, organic process of your mind and body, integration isn't really something that you do; it is something that you allow to happen. We can use boiling an egg as an analogy. To boil an egg, you must bring together the egg itself, sufficient water, a heat resistant container that can hold the egg and the water and sufficient heat to boil the water. Once you have established the proper conditions, additional intervention on your part will not boil the egg any faster or any better. In fact, pulling the egg out of the water to check its progress will actually interfere with the result you intend.

Vivation creates rapid and wide ranging self-improvement. The improvement that it creates is a result of the integration which occurs, which could be described as the willingness to give up the struggle to change what you are feeling.

Integration of any suppressed feeling occurs instantly in momentary time. However, it does not necessarily follow that everything that you have suppressed will be integrated in one Vivation session simply because most of us have suppressed a very large (nevertheless finite) number of feelings. Vivation is like exercise is the sense that it is a challenging, delightful and on-going process. Willingness is the most important ingredient. You can learn to do Vivation or VIVE on your own in a few short sessions and will find that this ability is worth far more than the few hundred dollars that it may cost you to learn. Having learned the process, you can do it on your own, with your partner and the rest of the family.

Like suppression, integration is also FAR less selective than we think. For example, resolution of a childhood incident of rejection often results in an increase in income for businesspeople or a reduction in shyness; resolution of resentment about any authority figure can make it easier to pay your taxes or get along with your boss and resolution of shame from childhood sexual abuse causes sweeping changes in how people relate to members of the opposite sex. Integration has a cumulative, snowball effect in that each integration facilitates the next one.

Integration resulting from Vivation does not necessarily change your emotions, instead you learn to change what they mean to you, how they affect you and your attitude about them. Just as attitudes influence behavior, integration commonly produces spontaneous changes in behavior that you'll like.

Emotional resolution offers the possibilities of:

1. Substantially increasing your range of emotional comfort, enabling you to change unconscious habits and patterns that do not serve you.
2. Greater awareness of your body resulting in taking better care of it.
3. Relaxation in formerly stressful situations resulting in increased effectiveness with less effort.

4. Peace of mind about difficulties which have plagued you.
5. Courage and ability to express your important values.
6. Greater comfort discussing distressing feelings resulting in greater intimacy.
7. Getting free of past upsets and the need to control or manipulate others.
8. A genuine sense of self worth resulting from integrating feelings of shame.
9. Becoming a beneficial presence to the world with greater compassion for yourself and others.
10. Acceptance of your body and intense sexual feelings resulting in a natural enjoyment of sex.

Regarding to your love life, Vivation™ offers a practical alternative to the following unproductive behavior and attitudes:
1. Avoiding discussion of sensitive issues.
2. Worrying, pouting, sulking or any behavior which you may compulsively use to avoid activation.
3. Getting bored with your lover.
4. Being threatened by your lover's accomplishments.
5. Having to find a new partner every time there is an upset.
6. Allowing your love life to be controlled by unresolved jealousy or mistrust.
7. Having affairs to relieve the boredom.
8. Manipulating others or allowing shyness to rule your social life.
9. Being driven apart by unresolved disagreements.
10. Allowing your behavior and desires to be governed by upsetting past experiences.

VIVATION AS APPLIED TO YOUR LOVE LIFE

Vivation provides couples and individuals with an effective method for dealing with the uncomfortable feelings that are often activated by your love life or by your unfulfilled desire to have one. Inability or unwillingness to deal with your own or your partner's jealousy, anger, shyness, fear and the other emotions that were described in detail in Chapter 9 often causes strife and separations in relationships. People withhold love from each other because of the fear (usually unconscious) that the intensity of feeling in love will trigger uncomfortable emotions. Lovers withhold truthful

265

communication from each other because of their inability to deal with suppressed feelings. Many sexual difficulties are caused by the inability to deal with body sensations themselves or their intensity. Vivation has been used to solve all manner of sexual problems.

Love may be enough to get you together but it's not enough to keep you together happily. Divorced people sometimes tells us, "I still love him (her), but we couldn't work it out." Vivation provides you with a sense of compassion about your emotional difficulties and for those of others. Since there is emotional content to every disagreement or problem, the ability to cope with your own and your partner's emotions in a compassionate way offers you a common framework and language for addressing it. This is of huge benefit when discussing your problems, allowing people to grow together (as individuals and as a couple) instead of growing apart.

Couples who learn to coach each other's Vivation sessions create for themselves a common method of emotional resolution, can actually contribute to each other's well-being in a very substantial way, allow the person who is closest to help them and experience growing trust for each other.

The responses to the confidential questionnaire completed by participants in our Love, Sex and Communication Seminars have shown us that people can identify their problems and often the causes of them, as well. Many have used various therapeutic methods to figure out the cause and effect of their past. Their most common complaint is, "I know intellectually why I behave like I do and I know what I could do to improve, but I just can't seem to change." The point here is that analysis can only bring you to understanding about yourself. Persistent personal problems are caused by the often unconscious struggle to keep suppressed the emotions that you make-wrong. Since this struggle is often unconscious, it is unwise to expect that the understanding of your conscious mind alone will bring resolution. Another way to say this is that the insights that you have about your past and your problems are valuable in learning about yourself, about how your past has affected you, and in increasing your compassion for the problems of others; but insight, by itself, usually is not sufficient to motivate you to change your behavior, if the associated sensations are not resolved.

We mentioned earlier that results of suppression are: your mind distracts you from the discomfort, in your body armors or tenses to control the discomfort, your breathing becomes inhibited, and an internal conflict is created. Knowing this, you can use any of these results of suppression to free yourself from it. The effectiveness of Vivation comes from the fact that it deals with all four of these results of suppression simultaneously.

Skill with Vivation enables you to establish conditions that result in integration of suppressed material in every case.

There are many methods of self-improvement that enable the practitioner to resolve the results of suppression. Psycho-analysis and most forms of meditation resolve the tendency for our mind to be distracted from our problems. Body work (massage, Rolfing) and most forms of yoga resolve the tendency for our bodies to to armor or tense up to avoid feeling uncomfortable sensations. Some forms of yoga and breathing exercises of all kinds, including vigorous exercise, resolve the tendency for the breathing mechanism to become inhibited as a result of suppression. Vivation combines the effectiveness of all of these methods, because its use involves the breath, the mind and the body simultaneously.

WHAT VIVATION IS NOT

Vivation is not therapy, regression, religion, psychology, yoga, medicine, hypnosis, anything to join and it is not a substitute for any of these things. You are not required to dress differently, behave differently, act out your emotions in an intensely cathartic way, join a club or anything like that; although you could do any of these, if you wanted to.

LEARNING VIVATION

Learning the Vivation process can be compared to learning to fly an airplane, although learning Vivation is much less dangerous, much less complicated and much less expensive. At first, you would want an instructor to teach you about the aircraft controls and the characteristics of flight and to provide you with confidence and guidance on your initial flights. After you get the hang of it, you would not want to have to take the instructor along every time you wanted to fly somewhere. To continue the analogy, the challenge of learning to fly a plane involves learning that the airplane flies itself and all you have to do is guide it. The novice pilot tends to over-compensate, flying all over the sky. If you pull too far back on the stick, the plane stalls and if you push too far forward, the plane crashes.

Learning Vivation has a similar challenge: that of maintaining awareness of the sensations in your body and balancing the tendency to lose awareness of them with the fear that they will be overwhelming. A big part of learning Vivation is learning THAT you can do it. Vivation is a natural, organic process of the mind and the body. A little practice and some willingness are the primary requirements for learning.

Our description of the Vivation process may seem intellectual to some. To a certain extent, that is the nature of writing. We will teach you everything you need to know; however reading a book about Vivation is very different from Viving, just as reading a book about exercise is just the first step toward improved physical fitness. In its application, the Vivation process is 99% about the sensations in your body and produces integration or alignment of the mind and the body to produce results that you want. It is a kinesthetic process. By kinesthetic, we refer to our internal feeling sense. This is not the external feeling sense which enables us to distinguish between wool and silk by touch; but rather is the awareness about our body which, when we raise our arm and close our eyes, lets us know that our arm is raised.

Integrating our feelings is a far faster and more effective method of dealing with problems than talking about them for several reasons.

1. Kinesthetic processing is faster. Our feelings are far richer and more complete than our thoughts, which are experienced one at a time. Just as a picture is worth a thousand words; it could be said that a feeling is worth a thousand thoughts.

2. Kinesthetic processing is more honest. Your mind can fool you or lie to you about a specific issue for decades, but the feelings about it are harder to deny.

3. Kinesthetic processing allows the process to be self-applied eliminating the requirement for the aid of another person.

The Five Elements of Vivation were originated by Jim Leonard in the late 1970's, as a result of his diligent research and experimentation with the Rebirthing process, the then rather crudely defined forerunner of Vivation. The Five Elements make the process extremely simple and easy for you to learn. They are the only elements that are necessary for you to have emotional resolution. Most people report that they are surprised at the straightforward simplicity of this method. This in fact is one of its most important advantages, despite our tendency to be impressed by complex technology. Since the process is natural and organic, it will enhance any other self-improvement methods that you are now using such as exercise, meditation, bodywork, therapy or yoga. If you now participate in a 12-Step Program, you'll be delighted with how much quicker your recovery will be when you learn to resolve your feelings. Vivation also works fine as your only self-improvement method.

The Five Elements of Vivation are:

1. Circular Breathing
2. Complete Relaxation
3. Awareness in Detail
4. Integration into Ecstasy
5. Do Whatever You Do — Willingness Is Enough

At first the Five Elements of Vivation may seem to be steps to be used in the order presented. The process will work fine for you, if you think of them that way, although it is more accurate to consider them as ingredients in a recipe where you have to remember to include everything to obtain the result, but the order doesn't matter. The Five Elements work together and each supports the others to cause integration. The function of the first Three Elements is primarily to aid you in getting in touch with the feelings that you have suppressed. The Fourth Element provides the kinesthetic context shift that is integration and the Fifth Element reminds you that Vivation is so personal and so individual that there can be no externally determined way to do it right (or wrong); but rather that your willingness is the essential ingredient.

The Vivation process is completely safe and completely natural. The writers of this book have personally taught this process to thousands of people of all ages and in all parts of the world. The Five Elements which we will describe below are the entire methodology involved in the process.

Circular Breathing cannot hurt anyone. You are breathing already and breathing in the circular fashion is the way that most people breathe while sleeping or when relaxed. Circular Breathing also provides the benefit of increasing the oxygen supply to every cell in your body, which is a definite health benefit.

Complete Relaxation cannot hurt you. Even in stressful situations, it is good to relax and, even when engaged in strenuous activities, you'll perform better if you can relax the muscles that are not in use. Anyone can respond more quickly when relaxed than when stress must be overcome for movement to occur. Relaxation is the natural state of our body. Many people seem to have forgotten this and Vivation enables you to develop relaxation as a skill and a habit.

Awareness in Detail about the sensations in your body definitely makes life safer, rather than more dangerous, because you will more promptly and clearly hear what your body is telling you. Our five senses are constantly feeding us with information on our state of mind and the world around us. Increasing your awareness of your feelings enables you to enjoy the pleasant sensations even more fully, enables you to act on your body's natural warning signals, and provides you with accurate knowledge and observation about yourself, reducing the self-delusion and disassociation that your mind has constructed about your feelings. Even the worst sensations that come up may hurt, but they won't hurt you.

Integration into Ecstasy means finding and feeling the good that already exists by accepting what you are experiencing without denial, instead of wishing it were different or better. All of us have placed unconscious limitations upon our happiness and success. Stepping back to give yourself an objective re-appraisal of the unfavorable judgments that we have made cannot hurt anyone and this is something that any person who makes improvements in his life does naturally and regularly.

Do Whatever You Do — Willingness is Enough is the element that allows for the individual to apply the process in his own way and at his own rate. Since Vivation involves changing the way that you relate to your feelings, the specific results for each person vary greatly, because we all have different desires, different problems and different personal histories. Intentionally increasing your willingness is something that everyone can do and clearly there is no danger is being more willing to have what you want. Increased willingness stems from the nature desire that we all have to improve our lives.

Application of the Five Elements has the potential of supporting you with increased happiness and success in every area of your life. The thousands of people that we have taught have discovered that the process is hazardous only to our misery.

THE FIRST ELEMENT OF VIVATION
CIRCULAR BREATHING

Circular breathing is any breathing that meets the following criteria:
1. The inhale and the exhale are connected with no pauses anywhere.

2. The exhale is completely relaxed and not controlled in any way. (The relaxed exhale distinguishes Circular Breathing from hyperventilation.)

3. The breath comes in and out the nose; or in and out the mouth.

Circular breathing requires some practice. It is easily learned because it is the most natural way to breathe. Circular breathing is how most people breathe when sleeping, that is with the suppressive inhibitions removed from the breathing mechanism. Circular breathing provides access to suppressed sensations as well as removes inhibitions from the breathing mechanism. At first you may experience a certain amount of tension in your breathing muscles, just as you would feel a little stiff at the beginning of an exercise program.

The circularity increases your awareness of the sensations in your body. It is neither desirable nor necessary to do any work at all on the exhale. When you inhale, the increased pressure inside your lungs, the tension in the breathing muscles and the force of gravity act together to propel the exhale and for this reason it is not necessary to do any work when exhaling. The circularity of circular breathing refers to the connectedness of the inhale and the exhale. The length of time for the inhale and the exhale may be different from each other or they may be the same. Another way to describe circular breathing is that you pull gently on the inhale until your lungs are about full and then abruptly relax on the exhale and continue the exhale, until just before it would have ended because all the air was gone.

Breathing in and out of the nose produces different results than breathing in and out of the mouth. Since the mouth is bigger, it is easier for most people to breathe faster through their mouth. Additionally breathing through the mouth ensures that the jaw is relaxed. You can switch from nose breathing to mouth breathing or vice versa whenever it seems right; however, if you switch too frequently the awareness that you place on switching back and forth may reduce your awareness of the sensations in your body.

The speed and the fullness of the breathing each have an effect on the sensations in your body. By the speed of your breathing, we refer to the speed of the inhale. In all cases the exhale is relaxed and its speed is neither controlled nor managed. Generally, the more slowly that you breathe, the easier it is to focus on the details of what you are feeling and the faster that you breathe the less that you notice the details and the more you tend to notice the overall feeling of aliveness in your body. The speed of your breathing can be compared to the lens control on a zoom camera, which governs the degree of detail that is perceived. Generally the more fully that you breathe the more intense that the sensations become and the more shallowly that you breathe the less intense the sensations become. The fullness of your breathing can be compared to the volume control on your stereo, governing the perceived intensity of your feelings

FULL AND SLOW CIRCULAR BREATHING

The slowness results in increased focus on the details of the sensations in your body and the fullness increases the intensity of the sensations. Full and slow circular breathing is advisable at the beginning of a Vivation session when you want to tune in the feelings or whenever, during the session, you are feeling great.

FAST AND FULL CIRCULAR BREATHING

The speed of the breathing puts you in touch with the overall feeling of being alive and the fullness turns up the intensity of the sensations so that you can feel them. Fast and full circular breathing is recommended in any situation where you want to increase the intensity of the sensations in your body. In particular, fast and full circular breathing is recommended whenever you are experiencing unconsciousness. Here we mean unconsciousness in the broadest sense, including sleepiness, the tendency to drift off into daydreams instead of paying attention to the sensations in your body, talking constantly (chit-chat-ananda) or compulsively fidgeting.

A common problem that people have with fast and full circular breathing is the tendency to associate it with hard work. Our breathing mechanism responds to unconscious and to conscious instructions. If you picked up your coffee table and made three laps around the block at full speed, you would be breathing fast and full when you got back home whether you consciously chose to or not, simply because your unconscious nervous system responds to the demand for increased oxygen by breathing faster and fuller. For this reason, we tend to associate fast and full breathing with hard work. It is possible however to breathe as fast and full as you would if you were running around the block and yet be completely relaxed at the same time. In learning the fast and full breathing rhythm, it is necessary for most people to disregard the messages about hard work that their mind is sure to deliver. In general, it is a good idea to breathe faster and more fully than you think is necessary.

Although you can breathe faster by rushing the exhale, relaxation on the exhale is more important than breaking a speed record.

FAST AND SHALLOW CIRCULAR BREATHING

The speed of the breathing keeps you in touch with the overall feeling of aliveness and the shallowness reduces the intensity of the sensations. Fast and shallow circular breathing is recommended in situations where the intensity is so great that your awareness is focused more on the intensity of the sensations than on the details of the sensations. Fast and shallow is similar to panting. Once again relaxation on the exhale is more important than breaking any speed records.

SLOW AND SHALLOW CIRCULAR BREATHING

Slow and shallow breathing is not recommended for Vivation. The shallowness of the breathing reduces the intensity of the sensations until sleepiness becomes the most prominent pattern of energy and the slowness of the breathing results in focus on the sleepiness. Slow and shallow

breathing is in fact how we fall asleep each night, although most people don't think of it that way.

HOW TO KNOW WHETHER YOU ARE ENGAGING IN THE FIRST ELEMENT OF VIVATION

1. The inhale and the exhale flow in and out of each other with no pauses between them.
2. There is virtually no noise caused by tightness in your throat, jaw or lips.
3. There is no effort on the exhale. Another way to say this is that you place your emphasis on the inhale and then abruptly relax and let gravity take care of the exhale.
4. Your body is tingling at least somewhere. If there is no tingling, then it is more than likely that breathing more fully will serve you. The tingling sensation is common to the Vivation process and is the energetic experience of the increased oxygen supply. *It feels great to breathe like this.*

THE SECOND ELEMENT OF VIVATION
COMPLETE RELAXATION

Complete relaxation means resting all the the muscles in your body except for the ones that are required to inhale. By relaxation we mean resting with alertness about the sensations in your body; not going to sleep. The word relax is a verb and verbs are action words; however, the word relax is an exception to this rule. Therefore to relax you don't have to do anything. Relax means not doing. The more that you relax, the more you will be able to feel the sensations in your body. Relaxation involves a paradox, which is that the more that you relax, the more tense the parts of your body that will not relax seem to be, simply by comparison. So, Complete Relaxation could be described as, relax as much as you can and relax about the parts that won't relax. The most important parts of your body to relax are the jaw and the throat. The jaw muscle is the strongest muscle in our body and a place where tension is often held. Complete relaxation means that it is not necessary, or even advisable to act out or express emotions as they come out of suppression into your awareness. Acting out emotions requires the tensing of muscles beyond those that are used to inhale. For example, some people when they are angry, pound their fist on the table to express their anger. What happens in this situation is that the feelings of anger are uncomfortable, so the person pounds his fist on the table, harder and harder, until the feeling of the fist hitting the table becomes more prominent than the anger, causing the anger to go back into suppression.

Sobbing results in a similar sort of suppression. When sadness becomes activated, the closing of the throat and the inhibition of breathing associated with sobbing tend to put the sadness back into suppression. A person that is sobbing heavily pushes strenuously on the exhale and barely inhales at all. A bit of practice is required to learn to breathe in a circular manner when experiencing sadness. After a few Vivation sessions, people become accustomed to relaxing while they cry.

Compulsively scratching, itching and fidgeting all tend to suppress sensations by providing activity to distract you from what you are feeling. The more complete relaxation enables you to feel the sensations and integrate them at a more subtle level.

HOW TO KNOW WHETHER YOU ARE ENGAGING IN THE SECOND ELEMENT OF VIVATION

1. All of the muscles are relaxed except for the ones that you are using to inhale.
2. Especially the jaw is slack, throat is loose enough to allow unhindered passage of air and no sound is caused by tightness in the throat, and the lips are not pursed or tense.
3. You are lying down without undue twitching, fidgeting or talking.

Since you can't win by fighting against your feelings, it feels great to just relax and let them be.

THE THIRD ELEMENT OF VIVATION
AWARENESS IN DETAIL

During a Vivation session, you want to focus your awareness on the sensations that are present in your body. You are always feeling something. Most of the time, your body will not bring sensations to your awareness in the same order or in the same way that you expect them. Awareness in Detail implies the willingness to accept this paradox and focus your awareness on the sensations in your body whether they make sense to your mind or not. (Especially when they do not make sense.) You are always feeling something. When people tell us that they are not feeling anything, we ask them how they know this. The important part of the Third Element is to let yourself be aware in detail of the most prominent pattern of energy that already exists, no matter what it is. The feeling of the floor holding you up, outside noise, the work you are doing to experience your feelings more and even the work you may be doing to avoid your feelings are no more or less are worthy of your attention than the more intense and troubling emotions which were described in Chapter 9.

Awareness in detail means focusing your awareness on the most prominent sensation or pattern of energy in your body. The sensation that is most prominent changes in every moment during a Vivation session, just like it does the rest of the time. The difference is that in a Vivation session, you notice the changes more quickly. For example, it is likely that the most prominent pattern of energy that you feel is different when you first wake up in the morning than it is just after lunch, although you may not be paying close enough attention to perceive the change.

Energy patterns of unconsciousness sometimes arise during Vivation sessions. Unconsciousness means any pattern of energy that tends to reduce your awareness of the sensations in your body. It is important to understand that unconsciousness is not a LACK of energy that you must fight against or resist; but is in fact a pattern of energy like any other, except that it has the unusual tendency of reducing your awareness of what you are feeling. The trick to integrating unconsciousness is to develop the ability and willingness to remain in touch with the sensations in your body while experiencing a pattern of energy that tends to reduce your awareness. Fast and full breathing is invaluable in integrating unconsciousness, and sitting up or standing up may be necessary while continuing to engage in a fast and full breathing rhythm. With some practice at integrating unconsciousness, you can actually feel your desire to engage in habitual suppression.

Energy patterns known as tetany sometimes arise during Vivation sessions. Tetany is an involuntary, temporary tightening of the muscles in the hands, feet and sometimes mouth that occurs when there is a profound shift in the carbon dioxide and oxygen balance in the body, resulting in build up of lactic acid. Tetany is not solely related to Vivation and is sometimes manifested as a reaction to strong tension or stress. Tetany may be frightening for you when it first arises in your Vivation session, if you

276

cling to the context of trying to make it go away or wishing that it were over. It seems to persist until the chemical balance in your body naturally restores itself. We have discovered 'that tetany no longer occurs once people have learned to relax on their exhale, no longer pushing or rushing it, and thereby maintain a carbon dioxide and oxygen balance.

Awareness in Detail could be called immersing yourself in your feelings. Anyone who has enjoyed a massage, a moving musical concert or making love already knows how to do this well enough to have Vivation work for them. Anyone whose lack of body awareness limits full enjoyment of these experiences will find that he enjoys them more as a result of Vivation.

HOW TO KNOW WHETHER YOU ARE ENGAGING IN THE THIRD ELEMENT OF VIVATION

1. The sensations in your body have your attention.
2. You can feel the sensations in your body changing.
3. The sensations in your body are a more prominent experience than the thoughts in your mind. In general, fuller breathing will turn up the intensity of the sensations in your body and make it easier to tune in to them.
4. You are taking responsibility for activating the sensations that are below the surface of your awareness, rather than going unconscious or giving up.
5. When you notice that you have more awareness on your thoughts than on your feelings, you investigate what you are feeling about what you are thinking.

Since suppression is such a habit for most of us, it feels wonderful to let yourself feel in a gentle way all the things that you had thought were wrong with you.

THE FOURTH ELEMENT OF VIVATION INTEGRATION INTO ECSTASY

The purpose of the Fourth Element is to remind us that it is our responsibility to shift contexts about the sensations that are too uncomfortable or too pleasurable and which have been brought to our awareness by Circular Breathing, Relaxation and Awareness in Detail. It could be said that the Fourth Element is about discovering and resolving self-

277

established limits: limits about your willingness to accept responsibility for the sensations in your body and limits about how good you are willing for your life to be. Wishing that the sensations would go away or trying not to feel them, simply leads to more suppression. Integration means offering yourself a new way to interpret your emotions, thereby changing the way that the content of your emotions govern your behavior. In this section, we will be describing various applications of the Fourth Element, which we call "Fourth Element Techniques". Because everyone relates to their emotions differently, we will present a list of 33 different ways to shift the content of your emotions to a positive context. This list was selected as the most universally useful methods of shifting contexts, based on our experience of teaching Vivation in our seminars. Clearly there is an infinite variety of ways to shift contexts about anything.

The application of the Fourth Element during a Vivation session corresponds to the conscious pre-selection of a context in which to place the sensations that will arise from suppression. This is a more natural thing to do than appears at first glance. All of us pre-select contexts about things all the time. Prejudice is an example of a pre-selected negative context about specific kinds of people. Unconditional love is an example of a pre-selected positive context about a certain person.

It will be obvious to many readers that if the Fourth Element were all that there was to the Vivation process, then the process would be little more than positive thinking. The distinction between Vivation and positive thinking is the awareness of the sensations produced by the first Three Elements.

We suggest that you read over the list that follows and identify the particular techniques that feel most appropriate to you. As you gain experience with the Vivation process, you will develop your own favorite Fourth Element techniques from this list or that you compose yourself. It is likely that you'll discover that one particular technique will not work in every case, which is another reason that we have offered you a variety. It is not necessary for all of the Fourth Element techniques that we list to work for you, in order for you to integrate suppressed emotions. There may even be some phrases that you disagree with. This is fine. Simply use the ones that cause your sensations to change or perhaps cause you to laugh. You will notice that some of the phrases contain the indefinite pronoun "it". It in every case refers to the most prominent sensation in your body at the moment.

These Fourth Element Techniques differ greatly from attitude builders which we described earlier. The Fourth Element Techniques are not thoughts that you run through your mind; rather they are things that you do. For example, the first one in the list is "Find a way to enjoy it." This does not mean think the thought "Find a way to enjoy it" instead it means actually find a way to enjoy it.

1. Find a way to enjoy it.
2. Notice that what you are experiencing is not infinitely bad.
3. Be grateful that it is as good as it is.
4. Open up to it as though it were pleasurable.
5. Notice the benefit that you are getting from it.
6. Be grateful for your ability to feel it.
7. Be grateful that it is coming up at such an appropriate time.
8. Forced surrender.
9. Bliss out on the miracle of its existence.
10. Compare it only to itself.
11. Give all parts of yourself and your experience unconditional love.
12. Enthusiastically exaggerate your feeling.
13. Notice that what you are experiencing is at least somewhat funny.
14. All is not lost.
15. Enjoy the challenge of being at the starting point of changing it.
16. Expand your compassion for all people who experience similar things.
17. Experience every sensation as an expression of God's love for you.
18. Turn the entire session over to God.
19. Obviously the Creator of the Universe thinks it's supposed to be exactly like this.
20. The same God who gave you life and every wonderful thing you have ever experience is in charge of this also.
21. Acknowledge that whether it is good or bad is completely up to you.
22. Acknowledge that you won't win by fighting against your feelings.
23. Be open to it making a contribution to you somehow.
24. Trust that you are strong enough to handle even the worst of this.
25. It's not as bad as your worst thoughts about it.
26. Appreciate that it helps you to get to know yourself better.
27. Be gentle, patient and caring with yourself in the presence of the feelings.
28. Be enthusiastic about integrating it.
29. Imagine what it would feel like for it to be exactly the way that it is, but for you to feel integrated about it.
30. Trust that everything works out, so it must be working out now.

31. Other people have made it through this, and so can I.
32. At least it educates you about your own values by letting you know what you don't prefer.
33. Cultivate a sense of fascination with it, acknowledge that it is at least interesting enough to have gotten your attention.

Some of the Fourth Element Techniques that we have listed will benefit from an explanation to give you an idea how they work.

FIND A WAY TO ENJOY IT.
We enjoy different things in different ways. You enjoy dinner with your partner in a different way than you enjoy reading this book. Additionally, some people find that they must develop or acquire their taste for something that they did not like at first.

NOTICE THAT WHAT YOU ARE EXPERIENCING IS NOT INFINITELY BAD.
Since make-wrong and suppression always involve comparison, if you compare what you are experiencing to something worse then you will tend to cease making it wrong and integration is facilitated.

BE GRATEFUL THAT IT IS AS GOOD AS IT IS.
The explanation is similar to preceding one. Additionally, gratitude represents a strongly positive context as well as the awareness that it could be worse.

OPEN UP TO IT AS THOUGH IT WERE PLEASURABLE.
The majority of the discomfort that we experience with any given sensation is the result of the struggle not to feel it. When you are willing to give up this struggle this Fourth Element Technique becomes a self-fulfilling prophecy.

NOTICE THE BENEFIT THAT YOU ARE GETTING FROM IT.
Everything that you do provides you with some benefit, even if it may be only a secondary gain, or you wouldn't do it in the first place.

BE GRATEFUL FOR YOUR ABILITY TO FEEL IT.
Suppression is far less selective than most people think. If you suppress certain unpleasant feelings, you can be certain that you are also suppressing pleasant feelings. If you feel it, you can heal it. Your previous lack of

awareness of the sensations that you are now experiencing is what gave them the power to control your life without your knowledge.

BE GRATEFUL THAT IT IS COMING UP AT SUCH AN APPROPRIATE TIME.

Let's say that you are experiencing intensely upsetting feelings about the fact that your lover has left you. You can be grateful that the sensations are coming up in the privacy of a Vivation session, rather than while you are making an important presentation at work.

FORCED SURRENDER.

There are some things in life over which you have no power or control. Some examples are other people, the weather and the stock market. An essential step to peace of mind is the ability to recognize and acknowledge those things that are not within your power to change. In these situations, it is to your benefit to develop the ability to make the best of it. It's just like this or it is the way it is. Anyone who has ever visited a dentist has exhibited a degree of Forced Surrender.

BLISS OUT ON THE MIRACLE OF ITS EXISTENCE.

For anything to be just like it is right now (including the feelings in your body), many, many very long and complicated chains of cause and effect events had to occur exactly as they did. If your parents had had sex at a different time when you were conceived, you would be someone else. Surely all of our lives would be different if the Allies had been defeated in World War II.

COMPARE IT ONLY TO ITSELF.

As we mentioned earlier, make wrong always involves comparison. Although your mind may not be accustomed to comparing something to itself, you will discover that it can do it and that this will eliminate make wrong.

GIVE ALL PARTS OF YOURSELF AND YOUR EXPERIENCE UNCONDITIONAL LOVE.

Love is a strongly positive context. The loving acceptance of the sensations in your body will eliminate make-wrong.

ENTHUSIASTICALLY EXAGGERATE YOUR FEELING.

Exaggerating what you are feeling is especially good for integrating depression, because one reason that people remain depressed is that it is not worth the effort to try to cheer up.

NOTICE THAT WHAT YOU ARE EXPERIENCING IS AT LEAST SOMEWHAT FUNNY.

Sometimes the funniest jokes are about the most distressing topics because jokes allow us to see something differently. This does not mean that it is a good idea to laugh at everything, but willingness to see that it is at least a little funny will reduce the gravity of any situation.

ALL IS NOT LOST.

This is especially useful for coming to terms with intense sadness.

ENJOY THE CHALLENGE OF BEING AT THE STARTING POINT OF CHANGING IT.

When suppressed sensations come to your awareness for the first time, you may think that they are something that you should have handled long ago. This technique is to enable you to develop rookie humility.

EXPAND YOUR COMPASSION FOR ALL PEOPLE WHO EXPERIENCE SIMILAR THINGS.

This Fourth Element Technique is especially useful for people who tend to be their own worst critic.

THE SAME GOD WHO GAVE YOU LIFE AND EVERY WONDERFUL THING YOU HAVE EVER EXPERIENCED IS IN CHARGE OF THIS ALSO.

If you have developed strong positive contexts about God, these techniques will serve you well.

ACKNOWLEDGE THAT YOU WON'T WIN BY FIGHTING AGAINST YOUR FEELINGS.

All discomfort is cause by holding the sensations in your body in a make-wrong context. Even pain is just sensation until you try to suppress it; so simply giving up the fight will enable you to experience pain for the sensation that it is.

HOW TO KNOW WHETHER YOU ARE ENGAGING IN THE FOURTH ELEMENT OF VIVATION

1. You are cultivating your willingness to accept even the most unfamiliar sensations.

2. You can feel the energy state shift from suffering or lack of awareness to acceptance.
3. You are taking responsibility for your reservations about the process that your conscious mind may be reporting to you.
4. You have compassion for yourself and a sense of humor about your previous struggle to make the sensations wrong.

It feels wonderful to discover that you can do something about the limits you had placed on your well-being, happiness and accomplishment.

THE FIFTH ELEMENT OF VIVATION
DO WHATEVER YOU DO; WILLINGNESS IS ENOUGH

Integration is the result of Vivation. Integration is a natural, organic process of the mind and body and is, therefore, not something that you do. The first Four Elements establish the conditions which ALLOW integration to occur. Integration does not happen as a result of trying to do it better or trying to do it right. The Do Whatever You Do part means that the process is so personal that you can only do it your way. Sometimes the way that you are engaging in the other Four Elements will not conform to your own standards of how you should be doing it. Your willingness for emotional resolution matters far more than trying to live up to a predetermined standard or expectation about what you should be feeling, what you should be clearing up or how fast your progress should be.

HOW TO KNOW WHETHER YOU ARE ENGAGING IN THE FIFTH ELEMENT OF VIVATION

1. You are willing to allow the sensations in your body to guide your session.
2. You are willing to let your session be like this, instead of how you may have expected or have heard that the session may be.
3. You are willing to stay with it until you feel resolved and complete.

It feels great to give yourself permission to be and do exactly the way that you are without consideration of any externally created standards.

ANSWERS TO THE MOST COMMONLY ASKED QUESTIONS ABOUT VIVATION AND INTEGRATION THAT WE HEAR IN OUR SEMINARS.

Can I do Vivation on my own? Yes. Most people find that they can learn most quickly and easily with a trained Vivation Professional, who can teach you to do the process on your own in 3-5 sessions. There is no danger in trying it on your own first; however, most people who have tried it on their own before obtaining guided sessions, report that they got only limited results because of the unfamiliarity with the sensations that were activated. Like learning any new skill, practice is required and instruction is beneficial.

How long does a session last? There is no prescribed length. Usually individual sessions with a trained Vivation Professional last from 1 1/2 to three hours. Generally after your skill increases the sessions become shorter.

What changes can I expect? Since Vivation eliminates make-wrong you can expect greater relaxation in formerly stress producing situations, reduced tendency to suppress your formerly uncomfortable feelings, improved sense of humor, freer flowing creativity, elimination of the need to engage in self-destructive patterns, willingness to take action to resolve the situations that you have been putting up with, greater self-confidence.

How often should I do Vivation? There is no standard frequency. One session will serve you. At the beginning, we suggest intervals of 5 to 21 days between sessions. After they have learned, some people like giving themselves daily or weekly sessions. Additionally, with practice you can learn to give yourself a session anywhere anytime.

How long should I keep doing Vivation? Once you learn it, Vivation becomes a life long process that you may use whenever you wish to increase your enjoyment of life and your effectiveness.

Is Vivation dangerous No. Vivation is dangerous only to your misery. Vivation consists of the Five Elements as we have described. Clearly, there is no danger in breathing, or in relaxing or in feeling what you are already feeling or in accepting what you are feeling or in being willing to do it your way. The changes that occur in you may be perceived as confusing or upsetting by others who have consciously or unconsciously manipulated you by taking advantage of your desire to suppress certain emotions.

Is Vivation like_____? This is a common question, where the method of self-improvement that the questioner already either knows about or is using occupies the blank space. We know of nothing that Vivation is like (although many readers undoubtedly notice similarities between the theories that we have presented and other philosophies). We have discovered that Vivation enhances the effect of any other self-improvement method; meditation, yoga, therapy, exercise, religion, 12-Step Programs or any other effective method of self-improvement.

Where is the best place to do Vivation? At first you will make the most progress with a trained Vivation Professional in a location that is quiet and free of distractions. Once you have increased your skill at tuning in to the sensations in your body, the process can be done anywhere, even while engaged in other activities.

How do I know if I integrated something? The shift of energy in your body is very evident, although people experience integration differently from each other and differently at different times. Sometimes people feel more alive, sometimes they have a profound sense of relaxation, sometimes they feel stronger, quite often they laugh, and feel peaceful and alert. The experience of integration is most often so evident that if you have doubts about whether you integrated, it is likely that you did not. If the uncomfortable feelings that come up recede slowly into the background of your experience, then it is likely that you chose to re-suppress them. If they shift quickly, then it is most likely that you integrated them.

Will I know what I've integrated? Sometimes you will have conscious insight or memory associated with the sensations that have been resolved for you. On other occasions, it will be a strictly kinesthetic experience without any cognitive insights. The resolution of the sensations is what matters. Additionally, in some cases you will not know what the session was about until later when you notice how your life is different. Every session will be different, because different suppressed material becomes activated. Additionally, each integration facilitates the next one.

Will integration give me an irresponsible attitude about things that matter? No. The resolution of sensations that you had been struggling to avoid leaves a whole lot more energy for devoting yourself to the values and causes that matter to you. Your increased self-reliance and sense of purpose will empower you to create the life that you want.

Will integration change my emotions? No. Nor will it make you less emotional, most people report that they feel their emotions more. Integration changes the way that you relate to your emotions and it changes the negative effect that your emotions have on you, enabling you to consistently use them to your benefit.

Is integration permanent? Yes. Making the sensations in your body wrong requires effort and therefore once any particular pattern of sensations is resolved, it becomes natural for the mind and the body to continue to relax about the same sensations, if and when they occur in the future.

How do I know when my session is complete? You will feel calm, peaceful and alert with no intense sensations remaining. In your early sessions, it is possible to feel somewhat disoriented for a short time (usually caused by unfamiliarity with feeling your feelings so directly and honestly). If you are wishing the session were complete, asking your Vivation Professional if it is complete, or thinking about all of the important things you must do when you get home, then your session is not complete. Keep going.

How do I find someone to teach me? Associated Vivation Professionals is a network of more than 100 trained Professionals located throughout the United States and the rest of the World. Some of the members are listed in the back of this book. For a listing of Professionals in your area, you can call TOLL FREE from the 50 United States, Puerto Rico, the Virgin Islands and Canada

1-800-829-2625

or write to:
Associated Vivation Professionals
PO Box 8269
Cincinnati, OH 45208 USA

How do I learn to be a Vivation professional? We offer two or three 17 day long Professional Trainings per year and the people who we have trained often train others. There are no pre-requisites for taking our Professional Training. We will teach you everything you need to know when you arrive. Being a Vivation Professional is a highly flexible and rewarding career. Some people work part time at home, some work full time and others travel throughout the world teaching others. Please phone or write to above phone number or address for a schedule of events.

286

28 ADVANCED VIVATION TECHNIQUES

There are many ways to apply the Vivation process beyond lying down in a relaxed position, which may be considered the most basic method. Lying down in a relaxed position is the best way for a newcomer to start with the process, because it allows maximum access with the sensations in your body by eliminating distractions and provides a sense of safety which facilitates dealing with the sensations that may be initially uncomfortable for you. Once you have some practice with the Five Elements, you may wish to experiment with some of the additional methods that we will describe. In all of the additional methods, The Five Elements are the same as we have described them.

Warm Water Vivation Warm water Vivation, as the name implies, is done immersed in warm water—either a bathtub, hot tub or warm spring works fine and a temperature of 98 to 102 degrees Fahrenheit (36 to 39 degrees Celsius) is best. This can be done with the aid of a Vivation Assistant or on your own, although it is beneficial that you have an Assistant for your first warm water session. It is likely that you will discover that the warm water acts as a stimulant to your circulatory and nervous system, making sessions in warm water both faster and more efficient.

The warmth of the water, the feeling of weightlessness imparted by the water and the pressure of the water combine to simulate life in the womb, so that warm water Vivation has the tendency to stimulate feelings and memories related to our experience of birth. Incidentally, this method is how Rebirthing, the forerunner of Vivation was done in its early days and hence the early name "Rebirthing".

Warm water Vivation can be done in various body positions which will vary the intensity of the emotional activation that you experience. Least emotionally activating is sitting up in the water with your body immersed, but your head out. More emotionally activating is lying back in the water with just your nose and mouth out of the water. Most activating is submerged with a snorkel and nose clips to permit underwater breathing. We teach warm water Vivation in our Professional Trainings, so most Vivation Professionals can teach you this method, or you may attend one of our Trainings.

Cold Water Vivation Cold water Vivation is the same in application as warm water Vivation except for the water temperature. The water must be colder than the surface temperature of your body, so that it feels cold but not so cold that you can't relax in it. We suggest that you start with water between 55 degrees Fahrenheit (13 degrees Celsius) and 70 degrees Fahrenheit (21 degrees Celsius). After some practice at these temperatures, Phil was able to give himself a Vivation session in the glacier flow at Lake Louise in Banff National Park in the Canadian Rocky Mountains. Others have done similar things and have reported resolution of feelings of dread and hopelessness, and memories of near drownings, producing a dramatically increased sense of well-being and confidence. It is useful but not essential to have your first Cold Water session with a Vivation Professional.

Self-Vivation Self Vivation means doing Vivation on your own without a coach. We consider that Self Vivation is the most important goal of learning Vivation and providing an enduring and valuable sense of emotional independence. The Five Elements are the same as we have described. The challenge for almost everyone with self Vivation is to stay conscious, simply because we have all used unconsciousness to avoid feeling distressing feelings. Leaning against a wall, sitting up or standing up, or setting a timer to buzz and wake you up if you have gone unconsciousness will aid you in maintaining awareness of the sensations in your body. Learning Self Vivation is essential step to learning Vivation in Action, which makes emotional resolution a continuous experience.

Mirror Vivation Mirror Vivation or Image Vivation means Viving while meeting your own gaze in a mirror. This can be done with a professional coach or as Self Vivation. The especially brave do it unclothed. Your reflected expression will show the feelings as they become activated and then integrated, providing the experience of HAVING rather than BEING your emotions. You will probably discover that the resolution of your dissatisfaction with your appearance and your self-hatred about your body will produce dramatic changes in your opinion of yourself.

Vivation with Your Partner and Family Vivation can provide you with a joint method for resolving and preventing the upsets that are a natural part of family life. Your partner and family members can become built in Vivation coaches with a little bit of practice. Since Vivation is a self-directed technique, it is futile to try to make someone do it that is not willing. You'll make more satisfying progress by Viving and letting family members notice the changes in you.

Unacknowledged control patterns are the biggest problem in coaching Vivation sessions for the people that are close to you. All of us want to control others to some degree. Thinking that you are certain what is best for someone else involves controlling them. Control patterns will not interfere in coaching the Vivation session of a loved one if they are acknowledged. For this reason, a simple acknowledgement of control process will aid greatly. One person talks first and says:

"Something I do to control you is" and the other simply says "Thank you."

Then the first person says, "Something I am afraid that you will do if I don't control you is " and the others says, "Thank you." THEN SWITCH.

It is essential to remember that it is the Vivationer and not the coach who has primary responsibility for the results produced in the session.

Trading Vivation sessions with your family members will undoubtedly contribute to the intimacy and closeness of all.

Eye Gaze Vivation Eye Gaze Vivation means Viving while meeting the gaze of another person. Thus, it is somewhat like Mirror Vivation and

289

somewhat like Vivation with a loved one. The intensity of the sensations is greater, likely because Eye Gaze Vivation violates social admonitions about staring. You will probably discover that it is necessary to breathe more fully than in sessions where your eyes are closed, in order to maintain present time awareness of the sensations in your body with the distraction of the visual input. Eye Gaze Vivation is excellent for couples during sex or after an argument.

Vivation in Action Vivation in Action means Viving while engaging in some other activity simultaneously. This makes the Vivation process portable and usable in almost every situation in life. Viving while waiting in line at the bank, while walking, writing, exercising, at work and at play will make all of these activities more enjoyable as a result of handling the associated feeling right on the spot; rather than stuffing them until there is an appropriate, safe place to feel them. Another important advantage of Vivation in Action is that you have far greater awareness of the feelings of frustration about waiting in the bank line, for example, while you are at the bank than you ever will engaging in Vivation at home or some other place.

We suggest that beginners not engage in Vivation while driving or operating heavy equipment, until they have developed their skill at managing the sensations in their body.

RESOLVING INCEST OR SEXUAL ABUSE WITH VIVATION™

Vivation enables you to resolve suppressed feelings from any period of your life. Vivation is likely to activate feelings or memories of childhood sexual abuse if you experienced any. You can accelerate your integration of sexual abuse with a small modification of the Vivation Process involving talking. This modification appears to work especially well for survivors of sexual abuse because of the admonition "Don't tell" which is often stated by the perpetrator or implied by family members. This de-briefing is essential both for the activation of the feelings associated with sexual abuse and for their resolution. It is not the News to say that survivors of childhood sexual abuse experience substantial fear and denial associated with their experience. It works well to remind them they are safe now, that the memories cannot hurt them and that it is OK not to remember.

HOW TO DO THIS

The Vivation Professional says, "please tell me what happened." The Viver then recounts the story of his or her sexual abuse as best that can be remembered. Survivors often have doubts about the truth of what they are saying, as a result of long held denial. The Vivation Professional offers no comments or analysis, except to say things like, "OK, and then what happened?" As the story proceeds, the suppressed feelings of the survivor will become more intensely activated. When they are activated enough, the Vivation Professional says "OK, please stop talking and start Viving." Once the activated feelings are integrated the Viver picks up the story where it left off or goes back to the beginning if it had been completed. The survivor's memory of what happened is almost never the same in successive tellings of the story, because feelings have been integrated and previously suppressed memories are revealed. It is common for the Viver to experience the disorientation, dizziness and disassociation that are tendencies with survivors of sexual abuse and to resolve these with the Vivation process. Most Vivation Professionals have been trained in this method of resolving sexual abuse and can aid their customers with it.

Because of the simplicity of this method, hundreds of people in all parts of the world have accelerated their recovery from sexual abuse by using it either in conjunction with traditional therapy and support group techniques or by itself.

IMMORTALIST PHILOSOPHY AND ITS RELATION TO THE VIVATION PROCESS

Immortalist Philosophy is a context or a way of thinking about life and death. Its purpose is to offer an alternative to Deathist Philosophy which is the system of ideas and beliefs about life and death that is so popular and widely held that almost no one seems to notice, let alone challenge its validity. The basic idea of Immortalist Philosophy is that death, if and when it occurs, is the result of unconscious intention on the part of the individual; whereas the basic idea of Deathist Philosophy is that death is inevitable, no matter what.

The purpose of Immortalist Philosophy, as related to Vivation, is to aid you in taking responsibility for resolving the sensations in your body that are related to your unconscious desire to die. Death, despite its statistical popularity, is the result of an unconscious desire on the part of a person's

291

mind to make things better; to avoid pain, to be with deceased loved ones or to go to heaven or be with God, for example.

Since death could be termed the ultimate in suppression or lack of body sensation, it is not unreasonable to conclude that every integration of a formerly suppressed sensation results in an integration of one's unconsciously held desire to die and results in making one feel more alive.

It is likely that sooner or later sensations associated with your unconscious desire to die will come to your awareness during your Vivation sessions. If you believe that feeling these sensations will kill you then the tendency will be to stop and return the sensations to suppression, at which point the struggle to maintain the suppression may eventually kill you. It is completely safe to feel your feelings about death. This is because it is the struggle to keep feelings suppressed that kills most people modern society who tend to die from lifestyle diseases like cancer, heart attack and high blood pressure; rather than from infectious diseases or accidents. There is far more substantial evidence that you are alive than that you are dead, so you can resolve feelings about death with the Five Elements of Vivation in the same way that you can resolve any other feelings that come to your awareness during your Vivation sessions.

29   LIVING HAPPILY EVER AFTER

There are three requirements for living happily ever after. These are willingness, skills and recovery of your inborn ability for giving and receiving love. Living happily ever after is not something that happens to you, instead it is something that you do. Willingness is by far the most important so we'll discuss it last.

Recovery is a word commonly used by people who are taking responsibility for their lives. It implies that you already HAVE what is required for happiness. It's already yours, it just needs to be reclaimed; like recovering something from the lost and found department, which is right inside you. Most of us were disillusioned years ago and started believing that it's hard to love and good things don't last, based on the evidence from our family of origin. Recovery involves risks and you'll notice that sometimes you will want to give up. Find friends that are recovering too and develop a support system. A sense of humor about it helps a lot.

Be willing to experiment and break with your family tradition. Most traditions are the unwritten rules that were laid down and followed by dead ancestors. Getting out of denial is a first step. Once you recover a little, it's easy to keep going because the outcome is assured. You'll find that recovery is a life long process but you'll start feeling better immediately.

To a large extent living happily ever after is a skill that can be learned. More people would do it, if they knew how. Living happily ever after is similar to riding a bicycle, everyone has the ability, but not everyone has developed the skill. Surely you will discover that you have already developed

some of the skills that we offer in this book, but that others will require some work and attention. You can have a love life that nurtures you—a partner with whom there is mutual respect—where you contribute to each other and bring out the best in each other. The content and the severity of your personal history and the apparent hopelessness of your current situation will not stop you if you follow the easy to use methods in this book. The love life you want, where feelings are OK and respected can be yours. A partnership where the focus is on benefiting each other, instead of taking from each other can be yours. For some, this may not be with the person you're with now.

In your recovery, you may discover that you and your partner will progress at different rates. This is natural and definitely should be discussed. If the difference in progress becomes so great that partners are unwilling or unable to help each other, unresolvable difficulties can arise. Divorce is not necessarily shameful and can greatly benefit both people.

Recovery and skills will never take the place of willingness. We know some couples whose willingness extends only to their willingness to stay together. They say, "We have been married for XX years," as if to imply that the passage of time is their major accomplishment. Obviously the QUALITY of the time together matters for more than the quantity. To live happily ever after, willingness is required to apply the skills we offer. Willingness is required to talk about those feelings that you don't want to talk about and to break through the legacy of denial, suppression and justification left unresolved from your family of origin. Willingness will be required from time to time to get up and start over again. Willingness implies determination, self-direction and deliberate action.

There are no external limits to human happiness. Everything you need is right inside you now.

About the Love, Sex and Communication Weekend

Unlike many self-development seminars, this is not about motivating you or confronting you. There is no nudity or sexual activity and it is appropriate for all ages. People aged 18 and under are admitted free with their parent(s). We teach you communication and emotional resolution skills that you'll use forever.

For a schedule or more information, write or phone us:

Jeanne Miller and Phil Laut
PO Box 8269
Cincinnati, OH 45208 USA
513-321-6411
513-321-4405
1-800-829-2625

A beautiful, 8½" by 11" printed poster of this Fourteen Point plan for Preventing Domestic War, suitable for framing or posting on your refrigerator is available for $ US 2.00 postpaid. Send you name, address and phone number to:

Miller/Laut Trainings
PO Box 8269
Cincinnati, OH 45208 USA

ABOUT THE ILLUSTRATOR

George Longfellow

1939, Macksburg, Ohio

Education:
Art Academy of Cincinnati 1957–1962
Cleveland Institute of Art 1963–64 BFA Degree

Professional experience:
U.S. Peace Corps, Peru 1964–66
Audio Visual Productions, staff artist and photographer, Lima, Peru
  1966–69
Freelance art work, Cincinnati, 1969–71
Staff artist Cincinnati Enquirer 1971–present time

Awards:
Yale-Norfolk Summer School Scholarship 1960
Wilder Traveling Scholarship 1962 (travel and study in Europe)
Bronze Award of Excellence, The Society of Newspaper Design, 1982
First Place, Graphics, Best of Gannett, 1985
First Place, Graphics, Best of Gannett, 1986
Award for Excellence, The Press Club of Cleveland, 1987

SUGGESTED READING

Vivation: The Science of Enjoying All of Your Life
   by Jim Leonard and Phil Laut
Money Is My Friend
   by Phil Laut
Your Fondest Dream: How to Master the Power of Creativity
   by Jim Leonard
Healing the Shame that Binds You
   by John Bradshaw
The Courage to Heal
   by Laura Davies and Laura Bass
Healing Your Sexual Self
   by Janet G. Woititz
How to Live with Another Person
   by Dr. David Viscott
Co-Dependent No More
   by Melody Beattie
I Just Got Tired of Pretending
   by Bob Earll
Out of the Shadows
   by Patrick Carnes Ph.D.
Loving Relationships
   by Sondra Ray
Women who Love Too Much
   by Robin Norwood
The Hazards of Being Male
   by Dr. Herb Goldberg
The Challenge of the Heart
   by John Wellwood
How Can I Help?
   by Ram Dass

Available from your local bookstore
or
The Creative Source
PO Box 11024
Costa Mesa, CA 92627 USA
714-458-7971

ABOUT THE AUTHORS

Jeanne was born in Memphis, TN in 1952. At the age of ten, she knew she wanted to do massage and to help end suffering, At nineteen she began doing just that. In 1976 she received her massage license from the Ohio State Medical Board and started her own business, Miller Health Service. She then started teaching seminars about the relationship between the body and the emotions and has been teaching ever since. This is Jeanne's first book and represents what she has learned about herself and the thousands of people she has worked with.

Phil was born in 1942 in Flushing, NY. In 1964, he graduated from the U.S. Coast Guard Academy in New London, CT and served as an officer in the Coast Guard until 1968, including a year as Commanding Officer of a patrol boat in Vietnam. Upon graduation from Harvard Business School in 1970, he worked at Digital Equipment Corporation until 1976. After three years of teaching seminars about personal financial success, he published his first book, "Money Is My Friend" in 1979. His second book, now entitled "Vivation — The Science of Enjoying All of Your Life" was published in 1983 and written with Jim Leonard.

Jeanne and Phil met in 1981 and were married in 1986. They live in Cincinnati, where Jeanne maintains a private practice in massage and Vivation and Phil maintains a private practice in Vivation and manages Vivation Publishing Co. They travel widely conducting their Love, Sex and Communication Weekend, the Money Is My Friend Weekend Seminar and training Vivation Professionals.

These are highly dynamic seminars that are frequently updated to include new things they learn and focus on practical tools that anyone can use.

Books and Tapes from
VIVATION PUBLISHING CO.

BOOKS

Money Is My Friend by Phil Laut $9.95
    ISBN: 0-9610132-2-2
    You can make more money doing work that you love. This
    100,000 copy bestseller teaches you how to increase your
    income, how to budget, save, sell and invest.

Your Fondest Dream by Jim Leonard $15.95
    ISBN: 0-9610132-1-4
    The techniques described teach you to tap your creative
    genius in two minutes a day and how to apply this genius
    to every aspect of your life.

Love, Sex and Communication: Skills for Recovery $12.95
    by Jeanne Miller and Phil Laut
    ISBN: 0-9610132-3-0
    Find and maintain the love life that you have always wanted,
    by learning how to resolve disagreements and how to make
    profound contributions to each other and how to resolve
    the emotions that stand in your way.

Vivation: The Science of Enjoying All of Your Life
    by Jim Leonard and Phil Laut $12.95
    ISBN: 0-9610132-4-9
    Over 50,000 sold. Teaches Vivation, the self-directed skill of
    emotional resolution.

TAPES

Money Is An Intentional Creation of the Mind with Phil Laut $20.00
    Two hour seminar recorded at Unity Church in Minneapolis
    covering forgiveness, service, gratitude, certainty and integ-
    rity as applied to your financial life.

Principles of Personal Financial Success with Phil Laut $20.00
    Two hour talking work book that offers the listener the
    writing processes necessary to organize his purpose in life,
    and his goals and plans.

Reclaiming Your Personal Power
    (Unraveling Infancy Patterns) $10.00
    One hour seminar with Phil Laut describing how to resolve
    patterns of struggle, dependency and helplessness.

Available at your favorite bookseller or from:
VIVATION PUBLISHING CO.
PO Box 8269
Cincinnati, OH 45208 USA
Please add $1.00 per item for postage.
Ohio residents, please add 5.5% sales tax.

A Worldwide Listing of Vivation™ Professionals

ARKANSAS
Herb Pablo, AVP
PO Box 2751
West Memphis, AR 72301
(501) 732-1238
(501) 732-1154

CALIFORNIA
Patricia Bacall, AVP
400 S. Beverly Dr. #214
Beverly Hills, CA 90212
213-937-7437

Randy Hillner, AVP
500 S. Eliseo #37
Greenbrae, CA 94904
415-461-2123

Nancy L. Hopper, AVP
508 Sunnyoaks Ave.
Campbell, CA 95008
408-370-7908
408-370-0211

Eve Jones Ph.D., AVP
140 S. Norton Ave.
Los Angeles, CA 90004
213-461-5774

Lee Kuntz, AVP
3627 Keystone Ave. #2
Los Angeles, CA 90034
213-839-4378

ARKANSAS *(continued)*
Robin Savage, AVP
40824 Gibbel Road
Hemet, CA 92343
714-766-8419

GEORGIA
Jim Leonard, AVP
PO Box 567713
Atlanta, GA 30356
(404) 551-8626

ILLINOIS
Pat Murrell, M.S.W., AVP
187 W. 19th
Alton, IL 62002
(618) 462-4051
(314) 569-5795

Steven Strauss, AVP
RR 2 Box 173
Pleasant Plain, IL 62677
(217) 487-7104

MARYLAND
Jonathan & Laura Bosch, AVP
805 Horton Dr.
Silver Spring, MD 20902
301-649-5813

Susan R. Cox, AVP
414 Fourth Ave., Box 277
Washington Grove, MD 20880
(Gaithersburg area)
301-258-0870

MARYLAND *(continued)*
M. C. Delahanty, AVP
1 South Woodington Rd.
Baltimore, MD 21229
301-644-3669

Mary Kent Norton, M.Ed., Ms.T., AVP
398 Ridgely Ave.
Annapolis, MD 21401
301-268-2322

David Pierce, AVP
11602 Highview Ave.
Silver Spring, MD 20902
301-949-3686

MASSACHUSETTS
Linda & David Jackson, AVP
PO Box 1065
Stockbridge, MA 01262
413-298-4435

Sande Sharlat, AVP
Tom Streit, AVP
218 Thorndike Place #104
Cambridge, MA 02140
(617) 494-6544

MISSOURI
Pat Murrell, M.S.W., AVP
PO Box 23305
St. Louis, MO 63156
(618) 462-4051
(314) 569-5795

NEVADA
Norma Viergutz, AVP
381 W. Berry Creek Ct.
Elko, NV 89801
(702) 738-7574

OHIO
Phil Laut, AVP
Jeanne Miller, AVP
PO Box 8269
Cincinnati, OH 45208
(513) 321-4405
(513) 321-6411

Marsha Beach, AVP
2120 Wyoming Street
Dayton, OH 45410
(513) 253-8141

OREGON
Barbara Wayne, AVP
1804 NW Second St.
Bend, OR 97701
(503) 389-3977

PENNSYLVANIA
C. John Hobe, AVP
6401 Park Line Dr.
Philadelphia, PA 19119
215-242-0522

PUERTO RICO
Raul G. Gaya, Jr., AVP
103 Mallorca
Floral Park, PR 00919
(809) 754-7772

TEXAS
Joan Bolmer, AVP
One Woodbranch Center
11931 Wickchester #200
Houston, TX 77043
(713) 784-1811

VIRGINIA
Shawn Moore, AVP
2212 Parkside Ct.
Virginia Beach, VA 23454
804-481-7670

CANADA
BRITISH COLUMBIA
Karen Lindsay, AVP
PO Box 6535
Victoria, BC V9A 1P6
604-389-0878

Amanda Vaughan, AVP
3588 W. 18th Ave.
Vancouver, BC V6S 1B1
(604) 736-4665

ASSOCIATED VIVATION PROFESSIONALS
PO Box 8269
Cincinnati, OH 45208 USA
1-800-829-2625

A referral service for Vivation Professionals. You can receive a list of Vivation Professionals in your area and additional information about Vivation by phoning: (800) 829-2625 in the United States or Canada or (513) 321-4405.

Vivation is a service mark and publishing trademark of Jim Leonard, Phil Laut, Jeanne Miller, and Anne Leonard, doing business as Associated Vivation Professionals.

Some of the members of Associated Vivation Professionals are listed above. They are indicated with AVP next to their names.

The following people, although not Vivation Professionals, are professional rebirthers who use methods similar to Vivation:

CALIFORNIA
Jane S. Cattell, RN MA
3520 Third Ave. Apt #109
San Diego, CA 92103
619-295-9416

Bob Frissell
5155 Simoni Ct.
El Sobrante, CA 94803
(415) 222-4059

NEW YORK
Rosetta DeGillio
525 E. 88th St. #1B
New York, NY 10128
(212) 734-9060

UTAH
Barbara & Dennis Bellows-
Terranova
2896 S. 2300 E.
Salt Lake City, UT 84109
801-487-8438

VIRGINIA
Ken & Renee Kizer
10613 Patterson Ave.
Richmond, VA 23233
(804) 740-9239

ENGLAND
Hilary Newman
79-A Acre Lane
London, SW2 5TN
(01) 733-9774